Creating your own library

PLANNING AND DESIGNING LIBRARIES FOR CHILDREN AND YOUNG PEOPLE

Erratum

Planning and designing libraries for
children and young people
Michael Dewe

Please note that the photographs for Figures 12.10 and
12.11 on pp 194 and 196 have been transposed.

PLANNING AND DESIGNING LIBRARIES FOR CHILDREN AND YOUNG PEOPLE

Michael Dewe

Lecturer
Department of Information and Library Studies
University of Wales, Aberystwyth

LIBRARY ASSOCIATION PUBLISHING

LONDON

Published by
Library Association Publishing
7 Ridgmount Street
London WC1E 7AE

First published 1995

British Library Cataloguing in Publication Data
A catalogue record for this book is available from the British Library

ISBN 1-85604-100-X

Typeset in 11/13 Times and Avant Garde by Library Association Publishing
Printed and made in Great Britain by Bookcraft (Bath) Ltd

To

Kathy – at last!

———————

CONTENTS

LIST OF ILLUSTRATIONS, PLANS AND TABLES

Tables

PREFACE

Space is one of the basic resources required by library and information services and its appropriate provision must be a major concern for library and information managers. The nature of that provision is largely determined by the environment in which the library is located and the needs of the users. It seems right, therefore, to devote a book to the particular library and information space requirements of children and young people, whether as pupils in schools or as users of public libraries in the community. As far as the author is aware, this has not been attempted before. It is also apt to consider these two aspects of library service to children and young people together as there are a number of common space resource issues, such as the need to make provision for different age groups and the impact of information technology. Also, in the United Kingdom, there has been a long historical and continuing link between schools and public libraries.

It is within these two contexts that this book describes the process, principles and practice of planning and designing an appropriate library space resource. While mainly concerned with new, purpose-built accommodation, some consideration is given to the particular issues raised by the modernization of an existing library, the conversion of 'alien' space to a library, and to road vehicles used in providing library services to children and young people. As indicated in Chapter 1, the librarian's responsibility extends beyond a concern for the creation of new, modernized or converted library space, however, to one for its day-to-day, and long-term, utilization and maintenance: a complete space management approach is therefore advocated. Although it is hoped that readers will find this book of practical usefulness, it does not set out to be a technical one, as other publications fulfil that particular role, notably Godfrey Thompson's *Planning and design of library buildings*.[1]

Many people are involved in the creation of a library, and their roles, and the contribution they make are dealt with in this book, especially Chapter 5. However, particular attention is paid to the role and the creative planning input, from the managerial point of view, made by the school or children's librarian. Planning, in both the architectural and design sense, is clearly a contribution made by the architect and others, although this does not mean the librarian should not endeavour to acquire some basic knowledge of architectural planning and design in order to work successfully with them.

In a wide-ranging book such as this, terminology poses something of a problem.

Generally speaking, I have used the all embracing term 'library' to indicate, as appropriate, a department or area in a public library for children and/or young people, and the school library or learning resource centre (media center in the USA) in a school. Where helpful, I have used the latter terms.

While the use of the terms 'children' or 'pupils' can often imply those of all ages, I have used 'children and young people' where the inclusion of the latter, older group needs emphasizing, and 'teenagers' or 'young people' where that group is the focus of attention. I have qualified 'pupil', as primary or secondary, where appropriate, keeping the term 'student' for older pupils. However, it might be helpful to spell out how the age groups are determined in public libraries and in schools, although in neither case is there consistency throughout the United Kingdom:

Public libraries

   Pre-school children – under 5 years old
   Children – 5 to 11 or 12 years old
   Young people – 13 to 16+

Schools

   Primary school – 5 to 11 years old
   Middle school – 8 to 14 years old
   Secondary school – 11 to 18 years old
   Sixth form college – 16 to 18 years old

In a modern context, some mention of space provision for other associated user groups, such as parents, teachers and carers is also necessary.

It is expected that the contents of this book will give school and children's librarians the confidence to participate effectively in any library space resource project that may come their way. This will be because they will understand the space implications of library and information service; will be aware of the elements of planning and design for libraries, and will have developed a critical and evaluative attitude to their utilization, layout, appearance and environment. The case studies in Chapter 12, which provide brief accounts, floor plans and illustrations of recently completed school libraries and those for children and young people, will help to exemplify many of the points made in the body of the text.

This work is principally intended for school and children's librarians and library school students in the United Kingdom, but it is hoped that it will have an appeal for architects, school governors, teachers and all those involved in working with and caring for children and young people. The book's international flavour, particularly in Chapter 6, which looks at library guidelines and standards, should, however, broaden its appeal and make it useful further afield.

In my capacity as lecturer, consultant and writer on library buildings, I have been fortunate over the last 19 years to see many libraries of all kinds both at home and abroad and I have visited a number of school and public libraries in the UK as preparation for this book. In addition, I have relied heavily on the professional literature and on the information provided by colleagues about current building projects. The literature, especially that about work with children and young people in public libraries, is predominantly American, as in many areas of librarianship, and there is, I believe, a great deal to be learned from it. However, I should like to encourage British librarians to be more like their American counterparts and to write more often about their expertise in and experiences of the planning and design of library facilities for children and young people.

As already indicated, this book owes much to the readiness of colleagues to supply me with information and often to show me round their libraries. I have also been given every assistance by the staff of a number of library furniture and equipment suppliers. I am, therefore, indebted to many people, and would like to offer my thanks particularly to: Sarah Airey, SJS Publicity and Marketing Services, Eynsham, Oxfordshire; Manjot Bami, Librarian, Swanlea Secondary School, Whitechapel, London; Pat Brunt, Librarian, Waddeson Church of England Secondary School, Waddeson, Buckinghamshire; David Barker, Principal Librarian, Services to Education, Clwyd Library and Information Service; Roger Bray, Director, Point Eight Ltd, Dudley; Jan Butler, Teacher-Coordinator, Petersfield School, Petersfield, Hampshire; Angela Conder, Assistant Team Librarian, Gloucestershire Library, Arts and Museum; Brenda Constable, Central Library Manager, London Borough of Croydon; John Dunne, Assistant County Librarian, School Library Service, Hampshire County Library; Anne Everall, Principal Librarian, Children and Youth Services and Teresa Scragg, Libraries and Learning Division, Birmingham Leisure and Community Services; Brian Goodyer, Commercial Director, Reska Terrapin Products Ltd, Milton Keynes; Gabriele Harms, Einkaufszentrale für Bibliotheken GmbH, Reutlingen, Germany; Roger Hawkes, School Resources and Information Officer, Park Community School, Havant, Hampshire; Julie A. Jones, Assistant Director (Cultural Services), Cynon Valley Borough Council; Grace Kempster, Chief Librarian, Leeds Leisure Services, Lindsay McKrell, Community Librarian, and Margaret Park, Young People's Services Librarian, Monklands District Library Service; Mary Mabey, Resource Centre Manager, Bacon's College (City Technology College), Rotherhithe, London; Liz Maxwell, Librarian, Winstanley Sixth-Form College, Wigan; Jan Mountfield, Teacher-Coordinator, Riders Middle School, Havant, Hampshire; Sue Philpott, Librarian, Royal Grammar School, High Wycombe, Buckinghamshire; Stephen J. Stanyard, G.C. Smith (Coachworks), Loughborough; Barbara Stevens, Teacher-Coordinator, Hulbert Middle School, Waterlooville, Hampshire; Pam Sutherland, Librarian, Whitgift School, Croydon; Moira Taylor, Publicity Manager, Library Furnishing Consultants Ltd, Wellingborough, Northamptonshire; Valerie Wallace, District Librarian, Hounslow Library, Hounslow Leisure Services; Nigel Woof, Marketing Director, Linda Cooke, Don Gresswell Ltd, London.

My thanks are also due to my departmental colleagues, Gwilym Huws and Ray Lonsdale, who gave me my first opportunity to write about planning and design for these particular users, as a unit of a comprehensive module on school and young people's librarianship, part of a distance learning masters programme of the Department of Information and Library Studies, University of Wales, Aberystwyth. I would also like to thank Bob Williams of the departmental library, Tony Bamber of Matrix Library Management, Julie Evans of the department's Open Learning Unit (who helped with the production of the text), and the former head of the Department of Information and Library Studies, D. Hywel Roberts, who has provided encouragement and practical support for the completion of this book.

Reference

1 Thompson, G., *Planning and design of library buildings*, 3rd edn., London, Butterworth, 1989.

1 SPACE AS A RESOURCE

Increasingly librarians and information workers are expected to manage rather than just administer the resources under their control. While there has been a general recognition in the profession, however, of the need to manage resources such as personnel, money and library collections properly, the same attention has not been paid perhaps to managing the library space resource. A resource that, in schools and public libraries, manifests itself in a variety of ways from purpose-built facilities through to converted accommodation and road vehicles. This lack of attention may be due partly to the emphasis given in both theory and practice to the creation of new accommodation, with little thought being given to its subsequent use and management. While this book is largely concerned with the planning and design of new libraries, this opening chapter advocates a more wide-ranging approach to the library space resource in schools and for children and young people that will justify the description of 'space management'.

The effective management of the library space resource is not only important, however, from the point of view of making the best use of that resource, but because of what it says about the school it serves or the public library service of which the department or area for children and young people is part. Today's schools, both state and public, operate in a competitive educational environment. To attract pupils, schools must market themselves to appeal to both pupils and their parents and project a strong and successful image. Part of that strength and image will be evidenced by good facilities, of which an attractive, spacious and well-equipped library would be part. However, there is also a growing realization of the importance of a well-supported school library resource centre for a school's academic and other achievements. Falling rolls in some schools also mean that space, or more space, becomes available for the provision of a library service.

Public libraries, with their provision for children and young people, are in a different but equally competitive situation, but here the competitors are the many other attractions that engage the young. Public libraries can only begin to compete if they offer appropriate services to different age groups in a range of spaces that attract and hold them and encourage them to return often.

Space management

Space management,[1] or facilities management, as it is known in the commercial world, is variously defined, but taken at its broadest, it can be seen as being concerned with creating new buildings, making the best use of space in an existing building, and seeing that buildings are properly maintained. In a large commercial organization, or a library system, all of these types of activity may be under way at any one time. Certainly, as is argued below, the last two concerns should be ongoing features of the well-managed library space resource. Some local authorities, for example Devon, may monitor the success of space management within schools by the use of performance measures for library accommodation and all public libraries are encouraged to do this in the Office of Arts and Libraries publication, *Keys to success: performance indicators for public libraries*.[2] This subject will be more fully discussed in Chapter 3. Such monitoring implies a commitment to the provision of quality library accommodation. This commitment is given as part of the Library Association's model charter for public libraries and the need to provide seats, study areas and special facilities for children is listed under the heading, 'Environment and facilities'.[3]

Building maintenance

Once created, library accommodation has to be managed on a day-to-day basis; the micro-level of space management. Building maintenance[4] should concern itself, therefore, with such tasks as:

(a) ensuring that the library is maintained in good repair – everything from roofs to plumbing and upholstery to carpets

(b) the maintenance and safe operation of equipment and of electrical, mechanical and other systems

(c) the safety of staff and users, bearing in mind legal responsibilities under health and safety and other legislation

(d) the internal and external appearance of the library – for example, its cleanliness, the removal of graffiti, the accuracy and condition of library signs

(e) emergency preparedness and disaster recovery plans, whether relating to major events such as fire or flooding or disruptive children in the library.

While building maintenance may be a less onerous responsibility for librarians in schools and in children's libraries, where others may be charged with the overall upkeep and maintenance of buildings and equipment, it is nonetheless an important responsibility to draw attention to the need for such maintenance and remedial work and to ensure that it is carried out. One way of ensuring that maintenance work is not always a response to a sudden crisis, is to create a checklist of matters relating to the building and its equipment that should be inspected or carried out on a regular basis – daily, weekly, monthly, quarterly or annually. A number of such checklists have been published that provide a useful guide to what could be included in a school or children's library's own maintenance list.[5]

Clearly the work of maintenance is more manageable if easy-to-maintain materials, finishes and surfaces are selected in the first place for a library when it is constructed.

Where library service to children and young people is provided from a mobile library or other road vehicle, then similar matters of repair, maintenance, cleanliness, servicing and safety in operation, as well as preparedness for emergencies, are equally important. Not only is a poorly maintained vehicle a bad advertisement for the library service, it could lead to an accident involving children and young people.

Space planning

In addition to the above largely routine, but important matters, space management means that the librarian responsible for a building, a department in a building (such as a children's library), or part of a building in which the library is housed (as is usually the case in a school), has a duty to make the best possible use of the space resource under his or her control. This requires the librarian to be constructively critical of the current appearance of the library and the way its space is utilized. This activity is usually known as space planning.[6] Such an appraisal by the librarian could result at its simplest in any or all of the following:

(a) The redecoration and limited refurnishing of the library to take into account changing tastes in interior design and to meet new needs; a new issue counter and a repainting of the library interior, for example.
(b) Minor improvements, such as the provision of a carpet.
(c) The installation of new equipment, such as a display case.
(d) Minor rearrangements to the library layout, to improve supervision, for example.

Once the librarian identifies the need for more substantial space planning, necessitating the full modernization, reorganization, and refurbishment of existing space, then a complex and detailed process is entered into that is similar to the planning of a new building and should be approached in that way. Once again a checklist approach may be a useful way of evaluating existing library spaces prior to implementing changes.[7] As part of such a thorough remodelling, and bearing in mind the librarian is working with existing space, it will be necessary, for example, to identify redundant or underused space, decide how new services will be accommodated, and consider the possibilities of structural alterations and whether an extension is required and possible.

Both for building maintenance and space planning purposes, it is useful to maintain an inventory of the library's furnishings, furniture, shelving and equipment; this may be formally required by the parent body. If time permits, an annual review of all such items and their records should be carried out.

The librarian as space planner

In the planning and design process described in this book, whether for a new or replanned library, the librarian acts in concert with others, especially an architect, to create appropriate school or public library accommodation for children and young people. However, it has to be recognized that, sometimes, as in the case of the planning or replanning of a small library, the librarian may be on his or her own. The scale and nature of the task, the expectations of the employer, and the funds available do not warrant nor permit the employment of an architect. However, as described in Chapter 5, some specialist help may be available within or from outside the school or public library service which will help the librarian to implement his or her plans.

Even in what are likely to be small-scale situations such as this, there is much to be gained by imitating the process used in the planning and design of purpose-built accommodation, including the use of an architect if at all possible. Otherwise there is a danger of thinking in terms of solutions – where should individual library areas be placed and how can the shelving, furniture and equipment be arranged? – without, for example, properly identifying the space relationships and other requirements to be met by such an arrangement. The design process by which spatial relationships and the detailed library layout are determined is dealt with in Chapter 10.

The challenge of space management

Creating an independent library building or other space resource (such as a library within another building), follows the planning cycle that library managers are familiar with from their professional education and from handling other projects. However, the process has a number of features that, while not necessarily unique, characterize a building project. These relate to such matters as:

(a) The inexperience of the librarian and the funding body. Faced with what is often a once-in-a-lifetime opportunity, a librarian may anticipate its challenge with some excitement and pleasure, while also feeling ill-prepared, and lacking in experience for such a task.

(b) The nature of the documentation the librarian will be required to prepare. The librarian is unlikely to be familiar with the task of writing a brief for an architect, interpreting plans and drawings, and writing furniture specifications.

(c) The design dimension. The librarian is usually unused to visualizing and making judgements on design both in general terms (the arrangement of space, for example), and on specific matters, such as colour schemes.

(d) The range of people involved. The team nature of modern building projects means that the librarian has to learn to work with an architect and a range of other specialists, including those who will have a major interest as users of the library, such as students, teachers and parents.

While dealing with these matters represents a professional challenge to the librarian, other aspects of the project will impose pressures and constraints. For example: finding sufficient time to devote to a building project; maintaining a planning momentum; working within a proposed time-scale and a given budget, and the permanency of the results. Unlike some other projects, where later changes may be possible at an acceptable cost, major mistakes of library planning and design may have to be lived with long into the future. This places a great deal of pressure on all those concerned to 'get it right'.

Frustration can also set in if projects are delayed, put back or aborted, as can often be the case. On the positive side, however, whatever the immediate outcome, work will have gone into evaluating current library provision and thinking about the future which can be used later. The opportunities that are presented by a new or remodelled library give the librarian the chance to rethink the nature of the library service to be given in a school and to children and young people of a particular community. Some may see this as the biggest and most difficult challenge of the whole planning process.

Developing and demonstrating space management skills

Much of the literature about planning library buildings is concerned with creating new, independently sited buildings. However, with some exceptions, libraries in schools and for young people are rarely separate buildings but more usually part of another building, such as a public library, or part of a group of buildings comprising a school. Consequently, the school or young people's librarian will usually be called upon to make a specialist input into a building project rather than have responsibility for a complete building. This is somewhat different to other, and usually more wide-ranging, library planning situations, and is reflected in the contents and emphasis of this book.

Such a situation is, however, not without its problems. For there is no guarantee that the librarian will be consulted by those with overall responsibility for a school building or public library, except as an afterthought, when the project may have already developed in a way that may be difficult to alter and may be disadvantageous to school or children and young people's library services. Similarly, a librarian may be appointed to a newly completed facility for which there has been no appropriate professional input during its planning and design. Both of these situations are avoidable by school and library managers, and the first can be actively combated by the librarian in post who takes the trouble to understand the complete planning and design process, knows what their contribution should be, when to make it, and insists on doing so. Such an attitude does not guarantee consultation but, combined with obvious knowledge, the librarian will be difficult to ignore. Equally, if the librarian demonstrates good space management skills, in addition to knowledge and enthusiasm, with existing resources in the ways described earlier in this chapter, then once again it will be difficult (and somewhat silly) to overlook him or her in a new library space resource project of one kind or another. It helps also if the librarian endeavours to initiate new space resource developments rather than allowing others to take the lead.

Solutions to space limitations

There will be times when space management may seem too grand a name for continuing to attempt to accommodate a quart in a pint pot. Nevertheless, when everything possible has been done to facilitate improvement and make the best possible use of current space in the library (and knowing that no additional adjacent space can be made available in the foreseeable future), the librarian must look for other ways to solve the space problem. Such solutions may require changes to current

5

policy and practice, as well as a willingness to compromise on a preferred library design situation. These changes could include:

1 Changes to practice
   (a) arrange the collection by size; several parallel sequences may be required
   (b) weed the collection heavily
   (c) place greater reliance on the schools library service, other departments of the public library, or other cooperative arrangements
   (d) create an open plan office area with no personal offices.

2 Changes to policy
   (a) examine policy on space allocation for particular activities and allowances for gangways between shelving, readers, tables, etc.; it may be possible that further items of shelving and furniture can be accommodated
   (b) create or review the library's collection policy. Problems with accommodating the library's materials, as indicated by the solutions above, would seem to indicate the need for this step; the library may be attempting too much.

3 Investing in space-saving and flexible equipment
   (a) island shelving on castors will enable the rearrangement of space to suit various temporary purposes, such as, group work, story hours, or displays
   (b) replace existing furniture with items that may accommodate more materials or readers and take up less space themselves, for example, lateral filing units, carousel periodical storage units, or multi-user tables. If ceiling height (and finance) permit, install higher shelving in all or part of the library; or compact shelving if floor loadings allow. Some visual impact, convenience and atmosphere may be lost by such changes.

4 Using available technology
   (a) exploit the potential of microform technology to replace runs of periodicals, newspapers and other material
   (b) invest in online and CD-ROM technology to replace volumes of indexes and abstracts and reference works
   (c) invest in automated library housekeeping systems.

5 Off-site solutions
   (a) a part of the library service, for example the library administration, may be housed elsewhere in the school or public library building; in the latter instance, where centralized services are offered, possibly in another building entirely
   (b) older and less used library materials may be stored off-site or elsewhere in the school building, for example.

Funding the space resource

All planning situations are affected by various constraints. For the librarian as space manager, the nature of the existing structure and its spaces immediately imposes various physical limitations on what can be achieved by way of space planning change and improvement. Common to the planning of new premises and the replanning of old ones is the question of the financial constraints which have been set in the budget for capital expenditure. Even though a library's current plans do not require capital expenditure on buildings, it is usual, however, to include a sum of money in the annual budget for maintenance and minor building works. Without such an annual allowance, the management of the library space resource is likely to be neglected.

Fund-raising and sponsorship

American schools and public libraries have long been associated with fund-raising and sponsorship to support their activities, including the library building. In the UK, city technology colleges in particular, are expected to raise money through sponsorship and, the greater the success they have at it, the more money is provided by central government, which must influence what can be provided by way of library accommodation. Peter Kingham has described how John Cleveland College in Leicestershire, an upper school for 14–18 year-olds, set about raising £20,000 for its library resource centre's refurbishment. He demonstrates how to go about such fund-raising and emphasizes a thoroughly business-like approach, warning that: 'If you approach any likely sponsor with an idea for a project but have no definite plans, no detailed budget and no vision, you are likely to see your ideas gracefully acknowledged but thrown in the bin.'[8]

Schools can also often rely on the money-raising work of parents and pupils, which may be utilized for the library and its accommodation. One middle school library was built by parents over two years and paid for by sponsored events. Not all schools may be able to match this achievement but they and public libraries (possibly through library support or friends groups) may consider sponsorship or fund-raising for manageable library building and equipment projects for children and young people.

References

1   For a brief discussion of some aspects of space management and its importance, *see* Montanelli, D. S., 'Space management for libraries', *Illinois libraries*, **69** (2), 1987, 130–8.

2   Office of Arts and Libraries, *Keys to success: performance indicators for public libraries*, London, HMSO, 1990.

3   Library Association, *A charter for public libraries*, London, Library Association, 1993, paragraph 6.3.

4   A full discussion of this topic is provided in Lueder, A. C. and Webb, S., *An administrator's guide to library building maintenance*, Chicago, American Library Association, 1992.

5   Wozny, J., *Checklist for public library managers*, Metuchen, NJ, Scarecrow Press, 1989, 127–36.

6   This topic is dealt with fully in: Fraley, R. A. and Anderson, C. L., *Library space planning: a how-to-do-it manual . . .* , 2nd edn., New York, Neal-Schuman, 1990.

7   Sannwald, W. W. (ed.), *Checklist of library building design considerations*, Chicago, American Library Association, 1991. One of the goals of this publication is for it to serve as a means of evaluating existing library spaces. Points to consider when refurbishing the library resource centre are given in: Charlton, L., *Designing and planning a secondary school library resource centre*, [Swindon], School Library Association, 1992, 13–14.

8   Kingham, P., 'Something for nothing: every school's dream', *School librarian*, **41** (3), 1993, 98–9.

2 | TYPES OF SCHOOL AND PUBLIC LIBRARY SPACE PROVISION

General solutions

Whatever the nature of the accommodation provided for a school library or public library facility for children or young people, it is either newly purpose-built, makes use of space not originally designed for a library, is prefabricated, or is older library accommodation that has been modernized and refurbished and possibly extended. Where library services to children and young people are offered from road vehicles these too may not always be purpose-built and vehicles are also refurbished from time to time. Given that the librarian may sometimes have to evaluate and argue for or against particular general space solutions of this kind, it is worthwhile beginning this chapter by briefly discussing their pros and cons.

Purpose-built accommodation

A new, purpose-built library, especially where standing independently on its own site, can have many attractions for the librarian:

(a) It can be located probably in the best relationship to other buildings – on a school campus, for example.
(b) It can be designed to respond as closely as possible to current and projected library requirements.
(c) There are potentially fewer constraints on the design.
(d) There is an opportunity to create a fresh library image.
(e) Where a separate building, a generous site can allow for future expansion, and if well designed, it is likely to attract recognition and add significance to its work as a library.

Where a school library forms an integral part of a complex of buildings (Figure 2.1), or a children's library is part of a larger building, all of these advantages may not be so easily obtained.

Conversions

The conversion of a building or part of a building for school (Figures 2.2 and 2.3) or public library purposes has the advantage of:

(a) usually being cheaper and quicker to bring about
(b) conserving a building of architectural and historical interest in some cases. Such reuse can give a library building a special charm, as in the children's

9

Fig. 2.1 *Purpose-built library within Swanlea Secondary School, Whitechapel*

Fig. 2.2 *Royal Grammar School, High Wycombe – library in converted hall*

Fig. 2.3 *Riders Middle School, Havant, Hampshire – computer area of library in converted cloakroom*

library at Castle Gates Library, Shrewsbury, housed in a converted sixteenth century hall or the library of Old Palace School, Croydon

(c) the building or space available for conversion, such as a gymnasium or hall, may have useful characteristics, such as a high ceiling, that will permit the construction of galleries or a mezzanine floor.

Disadvantages of such a conversion can include:

(a) a poor location
(b) the hidden costs of unexpected but necessary structural and mechanical improvements
(c) constraints on the design leading to compromises over the layout and arrangement of the library
(d) insufficient space to accommodate everything, especially desired new developments
(e) the possible need for more staff to operate the library
(f) higher operating costs.

Prefabricated buildings

A solution to library space provision, that is neither purpose-built nor conversion, is the prefabricated library building. These buildings can meet demands for libraries in newly developed housing areas with lots of children, or in some school situations, such as increased pupil numbers. In addition to low cost, such buildings are quickly erected and theoretically reusable. Often considered as suitable only for temporary,

11

usually extra, accommodation, they tend to become semi-permanent. Drawbacks to their use as libraries relate to their utilitarian appearance and the reputation of mass-produced systems buildings for inadequate insulation, leaking flat roofs, etc. However, much has been done to improve such buildings in recent years and at least one company the Terrapin Group, has specialized in supplying, erecting and fitting out prefabricated buildings for libraries as a package deal.

Such prefabricated structures are also used in the United States and the smallest version, known as a kiosk library, can be located in covered shopping centres and could be dedicated to children or young people's services if so required. The advantages claimed for such facilities are that:

(a) a large bookstock, as well as audiovisual materials, can be accommodated for their size
(b) they operate with minimum staff
(c) they are cost effective – annual costs of operation are low and issues high
(d) they are highly visible and attractive
(e) they can be used as a centre for activities.[1]

Modernization, refurbishment and extension

There can be many sound reasons for not replacing an existing library, such as insufficient funds, a good location and adequate space, and opting to modernize and refurbish the present accommodation instead. Where space is an issue, but an extension to the existing library is possible, this may be yet another reason for modernizing and developing the current library rather than another solution.

Such an approach has many of the advantages of a conversion – in terms of cost and time, for example. Its success may depend on the structural adaptability of the internal spaces – to permit the combining of rooms, for instance – and the availability of an area for expansion, if additional space is required. Where there is a poor location of the library, no room for expansion, and interior spaces that are not adaptable, or too small, then this would suggest that some other alternative to the reuse of the current accommodation for children within a school or public library should be considered.

Mobile libraries

Not all library services to children and young people may be offered from static service points, but from a variety of road vehicles and, in some countries, from trains or boats, although not, as far as the author is aware, from aeroplanes. The mobile library, whether van or larger vehicle, has become a universal response to providing a flexible service to those who are at some distance from a static service point – usually in rural areas but not exclusively so (and including children and young people) – and the mobile library bookstock will be intensively used. Urban mobile libraries are also to be found in many British cities and overseas.

However, because of size restrictions, the traditional mobile library can only carry a limited stock for children and may call when all but the youngest children are at school. On the other hand, when children are on holiday, the usual mobile library service is likely to be inadequate for their needs. Some of these problems can be addressed by the use of:

(a) the trailer or container library (housing a larger amount of stock)
(b) holiday mobile libraries
(c) vehicles visiting schools and other centres.

Other disadvantages include the fact that the general mobile library cannot be used for community activities like a static service point; there may be no study facilities and little provision of periodical, audiovisual materials or community information, and there may be considerable gaps between visits, especially if one is missed or there are changes to the schedule for one reason or another.[2] These are further considerable disadvantages for children and young people.

The remainder of this chapter briefly discusses the emergence of various specific types of library space provision that have developed to meet the needs of children and young people and looks at some of their general advantages and disadvantages.

Provision in schools
School libraries: historical background

Prior to the beginnings of the state school system, following the Education Act of 1870, school libraries were to be found in public schools. Much earlier the school libraries were associated with religious foundations.

The first state school libraries were those provided by some public libraries – Leeds, Plymouth and Bootle, for example – during the 1880s and 1890s, as collections of books in schools. In some instances such arrangements overcame the financial problems of providing branch libraries, as the books were made available to local children and residents, as well as pupils.

Sheila Ray writes that little interest in school libraries was taken by the Board of Education until 1928, when it drew attention to the library as being as essential as a laboratory in all secondary schools.[3] By this time, the pattern of provision that had arisen in England and Wales in both municipal and county authorities (with the exception of London) was one where libraries and schools were run by the same local authority and often the same committee, and thus of school library collections provided or supplemented by the public library.

The continuance of this cooperative approach meant that by 1935, 138 English libraries provided for 1,997 schools, mostly elementary, rather than secondary schools. The provision in Wales and Scotland was not as good, although Cardiff continued to be a leading authority in its work with schools, and comprehensive provision was made by Edinburgh, where the local authority provided accommodation and equipment, the public library books and staff. In spite of these details, Ray feels that there was little real development of school libraries before the Second World War.[4]

During the postwar period, 1945–58, and as a consequence of the impact of the 1944 Education Act, many new primary and secondary schools were constructed. A survey of 1954 showed that many local authorities were providing a school library service usually at a cost to the education authority, although the financial situation was varied and confused, and this number increased by 1959. In about two-thirds of cases, the service consisted of a deposit collection changed from time to time. Thomas Kelly suggests that the numbers may underestimate the improvements in the quality of service that had taken place in both schools and public libraries.[5]

The school library was still not, however, the focal point of most schools in Britain and their provision today is still not a legal requirement. However, they have been compulsory for certain types of school in Japan since 1953; Sweden since 1962; Norway since 1935 and 1985; Iceland since 1974, and Denmark since 1983.[6]

The 1960s saw a number of developments that were to alter the concept of the school library. First, there was a fundamental change in educational philosophy, with a shift from a teacher-centred to a learning-centred approach, particularly in primary schools, leading, for example, to topic or project work. Secondly, the development and greater use of audiovisual materials for teaching and learning. Thirdly, the widening of services provided by schools library services, of which Wiltshire, with its emphasis on the supplying of books and other materials to support teaching, was an outstanding example. And, fourthly, the emergence of the library resource centre concept with 'some of the new schools designed towards the end of the 1960s . . . planned with the resource centre at the heart of the school'.[7]

In 1970 the resource centre approach was given fresh impetus when the Library Association published, *School library resource centres: recommended standards for policy and provision*, supplemented by a publication on non-book materials in 1973. Codsall School, Staffordshire was amongst the pioneer secondary comprehensive schools to create a learning resource centre, and Leicestershire and Nottinghamshire were considered front-rank education authorities of the early 1970s in encouraging the development of resource-based learning, with new schools designed so that learning was obliged to be strongly resourced-based. However, the Bullock Report of 1975 demonstrated that many secondary school libraries still did not provide an acceptable basic library service.

At local government reorganization in England and Wales in 1974, public library authorities were in general coextensive with education authorities and the larger library units permitted the employment of more specialist staff and the offering of more specialized services to schools from a schools library service. Reorganization in Northern Ireland in 1973 established five education and library boards each with a senior librarian responsible for both school and public library services to children and thus permitting an integrated approach to such provision. In Scotland, reorganization in 1975 destroyed the formal link between school and public libraries, although the regions retained the old county library headquarters as focal points for reorganized schools library services.

Hard on the heels of local government reorganization came the financial cuts leading also to cuts in school library service and the numbers of librarians working in schools. The late 1970s, however, saw a greater focus on the role of the library in the learning process, in addition to that of provider of materials, and the recognition of the need for library and study skills as a necessary corollary of resource-based learning.

The early 1980s opened with two contrasting examples of school library provision. The first, the purpose-built Learning and Resource Centre at Millfield School, containing television studio, cinema, viewing rooms and bookshop; the second the conversion of kitchen and dining room at Mountfleet High School, Stansted, to accommodate 6,000 volumes.

By the end of 1982, the year designated Information Technology Year, 90% of secondary schools possessed a microcomputer, compared with 1980 when only about 20% had acquired them. Computers are now found in both primary and secondary schools and are a major and developing aspect of the school library resource centre.

In *School libraries: the foundation of the curriculum*, published in 1984, the school library was recognized as having an essential and central task in the school curriculum and that library skills are its foundation.[8] The government's 1985 White Paper, *Better schools*, supported the inclusion of library services in a school's curricular policy but did not lead to any real government support for their provision. HMI reports of the mid- and late-1980s showed that the provision of school libraries in the UK still left much to be desired.

The Education Reform Act of 1988 introduced the National Curriculum and the local management of schools and the opportunity for schools to opt out of local government control. The implications of the National Curriculum 5–16 for appropriate resource provision to support its aims were endorsed by the School Library Association and the Library Association. The late 1980s, therefore, saw school librarianship at the crossroads of change, with provision in the UK overall still considered inadequate. However, pressure of GCSE requirements, an improved perception of the role of the school library, and the changed financial situation in some schools seems to have led to the refurbishment and remodelling of many school libraries in the early 1990s.

Primary and middle schools

In the post-Second World War period, consensus was in favour of classroom libraries in primary schools; they were considered particularly helpful to slow learners. 'However, a central library was sometimes successful and became increasingly useful in the junior school.'[9] There was, nevertheless, some controversy over the desirability of the central library concept in the 1950s, but today many schools will have both central and classroom library resources.

Sheila Ray draws attention to the importance of the 1958 School Library Association's publication, *The library in the primary school*, first published 'when the idea of the library in the primary school was becoming widely accepted and both reflected and stimulated this development'.[10] A second edition was published in 1966, giving some idea of its significance at the time; it is still considered a useful handbook.

Primary schools exist today to serve the educational needs of the 5–11 age group and some may be divided into infant and junior departments. In some instances a nursery school for the under-5s may be attached to a primary school. Some local authorities in England have established first schools for children aged 5 to 8, 9 or 10. Today's pupils work on their own a great deal with a variety of resources and are encouraged to follow their own interests. Even where there is a central collection, as in larger schools, most library materials will probably be found in the classrooms.

Middle schools are considered of primary level but accommodate pupils in the age-ranges between 8 and 14. Given the age-range, middle school pupils require a mix of primary and secondary school types of library provision.

Special schools may have handicapped children up to the age of 16 and 'they are likely to adopt a primary school approach towards their library provision, with books and other materials easily accessible in every classroom, and perhaps in a small central library'.[11]

Secondary schools

Following the 1944 Education Act the idea that every secondary school should have a library became generally accepted. 'However, the need to continue to make use of existing buildings and the failure of building programmes to keep up with the rising numbers of children meant that many schools had to make do. Even in the 1980s, when school roles are falling and some schools are actually closing, there are still some schools which cannot allocate a room entirely for library purposes.'[12]

Libraries in secondary schools are usually centralized collections; some schools may also have base, departmental or laboratory collections. Some schools may have a junior library for the lower and middle schools or accommodation within the library reserved for sixth formers.

The comprehensive schools, which developed substantially in the 1960s brought together the former strands of grammar, technical and secondary modern education into a common school and are attended by most of the secondary school population in Great Britain. Those in England and Wales can be organized to cater for the 11–18 age-range, as middle schools, or with an age-range of 11 or 12 to 16.

Sixth-form colleges

The sixth-form college concept dates from the early 1960s and, where adopted by a local education authority, provides a separate institution for those pupils aged 16 to 18 who are between school and higher education and may offer both academic and non-academic courses. Such colleges concentrate resources in fewer places and allow for a more adult environment for their students who need adequate independent study and social space.

City technology colleges

It was announced in 1986 that the government planned to set up city technology colleges (CTCs) in urban areas, and the first, Kingshurst, Solihull, opened in 1988. The CTCs are funded jointly by the government and private industry and the latter is encouraged to be involved locally in running the colleges. Pupils are between the ages of 11 and 19, representing a broad range of abilities, and their curriculum emphasizes science and technology, economic awareness, business understanding, and personal and social education.

There is extensive use of information technology throughout each CTC to support educational objectives, and the library, linked to the college's network, is seen as the most important resource area. Reprographic facilities are usually provided adjacent to the library.

Dual-use libraries

A dual-use library, known by various other names around the world, for example, combined library in Australia, is one that is usually located in a secondary school and serves both the school population and the local community. Because of the advantages it offers in terms of economies in respect of premises, staff and collections, it is a solution to library accommodation that is sometimes utilized in the UK, as well as in Australia, Canada, Germany, Iceland, Israel, Sweden, Switzerland and the USA. Potential disadvantages relate to the possible conflict of interests between children and adults, the site, and the dual relationship and loyalty of the librarian to school and library service. However, such combined facilities may be better resourced overall as they serve both pupils and the general public.

As demonstrated earlier, there is a long history of links in the UK between schools and their public library service. In Edinburgh, four distinct types of library provision in schools had developed by 1936. One of these was the school library branch that served both children and adults. Between 1934 and 1936, four such service points opened in elementary schools serving areas of new housing. Adults entered the library directly from the street, as did children when the school was closed, otherwise they entered it from the school. From 1928 libraries, which were to be used by children from other schools as well as evening class students were also established in schools in Leicester. In 1935 a public library branch was opened in a new school in Whitehaven.

Public library branches were established in comprehensive schools in Bristol and Egremont in 1962 and 1964 respectively and in a number of other schools since then. Examples include: Padgate Library, Cheshire (1982); Stoke Community Library, Suffolk (1986); Thornhill Branch Library, Kirklees (1988); Perronet-Thompson Library, Humberside (1989), and Peers Community Library, Oxfordshire (1991).

However, the dual purpose library has attracted a certain amount of opposition. The 1969 *Standards of public library service in Scotland* criticized the idea when it resulted in 'access to the public during school hours and in holiday time, adult books accessible to children, and restriction on the use of books by classes as groups'.[13]

The report conceded that a joint arrangement might work in a small community. The Department of Education and Science too had reservations in 1967 about an arrangement that 'always works to the detriment of the school', and stated that 'A better case can be made for a school library separate from but associated with, either a youth library or a branch of the public library in the same building, with appropriate safeguards.'[14]

However, as Barnes and Ray report, in 1970 the Department of Education and Science was officially encouraging dual-use accommodation for library services and for sports and educational facilities generally.[15]

In spite of widespread disagreement about the effectiveness of the dual-use library, both here and abroad, they continue to be established, but in the UK the local management of schools may limit further development. Where they appear to be most successful is in small, rural communities.

Schools library services

The long association of public libraries and schools in many areas led to the setting up of a department within the local public library system known as the schools library service, although not all are run by public libraries. Over the years, such departments have developed a wide range of advisory, training and supply services to help local school libraries and their staff. For example, Manchester and Sheffield maintained demonstration collections of books in the 1930s to assist teachers in their new book selection.

A service to schools was started at Bristol in 1954 supplying books for recreational reading and project work. One of the larger branches was used as an administrative centre and teachers were able to visit it to choose books; special attention was given to the needs of junior school children.

Alec Ellis comments, however, that 'Too few libraries maintained a more sophisticated service to schools than the loan of books . . . In 1959 only 11 per cent of libraries maintained demonstration collections, although this was a slight improvement on the facilities available in 1954.'[16]

Bourdillon reported in 1962 that most of the larger municipal and all the county libraries in its survey provided books to schools on behalf of the education authority (in fact one English county did not). Services to schools included talks to parties of children, the provision of booklists and the loan of material for special purposes. Wiltshire, as mentioned earlier, came to be seen as one of the outstanding service providers to schools for the range of its activities, which included, a basic collection of books, an agreed number of books exchanged each term and all books (including those purchased on behalf of the school) classified, catalogued, processed for use and rebound as necessary. This latter type of service was new and offered by very few libraries. An advisory service was also open to teachers on all aspects of school library administration. Many of these services were also available in counties such as Buckinghamshire and Hertfordshire, and Nottinghamshire planned school libraries cooperatively. West Riding County library was considered to have one of the finest exhibition collections, eventually in excess of 10,000 volumes.[17]

The period 1965 to 1975 saw important developments stemming from new teaching methods emphasizing project and discovery work and individual learning. These called for a wider range of support materials from schools library services, including non-book formats and the provision of 'kits' and learning packs.[18] The project loan collection, however, was perceived by teachers as the most important component of the schools library service.

In 1973 the DES set out in *The public library service: reorganisation and after* the requirements of a good library service to schools which it was hoped would be adopted in the reorganized local authorities. Among its many themes, the publication argued for greater coordination with teachers' centres.[19] In Hertfordshire, teachers' centres were used as bases for the divisional school library services.

While there may be some decentralization of a schools library service in a larger public library system, its headquarters should be closely linked with the central library or county library headquarters as the case may be. Given the range of services provided, and the staff and collections to be housed, a substantial amount of space is likely to be required in such a building.

Centralized support services of various kinds are also to be found in other countries, for example, in Germany, both at regional and local level, at municipal level in Norway and Sweden, at state and territory level in Australia, and at district level in Canada and the USA. Often such centralized services will provide advice on the planning and design of the school library. In a number of countries – Fiji, Israel, Norway, Sweden, for example – school and public libraries are able to make use of centralized services to libraries provided at a national level. In some instances, these central service organizations, such as those in Germany and Scandinavia, are able to supply library furniture and equipment and offer advice on the utilization and layout of the library space.

Given the changes in the ways schools are now funded in the UK and the way they use their funds, it has been pointed out that 'The changing context in which schools library services are now required to operate brought about by the Education Reform Act . . . poses a series of challenges [e.g. a commercialization of the service in some local authorities]. Children attending rural schools may be additionally disadvantaged where there is an increasing requirement for books and other materials but more limited funding available.'[20]

Vehicles for service to schools

In the 1890s a covered handcart was used in Bootle for the delivery and return of books from a local school in order that the collection did not remain static. The problem of maintaining collections in schools in various locations was facilitated in this century by the use of the library van or school mobile library. For example, in the 1950s, Hertfordshire used a library van to visit 450 educational institutions and teachers were able to select from collections of 1,500–2,000 volumes. In the 1960s Wiltshire used regular mobile library visits to exchange books at schools.

Writing in the 1980s, Sheila Ray says that, where teachers are unable to visit a centre to choose books, a termly visit of a schools mobile library for the exchange of stock can be scheduled. She says that the vehicle should be purpose-designed and more than one may be necessary in some areas. It may also be used for the delivery of project material if not sent through the regular delivery service. The mobile library can also be designed in a flexible way for use as a touring exhibition either permanently or for one or part of one term each year.[21] The ordinary community mobile library may, of course, also visit schools for use by pupils.

Public library provision

With a few exceptions, often found later to be mistaken, such as a city centre library mainly serving a business and commuter population, all public library accommodation in the UK will provide facilities for children. In urban areas, separately sited children's libraries have sometimes been provided but children usually make use of facilities provided for them in a library building or mobile library serving all the community. The extent of that accommodation will vary from a small section in a one-room branch library or mobile library to a room or group of rooms forming a separate department in a major building such as a central, district or main library.

The public library service to children and young people today targets particular age groups, such as pre-school children and teenagers (or young adults), is concerned with formats other than books, and offers a variety of services and activities within and outside the library.

Generally speaking, however, the early public libraries made no special provision for children and young people. Membership of the library was usually restricted to those aged 14 and over and young people were expected to find their reading in the adult lending library. This latter department constituted one of the three basic elements of the public library of the time, the others being the reference library and the reading room, or rooms, for newspapers and magazines. The emergence of separate departments or sections for children is described below and this was sometimes preceded by special provision for boys, the needs, indeed the existence of girls, apparently being disregarded.

Children's departments or sections

Among the early public libraries that had special facilities for children were Westminster from 1857, where there was a separate room, and Birmingham which, from its establishment in 1861, provided a children's section in every lending library. In the years from 1865 to 1880, Birkenhead, Plymouth and Newcastle are also known to have established children's sections.

In the USA, Pawtucket, Rhode Island set a corner aside for children in 1877 and children's rooms were provided in some libraries, such as those at Minneapolis and Denver in the 1890s; in the latter children were allowed access to the shelves. The Pratt Institute, Brooklyn, of 1897 claims the first purpose-designed children's room in America.[22] American library buildings, such as the Carnegie Library, Pittsburgh, contrasted with their English equivalents because of their spaciousness and high-quality equipment.[23] However, children's work in the USA did not go uncriticized, as it was suggested it was carried out at the expense of service to adults,[24] and a similar opposition to special provision for children was later expressed in Britain in the early twentieth century, where the 1880s and 1890s had witnessed improved facilities. This, as Kelly says, usually concerned 'children's lending libraries, children's reading rooms, and combinations of these two'.[25]

The central library (1907) and north branch library (1906) created at Islington by J.D. Brown, the advocate of open access libraries, probably symbolize all that was considered the best in children's provision in the first decade of the twentieth century.

In both libraries, the juvenile room, as it was called, was accessible from the entrance hall and consisted of identical arrangements: rows of long tables and chairs arranged across the room, occupying most of its space, and a small enclosed but open access area designated the lending department, complete with its own counter.

Kelly states that 'By 1914 the idea of special provision for children was widely accepted. A considerable proportion of libraries had children's rooms.'[26] However, the provision for children was often thought of in terms of social welfare and given the atmosphere of the schoolroom. An illustration of the children's reading room in Cathays Branch Library, Cardiff, shows a room centrally supervised from a counter by the entrance door, with long tables across the room providing seating for boys and girls, and shelving round the walls. Some attempt to relieve the formal atmosphere is made by the use pictures and flowers.[27] In the early years of the twentieth century it was possible to find libraries that had introduced a story-time, provided accommodation for homework or lent museum objects and stereoscopic views.[28]

Kelly comments that a separate children's department or departments were to be found in libraries serving towns with populations of more than 20,000 in the post-First World War period,[29] although Ellis notes some exceptions such as Brighton, Gloucester and Holborn in 1924.[30] Generally speaking, the 1920s provided many good examples of children's rooms in Britain, such as those at Croydon, Hove, Richmond (Surrey) and North Camberwell. By the time of the Kenyon Report in 1927, 151 public library authorities provided lending departments for children, some offering 'personal access to the shelves', and 87 authorities reading rooms for children.[31]

In 1919 Manchester created young people's rooms that endeavoured to get away from the schoolroom atmosphere by providing small tables, separate chairs, books in coloured jackets in low bookshelves and some flowers and pictures. By 1926, 11 such rooms had been provided in Manchester but they were for reading only; borrowing took place in the lending library. Several closed and were replaced by children's sections in the adult libraries by 1931.[32] This latter situation was reflected in Lionel McColvin's 1942 report, which found that in 40% of the main libraries visited there was no separate children's department; children were provided for by the lending library.

The period immediately prior to the Second World War had brought some improvement, however, with separate children's rooms being accepted and often provided in new libraries of the 1930s, particularly in the counties.[33] New buildings of the 1930s were often set in landscaped grounds and provided children's libraries that were comfortable, light and informal. Characteristic of these departments were: low open access shelving round the walls; a special corner shelved with picture books for the very young; suitably sized tables and chairs, the former in various shapes, varied seating; and fireplaces. Brighter colours were used for walls and curtains and lighter wood colours for furniture. Flowers, displays and friezes helped demonstrate the contrast to the old style children's room with double-sloped tables and backless forms in poorly lit rooms painted in sombre colours or tiled.[34]

In the postwar period, the basic elements of the public library were now seen as adult lending library, adult reference library, and the children's library, which combined the two adult functions. There was demand for study and reference books for children and this was reflected in the special study, homework and reference rooms provided in libraries of the period. There was a tendency towards an open plan, flexible, layout with all accommodation in a single space – much influenced by Scandinavia and America.[35]

In the latter half of the 1950s there was a continuing increase in the number of authorities that provided separate children's libraries as opposed to a children's section. This increase continued throughout the 1960s, which was a boom period for new public library buildings, both as additional and replacement service points. A variety of influences – official reports, legislation and economic growth – led to increased expenditure on libraries that benefited children, as it benefited others, but there was no targeted state grants for work with children as in other countries.[36]

Changes which took place during this period included increased extension activities; improved children's library decor; more provision made for the under-5s; children encouraged to treat the library as a club, and the disappearance of the separateness of adult and children's facilities in many instances. W. A. Taylor suggested in 1967 that a full programme of children's activities required space for very young children, a general lending area, a reference area or study room, and accommodation for extension activities. In a central children's department, this would mean a suite of rooms; in a small service point a few shelves, but both should provide the facilities first indicated. Many libraries also provided cloakroom and toilet facilities.[37]

Characteristics of library buildings of the period were: much use of glass, which also advertised the library service; varied shaped libraries which influenced the shape of the children's library; subdued decorations; a more informal atmosphere; kinderboxes and stools; carpeted areas; carpeted kinderpits, activities area, and metal shelving.[38] Some libraries provided gramophone records for children.[39]

A summary of the county library situation over the years since their beginnings in 1919 illustrates the great strides made for children in public libraries generally by the 1960s. In their early years, the counties made do with inadequate, often adapted, buildings. A few purpose-built libraries were erected in the 1930s and again in the mid-1950s, although mostly prefabricated. However, the number of new libraries grew steadily up to 1966 and then became a flood. Such libraries meant that specialist provision for children could be made.[40]

By the late 1960s, a Library Association survey showed that the number of separate children's libraries (rooms or premises) had risen to 1,227 (compared with 910 in the late 1950s) and the number of children's areas in adult libraries from 1,657 to 1,813 in the same period.[41]

A major development of the early 1970s was the desire to extend children's services to the children of immigrants, playgroups, children's hospitals and community centres. While during the 1960s the need for provision for pre-school children and their parents had generally come to be accepted.

The major children's library of the early 1970s was Birmingham Central Library. This was: 'Housed on the ground floor with access both from the main entrance and from the outside, it comprises a carpeted lending area with reading space, display areas and flexible storytelling facilities, and an activities room equipped for craft work and similar activities.'[42]

A feature of the 1970s onwards has been the regular budget reductions for public libraries, which at the same time have been urged by central government to run an accountable, customer-oriented, efficient, effective and economic service. Responding to the needs of children and young people – in deprived areas, for example – with reduced financial support has been difficult. Indeed, given decreased resources, children's librarianship in the early 1980s was said to be 'a specialism in need of redefinition'.[43] The rest of the decade seemed concerned with making this 'redefinition', culminating, perhaps in the publication of guidelines for work with children and young people in 1991.[44]

While Godfrey Thompson has shown that over 250 public library buildings were erected in the period 1970–75, he writes that the general picture for 1976–80 was of fewer being built than in the previous ten years.[45] Taking into account the financial situation noted earlier, it may therefore come as a surprise that in the 1980s in excess of 300 new public library buildings were constructed and that extensions and conversions accounted for around a further 300 projects. Most of these would have brought improved facilities for children and young people.

During the 1980s new designs for the shelving and display of library materials began to emerge, to encourage the informal atmosphere of the bookshop as well as to reflect more reader-orientated arrangement. Such a general change has also affected children's departments and a notable feature for younger readers has been the colourful and varied 'play and display' furniture the popularity of which seems to have replaced that of the carpeted pit.[46]

In the 1990s preliminary figures would seem to indicate a continuing decline in new library building projects for 1990–93. Whether this situation will continue, and its implications for children's facilities, remains to be seen.

Separate branches for children

The separate children's lending library, opened in Nottingham in 1882, is said to be the first of its kind in Britain. Similarly separate was the Powell Boys' Reading Room and Library that opened in Wigan in 1893, combining lending library and reading room. Boys' and Girls' House in Toronto, Canada (1924), next to the public library, provided a lending service, reading and story hour rooms and a theatre. In the same year a library built for children, L'Heure Joyeuse, opened in Paris. There were also a few American examples of separate children's library in the period 1914–41 in the New York area; none continued as such after 1965, mainly due to changes in their neighbourhoods.

A number of separate children's branch libraries were created in the 1950s and 1960s, mostly in the London area, for example: Lewis Carroll Library (Islington, 1952); Liverpool Central Junior Library (1958); Churchill Gardens Children's Library (Westminster, 1960); Dick Whittington Junior Library (Islington, 1962); Dover Central Children's Library (1963).

Another approach, that did not put the children's library on another site but kept it distinctly separate, was that demonstrated by the design of Crawley Branch Library (West Sussex) in 1963. Here the children's library, with its own entrance, was linked to the main building by a short corridor. While there are other similar design solutions to that at Crawley, no separately sited children's branch appears to have been built in the UK since those of the 1950s and 1960s, other than that in the Wiend Centre, Wigan and opened in 1987, and that at Cheltenham opened in 1988.

The separate children's branch library is, as already shown, used elsewhere in the world. Further examples include a children's library built in Accra close to the main library of the Ghana Library Board, and the municipal library system of Thessaloniki, Greece, which has a number of such service points, although they occupy a floor in a building devoted to other, non-library activities rather than their own separately sited accommodation. In the former USSR there was a large network of separate branch libraries for children, and teenagers, generously sized and well furnished.

While separate libraries for children may stem from a lack of space rather than a desire to provide a separate service, the advantages of such an arrangement are that they can be established where large numbers of children are to be found and are thus more easily accessible to them. The main disadvantage is said to be that it does not encourage the change from child to adult user.

Toy libraries

The provision of toys to children by public libraries can now be said to be a worldwide movement, with services being offered in many countries. Probably the first public library service was that given in California, through the Los Angeles County Toy Loan Program, in the 1930s, and continuing to the present day. Elsewhere in the world – Sweden, Switzerland and the UK, for example – provision is more recent, a phenomenon of the 1970s and 1980s.[47]

The first toy library to be housed in a public library in the UK was that at Whitehawk Branch Library, Brighton, in 1973. This move towards toy provision can be seen as a desire to provide an even wider range of library materials for children, although there is a continuing doubt among librarians as to whether toys are a public library responsibility. This doubt can be seen in the way that the development of toy provision has largely taken place outside public libraries, although a number accommodate toys on behalf of groups, while some, probably a small number, provide their own service. The following brief details indicate the variety of arrangements that have developed and the differing purposes of such collections.

Cunninghame District Toy Library, set up in 1989, offers a service for under-5s and/or children with special needs in areas of social deprivation through five branch libraries,[48] while the pioneer, Whitehawk Branch Library, tries to provide for all ages – children and adults. Muswell Hill Toy Library, an independent, registered charity, opened in 1986, operates a room adjoining the children's library, with staff to man the service provided by Haringey Council. The service caters for parents, carers, professional childcare workers and children. At Newton Le Willows, the community library provides accommodation, including heating and lighting, while a local charity, Disability Network UK, provides funds for the toys, and St Helens Community College the staff. This toy service, started in 1988, 'aims to provide a community service, a training place for students and a resource centre for college staff'.[49]

Advantages claimed for toy provision are varied, but significant ones are that it encourages borrowers to make use of other services, encourages greater use of other library materials, and is crucial to the proper development of children. Problems are largely those relating to inadequate resources – time, space, staff and money – to make toy provision a completely satisfactory service.[50]

Libraries for young adults

A development of the 1930s was the attention given to adolescents – the teenagers or young adults of more recent decades. The pioneer was Walthamstow in 1924, which created a separate 'intermediate section', with its own entrance, for those aged 14–17. The year before, however, Nottingham's northern branch library had instituted a section of books for young adults and, around the same time, Coventry had experimented with displays of books for adolescents but they were discontinued in 1932. In the London area in 1934, five libraries reported having intermediate sections for adolescents in addition to Walthamstow. The idea was also current of libraries acting as clubs for teenagers.

In 1936 Northampton opened a room for adolescents, placed between the children's and adult rooms, with entry from both, and this was generally thought better than a separate entrance. In addition to Northampton, 15 other places reported special sections or departments for adolescents in 1939; a development that the outbreak of the Second World War brought to an end.

Work with young people in the USA had begun at the New York Public Library in 1919. However, the Robert Louis Stevenson Room at Cleveland in 1925 was the first to be completely concerned with work with teenagers. In 1926 a library for teenagers was provided in the Los Angeles Central Library. Ellis considers that while work with teenagers started in Britain and the USA at about the same time, its progress was greater in the latter, especially after 1945.[51]

Preston opened a self-contained youth library in 1953, containing both reference and lending material, which functioned for almost 20 years, closing in 1972. In 1954 it was reported that 84 authorities made special provision for adolescents, mostly in the London area, and again in 1959 that the collections for teenagers in that area were usually kept in the children's library but sometimes in the adult library.

In the period from about 1958 to 1968, there were further attempts to get to grips with the question of service to teenagers. Leicestershire experimented in 1964 with the provision of books to youth clubs, with mobile libraries visiting some youth clubs when in session, and Walsall opened a teenage library in 1965. One teenage library that attracted a good deal of attention was that opened by Lincoln in 1968 and aimed principally at non-readers aged from 13–14, although older teenagers were attracted to it. Its Friday evening club, with music, dancing and coffee, was probably unusual for the times.[52]

A Library Association survey of 1968 showed that of 409 returns, only two libraries provided a separate teenage section or room; about 15% included books for teenagers in the adult library; 28% provided them in the children's library. This was thought to be a substantial improvement since 1959, although Ellis comments 'The youth service was vocal in the 1960s on the subject of cooperation with public libraries, but except in a minority of instances did not evoke an enthusiastic response from librarians.'[53]

In 1960 the American Library Association had recommended that work with teenagers in large public libraries should be organized as a specialized service on the same basis as work with children and adults and that a separate room was an asset. However, the Young Adult Roundtable of the California Library Association stated in 1964 that 'a separate room is not recommended except perhaps in extremely large library buildings'.[54] The Boston Public Library of the early 1970s was planned to provide 6,400 ft² (595 m²) for a young adult area on a mezzanine floor.

In Britain it was suggested that because the school leaving age would be raised to 16 in 1972/73, work among younger teenagers should be mainly the responsibility of schools. Certainly librarians have not accepted the challenge of library service to young adults; the reported limited developments of the 1980s and early 1990s for this group at Bradford and elsewhere are described later in Chapter 8.

Mobile libraries and other road vehicles

C. R. Eastwood has shown that it was the municipal library services in the UK that first took up and developed the mobile library in the early decades of this century. County libraries, while slow to accept the mobile library, rapidly adopted it as a feature of their post-1945 developments.[55] It is surprising, however, that, as late as the mid-1960s, librarians were still debating whether to provide a children's service on mobile libraries, and many did not do so.[56] Ellis notes that, by 1970, every county, except East Sussex, operated a mobile library service, but many only provided children's books for the under-5s.[57]

Other types of vehicle that have come to be used for mobile library services are trailer and container libraries. These are designed to take the place of static service points, as they stay in one spot for a few days and are then taken to another site. Their larger size means that they are able to carry bigger bookstocks and offer a wider range of facilities; usually this means much better services for children than can be provided on the standard mobile library vehicle.

Separate children's mobile libraries are known to have existed in the Netherlands, America, Sweden and in Bombay in the 1950s and 1960s, but Eastwood mentions only one UK example of the period, that of Bermondsey.[58] Two other children's mobiles, in Ealing and Southwark, were noted by Margot Lindsay, nevertheless, as being introduced in 1962.[59] In the UK, however, this development of separate provision has generally taken the form of the holiday mobile, the bookbus, and vehicles devoted largely to younger children.

Nottinghamshire is credited with pioneering the idea in 1958 of the holiday mobile to serve children while schools are shut. In the following years, the concept was taken up by others, including Wiltshire and Denbighshire, sometimes using spare mobile vehicles. Hammersmith and Fulham, however, launched a more obviously children's holiday mobile, touring the streets in the summer of 1975, whose exterior paintwork, painted flamingo pink, featured the darker attractive design of the Pied Piper followed by children in modern dress.[60] At other times it visited schools where access to library services was difficult. Shropshire's Pied Piper mobile was introduced in the following year and the library vehicle was said to look more like an ice-cream van.[61]

It was in the mid-1970s that the bookbus idea took-off. Leicestershire began with a converted, eye-catching, double-decker bus in 1975, which offered competitions, storytelling and film shows to children under 14 and their parents during the summer holidays. Southampton also put a bookbus on the road in 1975 – painted pink! Bookbus services that started a little later tended to move away from the holiday mobile idea to ones that 'have their roots in the need to reach traditional non-users and to overcome the prejudices and ignorance of traditional building-based library service'.[62] Derbyshire and Newcastle in 1978, Bradford in 1979 and Hackney in 1980 all began bookbus services. Where buses were double-deckers, it was usual for the library area to be on the lower deck and the upper deck used for activities, storytelling, or exhibitions. The purpose of such buses could be quite varied and not confined to work with children, although they were usually the principal target clients. For example: Newcastle – to reach children in 'stress areas'; Southampton – to play a community liaison role; Bradford – to provide informal and relevant library and information services to socially deprived communities that were not confined to book related activities; Hackney – to publicize all aspects of the library service to local people. Bookbuses also visit schools and play and other groups, in addition to their street stops.

Mobile library visits to schools were said by Eastwood not to be usual in Britain in the late 1960s, but seem to have become more common from the 1970s onwards, now that more specialized vehicles for children are in use. The various pros and cons of such visits are rehearsed by Eastwood, who points out that in spite of a long tradition of this in America, there was some disquiet voiced. Some American librarians felt that there was a danger that the mobile library visit to the school would be seen by the school as a cheap and convenient substitute for the provision of a proper school library, and presumably that danger exists in Britain too.[63]

This is perhaps the place to mention the work of the National Playbus Association, which promotes the use of mobile facilities for children and communities in need, and this includes bookbuses and toy library buses. The association recognizes that mobile resources constitute a flexible and responsive service to those suffering social isolation: 'Whether this occurs in communities in rural areas, new out of town housing estates or in troubled inner cities.'[64] This philosophy is very much in line with those library services offering bookbus facilities and which recognize that the needs of children, whether as individuals or groups, can be met by such vehicles.

However, in spite of the diversity of the bookbus concept, dedicated children's mobiles continued to appear and Kirklees' vehicle of the early 1980s had startling outside paintwork, a wheelchair lift, toilet, running water, worktops and display space. More recent road vehicles to serve children include those at Birmingham, Gloucestershire, Cynon Valley and Hampshire. Such vehicles can also be aimed at young adults and in 1985 it was reported that the mobile library 'can and is being used in urban areas to compensate for lack of existing library provision for young people [i.e., teenagers]'.[65]

References

1 For a discussion of kiosk libraries *see* Akin, L. and Dowd, F. S., 'A national survey of portable library structures', *Public libraries*, **32** (5), 1993, 267–9.

2 Capital Planning Information, *Library and information provision in rural areas in England and Wales*, London, HMSO, 1993, 37–8.

3 Ray, S. G., Library service to schools, 3rd edn., London, Library Association, 1982, 1.

4 Idem, 2.

5 Kelly, T., *History of public libraries in Great Britain 1845–1975*, London, Library Association, 1977, 399–401.

6 Lowrie, J. E. and Nagabura, M. (eds.), *School libraries: international developments*, 2nd edn., Metuchen, NJ, Scarecrow Press, 1991, 7, 53, 63, 65, 221.

7 Ray, op. cit., 4.

8 Shepherd, J., 'Children's librarianship and school libraries', in *British librarianship and information work 1981–1985* (ed.) D. W. Bromley and A. M. Allott, London, Library Association, 1988, 155.

9 Ellis, A., *Library services for young people in England and Wales 1830–1970*, Oxford, Pergamon Press, 1971, 110.

10 Ray, op. cit., 4.

11 Idem, 9.

12 Idem, 3.

13 Scottish Education Department, *Standards for the public library service in Scotland*, Edinburgh, HMSO, 1969, 32.

14 Department of Education and Science, *The school library*, London, HMSO, 1967, 22.

15 Barnes, M. and Ray, S., *Youth library work*, London, Bingley, 1968, 43.

16 Ellis, op. cit., 114.

17 Idem, 149–51.

18 Kelly, op. cit., 136–7.

19 Department of Education and Science, *The public library service: reorganisation and after*, London, HMSO, 1973, 17.

20 Capital Planning Information, op. cit., 39.

21 Ray, op. cit., 37–8.

22 Ellis, op. cit., 15.

23 Idem, 33, 34.

24 Idem, 34.

25 Kelly, op. cit., 195.

26 Idem, 198.

27 Idem, illus XIII a.

28 Ellis, op. cit., 42.

29 Kelly, op. cit., 239.

30 Ellis, op. cit., 46.

31 Idem, 48.

32 Kelly, op. cit., 256.

33 Idem, 293.

34 Ellis, op. cit., 66–8.

35 Kelly, op. cit., 371–2.

36 Ellis, op. cit., 120.

37 Idem, 122.

38 Idem, 126–7.

39 Harrison, K. C., 'Public libraries in London', in *British librarianship and information science 1966–1970* (ed.) H. A. Whatley, London, Library Association, 1972, 443.

40 Ray, C., 'Children's and young people's libraries', in *British librarianship and information science 1966–1970* (ed.) H. A. Whatley, London, Library Association, 1972, 480.

41 Kelly, op. cit., 436; Kelly's figures have been corrected from his quoted source.

42 Ray, C., 'Children's libraries', in *British librarianship and information science 1971–1975* (ed.) H. A. Whatley, London, Library Association, 1977, 182–3.

43 Shepherd, J., 'Children's librarianship and school libraries', in *British librarianship and information work 1981–1985* (ed.) D. W. Bromley and A. M. Allott, London, Library Association, 1988, vol. 1, 162.

44 Library Association, *Children and young people: Library Association guidelines for public library service*, London, Library Association, 1991.

45 Thompson, G., 'Building, equipment and conservation', in *British librarianship and information work 1976–1980* (ed.) L. J. Taylor, London, Library Association, 1982, vol. 1, 25–6.

46 Dewe, M., 'Trends in UK public library buildings during the 1980s', in *Petrification or flexibility*, Stockholm, Swedish National Council for Cultural Affairs, 1992, 31–6.

47 For an international perspective *see* Morgan, S. M., 'The role of public libraries in lending toys', (M.Lib. thesis), University of Wales, 1991, 57–80.

48 Idem, 46–7.

49 Idem, 19–20.

50 Idem, 53–4.

51 Ellis, op. cit., 56.

52 Idem, 146.

53 Idem, 145.

54 Idem, 146.

55 Eastwood, C. R., *Mobile libraries and other public transport*, London, Association of Assistant Librarians, 1967, 35–41.

56 Idem, 232.

57 Ellis, op. cit., 123.

58 Eastwood, op. cit., 234.

59 Lindsay, M., 'Mobile libraries – forward or back?', *New library world*, **79** (939), 1978, 168.

60 Ellis, op. cit., 123; Kelly, op. cit., 402, 436, illus XVI a.

61 Orton, G. I. J., *An illustrated history of mobile library services in the United Kingdom*, Sudbury, Suffolk, Branch and Mobile Libraries Group of the Library Association, 1980, 83–4.

62 'Books and buses: the librarian's roadshow', *PLG news*, **15**, 1983, 11.

63 Eastwood, op. cit., 236.

64 National Playbus Association, *Annual report 1992–3*, Bristol, National Playbus Association, 1993, 4.

65 Library Association, Community Services Group in Scotland, *Library services to teenagers*, [Glasgow], Library Association Community Services Group in Scotland, 1985, para. (d).

3 STAGES IN THE CREATION OF THE LIBRARY SPACE RESOURCE

This chapter provides an overview of the main stages concerned with the creation of a library building. The latter stages, however, are dealt with in more detail, as they are not developed further in this book, although some aspects of design are dealt with in Chapter 10. The first two stages, pre-planning and planning, are particularly important to the librarian, both because of the input he or she will make, and for their significance in laying the foundations for the success of the whole project. These two stages are dealt with more comprehensively, therefore, in the next chapter. Some indication is also given in this chapter as to how the planning and design process might be used for other space resource situations, such as remodelling a school library or children's department, or launching a road vehicle for use with children and young people.

Understanding the process

While, according to circumstances, the involvement and responsibility of a school or children's librarian may vary from one building project to another, it is vitally important that they understand the complete process that lies behind the successful creation of library accommodation in order to appreciate what the librarian's contribution is to be at the various stages that are involved. This understanding will also demonstrate that good library design results from a process of gradual refinement – of raw data about those to be served by the building to the opening and successful use of the finished premises. Without a knowledge of this complete process there is a danger that the librarian may pay more attention to the end result (the physical structure and what it will contain), rather than doing the information-gathering, analysis, thinking and planning that should precede that achievement. In other words, the librarian's approach may place the planning emphasis on what the library is to be like as a building, important as this might be, rather than on what purpose it is to serve and how this is to be properly and successfully achieved within it. An understanding of the planning and design process also emphasizes that the librarian must learn to work with a variety of specialists in an harmonious way, a collaboration discussed in Chapter 5.

This planning and design process can be helpfully illustrated perhaps by outlining the steps involved in the creation of a new public library, of which accommodation for children and young people will form part. A similar planning and design process will be necessary for a school, although a contrasting building type, of which the library forms a unique part.[1]

The librarian referred to in the outline below is the librarian responsible for the complete project, not the children's librarian, whose detailed contribution to such a scheme is considered in the next chapter. Other planning and design situations where the school or children's librarian might take a more central role and overall responsibility, such as a conversion or renovation, are considered towards the end of this chapter. Although not always the principal participant, the librarian with overall responsibility for a particular project has a role to play in all the stages of the creation of a library building.

The pre-planning stage

The process of planning a library building begins with someone, usually the librarian, recognizing the need for new or improved public library accommodation. In a public library system, that need may be documented to a greater or lesser degree as part of an audit or review of service point provision, with a schedule of priorities for action related to a capital programme. The need for a particular service point has to be thoroughly investigated and documented, including the estimated size and cost, and agreement for the proposed building project to go ahead obtained from the local authority. Such agreement may possibly be only in principle at this stage. The site of the library and its approximate cost may also be determined at this time. Any course of action which will have been recommended by the librarian will be based on an evaluation of the possible options, for example, whether a new or remodelled library is the best solution in the prevailing circumstances.

Another strand of the process at this initial stage is the improvement, where necessary, of the librarian's knowledge about library planning and design through, for example, reading, attendance at courses, visits to trade exhibitions (such as the Library Resources Exhibition) and to other libraries, the collection of library shelving and furniture suppliers' catalogues (and visits to their showrooms) and of plans, data, and photographs about existing library buildings, and familiarization with the appropriate standards and current building costs. Equally important these days is for the librarian to undertake a technology-update exercise to ensure an awareness of the latest developments in information and other technologies. Given what is involved, this updating process, as regards planning and design, and information technology, will extend into and be utilized in the next stages of the building project described below.

There will also be the task of educating others involved in the project about trends in library service and space provision both formally through the documentation prepared for the project and informally through consultation and discussion. At the end of this stage the librarian should know in sufficient detail what needs to be provided by way of library services and facilities in the proposed building to obtain approval for the project for funding purposes and then move to the next stage.

The planning stage

The major task for the librarian at this stage is to write the brief for the building for the architect. This is a document, which may be of considerable size for a large building, describing the requirements of the library in both quantitative and qualitative terms sufficient for the architect to commence the design process. It translates the details gathered in the pre-planning stage about the community to be served, its library and information needs, and the present library service and its necessary proposed future development to meet those needs, into a statement about the space requirements, functions and qualities of a building to fulfil such demands. It is important that both staff and library users are involved in making inputs to the briefing document.

At the heart of this document will be a description of the basic elements of the library building: space for users, for staff, and for the collection of library materials in a variety of formats. Increasingly in calculating what space is required, the librarian has to take into account that required by staff and users for equipment to work with and to access electronic information both within and without the library. To the total for these three elements must be added space for those parts of the building which have no library function, such as stairs, toilets, lifts, heating and ventilating plant, and an allowance for circulation space to allow people to move around the building. In the architect's plans such non-assignable space (or balance area as it is also known) should be kept to a minimum, certainly not more than 25% of the total space and preferably less.

The design stage

Based on the information in the brief, the architect should initially develop various broad possible design solutions or concepts, related to the given site and available funding, for consideration by the client. Such a concept, or schematic design, will demonstrate, for example, how the building will occupy the site, its shape, the number of floors, and the location of major elements of the library. Once a general design concept has been agreed upon, sketch plans will develop the design and working drawings will follow to provide constructional documents for the builder. Once the sketch plans have been finalized there should be no further modification of the brief or earlier work will have been abortive.

While the architect may design the interior and the layout of shelving and furniture, the former may be put in the hands of an interior designer and the latter made the responsibility of a specialist supplier of library shelving and furniture.

This stage will close with the preparation by a quantity surveyor of bills of quantity (a detailed statement of the quality and quantity of the materials to be used in the construction of the library), and a call for tenders. Such tenders will indicate at what cost the contractors can construct the building; one of the tenders will be chosen unless all are in excess of the funds available. In the latter case the proposed plans will need review and amendment and the design process repeated. Alternatively, increased funding can be requested or negotiations entered into over the lowest tender.

The construction stage

Unless there are specific problems to be resolved during construction, this can be the least demanding stage for the librarian but he or she should be kept informed of progress, inspect the building from time to time, and participate in checking the building towards completion. However, Bill Chase writes that design decisions are made during construction and warns that:

> A librarian who leaves the construction process to others will find some of his or her plans compromised (behind his or her back) by the exigencies of getting the facility built within budget . . . Few librarians should try to represent their institutions in the bargaining that goes on at the construction stage, but all should make themselves available for consultation . . . A good architect is especially important here, for the proposal of alternative, more expeditious designs than the original can turn a discouraging situation into a satisfying one.[2]

The librarian's nightmare is that there will be a cut in funding during the construction phase which will reduce the final amount of space available and/or affect the shelving, furnishings and fittings that can be afforded. As indicated by Chase, the resolution of these or other changes must involve consultation with the librarian and some modification of the original plan may be necessary. More optimistically, inspections of the building during the construction stage may suggest improvements, such as an exchange of function between spaces, the rightness of which may not have been fully apparent until the library's structure was in place. The committee and team structures discussed in Chapter 5 provide mechanisms for helping to ensure that problems and design issues occurring during the construction of the library building can be successfully resolved. Ruth Griffith recommends that the librarian 'Set priorities early so that, should cutbacks be necessary, you will know what is essential and what can be postponed or eliminated.'[3]

The construction will proceed from foundations, structure, enclosure, to the installation of services and the application of finishes. Construction work is regularly inspected by the clerk of works to ensure that the architect's instructions are being followed. Towards the completion of the library a list of unsatisfactory or unfinished work will be drawn up by the architect and the librarian for remedial action and completion. When this has been satisfactorily carried out, the building is handed over to the local authority.

The occupancy stage

Once the building has been completed, its library functions are made more apparent through the installation of shelving, furniture and equipment, including automated and mechanical systems, by their suppliers. Where furniture and equipment from the old building are to be reused in the new one, arrangements will need to be put in hand for their removal to the new location.

A major removal task will be that of moving in the book- and other stock from the old building, or receiving new stock for a new building. A library move, particularly of the former kind, needs to be planned in considerable detail if it is to be done quickly, smoothly and accurately.[4] Such a plan will include:

(a) quantifying what has to be moved – the collection of books and other library material

(b) selecting suitable assistance – deciding whether to use volunteers, hire professional movers or temporary staff, for example

(c) deciding on the most suitable time for the move – one that will avoid major disruptions to the library service

(d) publicizing the move to library users and others, including details of closure if necessary

(e) preparing written instructions – to include staff responsibilities and the order of the move

(f) preparing for the move – weeding stock (allocating a regular amount of time to this activity) and the marking up of new shelf locations, for example.

The move itself will probably involve using special packing boxes, and these may require road transportation between the old and new sites.

Other matters that will take place at this occupancy stage, and will need to planned in advance, include:

(a) a staff familiarization programme for the new accommodation, its equipment and procedures

(b) the formulation of new rules, regulations and processes for new services, arrangements and facilities

(c) arrangements for an opening ceremony[5]

(d) the preparation of publicity and printed information about the building, its services, facilities and their availability

(e) the planning for visits by librarians, architects and others interested in the new building.

The evaluation stage

The final stage in the process, which occurs after the opening of the finished library, is its evaluation for building and other faults, and for its functional success in use. In both cases remedial action may need consideration and appropriate steps taken. For example, it might be necessary

(a) to improve the accuracy and helpfulness of signs

(b) to arrange for the fine-tuning of mechanical and other systems and

(c) for the movement or adjustment of the issue desk location.

The architect, librarian and builder will inspect the building six to twelve months after completion, and the builder will be provided with a list of outstanding defects; once remedied the builder's account will be finalized.

Post-occupancy evaluation of the library, as part of a space management programme, is also worth carrying out when a longer period of time has elapsed after opening, perhaps two or five years later, although there seems to be little evidence of this occurring a great deal in practice. The information gathered from such an exercise, which could include the observation of users and staff, the use of questionnaires and interviews, and the measuring of temperature and lighting levels, may suggest appropriate building maintenance and space planning responses. Lessons learned can also be important for the future success of other libraries that are being or will be planned within a library system.[6]

Performance measures and indicators

One way of regularly and consistently evaluating the school or children's library's accommodation, both new and old, in order to demonstrate its achievements, maintain its quality and to help with its future planning and development, is through the formulation and use of performance measures and indicators. A.J. Meadows says that a 'performance measure provides a direct quantitative statement about an activity . . . the result necessarily consists of a numerical value'[7] – the number of users of the school or children's library at particular times of the day, for example. On the other hand, a performance indicator has been described as 'a statement of what is considered to be a good standard of performance or appropriate achievement in a particular field'.[8]

Using performance indicators, Devon Education and Devon Libraries have jointly created a handbook for evaluating a secondary school library in all its aspects – what it does and what it provides – which is also there to assist the librarian in the preparation of a short, standardized annual report (with recommendations) for supervisor or head teacher, as appropriate.[9] The Devon performance indicators include sections on: accommodation and ambience; physical access, and access to materials. Against particular indicators, for example, 'Leisure and formal seating capacity as a % of the total roll', minimum and optimum indicators are given (4% and 7% respectively in this case), with a column for comments on the present situation. Another column indicates the methods and sources to be used to arrive at an appropriate assessment of such matters as: justification for multiple libraries; lighting and ventilation, and wheelchair access. The methods include observation, and the views of students, teachers and library resource staff.[10]

Hertfordshire Library Service have produced a somewhat more simplified and reworded version of the Devon document, which also covers accommodation (including ambience, access and guiding), and precedes the list of indicators with the statement: 'For some [schools] the OPTIMUM column may take time to achieve but the MINIMUM should be the base level from which to work.'[11]

The international edition of *Indicators of quality for school library/media programs*,[12] is another useful evaluation tool. This has been drawn up to help facilitate the creation of local standards for school libraries at both regional and local levels. The listed indicators are goals, emphasizing the quality aspects of the library service, and can be rewritten to relate to a particular school or regional service. Using the document, each item in its seven categories, that include categories for staff, materials and equipment, and physical facilities, can be checked by a school library for its degree of acceptance and degree of implementation on a scale of 1–5 in both instances. For example: 'Space will be provided in the Library/Media Center for diverse activities, quiet and active, individual and group in an atmosphere conducive to learning.'[13] The publication suggests that once 'quality goals have been determined, standards (quantitative goals) can be written'. Following the formulation of local standards, long-range plans and estimates of costs necessary to achieve goals of quality, including those for accommodation, can be prepared.

For public libraries, the Office of Arts and Libraries publication, *Keys to success*, suggests ways of measuring input for facilities/premises and access to library equipment (the cost of building or acquiring library equipment, plus maintenance and associated administrative costs), and of developing various types of indicators. [14] For example:

1   Service output measures
    e.g. amount and quality of facilities; reliability of equipment; availability and accessibility of the library and its equipment.
2   Service effectiveness measures
    e.g. amount of and purpose of use of the library; numbers of uses of equipment.
3   Operational performance indicators
    e.g. cost per square metre of space; cost per item of equipment.
4   Effectiveness indicators
    e.g. user satisfaction with and importance of the availability of the library and reliability of equipment.
5   Cost-effectiveness indicators
    e.g. cost per visit; cost per use of equipment.
6   Impact indicators
    e.g. number of visits; number of uses of equipment per capita.[15]

These measures and indicators could be adapted for evaluating space and equipment provision for children and young people in particular libraries. The American publication, *Output measures for public library service to children*, addresses young library users directly, and, as far as space is concerned, indicates ways of measuring visits per child, use of the overall building by children, and their use of furniture and equipment in the children's room. It also shows the potential space, furniture and equipment implications of determining such measures: a building can be shown to be too small to handle more business; that more, or less, seating is required; that another OPAC terminal is needed.[16]

The work of Holly Willett in devising environmental rating scales for public library children's services provides librarians with a comprehensive tool for specifically evaluating aspects of children's provision, including physical facilities, rather than adapting more general formulations.[17] Use of Willett's environmental rating scales permits a comparison of the value system which guides public library service to children with actual provision; in other words performance indicators are used to ascertain the quality of children's services on a whole range of issues. There are over 200 questions to be rated in the version of the scales intended for large and medium-sized libraries. As with all evaluation systems, there is a necessity for a set of goals and objectives to be in place against which performance can be evaluated or rated. Willett's system allows rating on a seven point scale: inadequate; minimal; good, and excellent, with numbered mid-points between where all conditions of the lower level (stated in the ratings) are met but only some of the next. The scales suggest qualities rather than exact phenomena when considering particular questions about the library environment. For the physical aspects of the children's library, such questions can relate to:

    (a) staff availability when patrons enter the children's room
    (b) provision of locked storage for library equipment and supplies
    (c) the provision of bicycle racks
    (d) doors that can be used by young children
    (e) furnishings for routine use by young children and their adults
    (f) office and workroom space for staff.[18]

Performance measures and indicators and the way they are used and described can present an unhelpful and confusing picture, but there is no doubt that librarians, including school and children's librarians, must learn to use these techniques to defend, improve and advance the quality of their library service, including its accommodation.

Other space planning situations

The stages of the planning and design process described above, suitably adapted, could also be used, for example, to create a library facility (where none has existed before) out of redundant space in a school building, for the substantial remodelling of an existing school library or young people's accommodation in a public library, or for designing a road vehicle for library service to schools or work with children and young people. A similar situation to that of adapting existing space for library service is that of creating temporary, workable accommodation to be used while permanent facilities are being constructed or converted.

Adapting spaces

In her book, *Adapting spaces for resource-based learning*, Barbara Atherton provides a model for the adaptation of space for resource-based learning in schools that bears a similarity to the stages outlined above, although special emphasis is given to adapting space within identified constraints.[19] The model has the following stages:

1   Establish the facts – by analysing the present situation.
2   Identify the needs – by describing the ideal requirements.
3   Consider the constraints – finance, legal/health and safety regulations, staffing, the school building.
4   Design the adaptation – this involves redefining the requirements, discussion with staff and advisors, preparation of the final brief, and the commencement of the adaptation.
5   Evaluation – to ensure it is meeting the identified needs and to assess its effect on the use of resources, and thereby identify matters for corrective action and future development.

The model is followed by a series of discussion points under each of the above stages with some indication of possible actions and implications. Some of these discussion points are, for example:

(a) What major factors (i) encourage use (ii) inhibit resource use?
(b) Are there any special areas, e.g, use of film or TV, you would like to develop?
(c) How satisfactory are the facilities for staff to prepare materials?
(d) Can any changes be made in the existing allocation and use of space within the school?[20]

These discussion points could be used by school librarians as the basis for planning local adaptation projects and providing input to the brief. The book is rounded off by a case study of this 'approach in action' in an infant school of 200 children with nursery attached, and helps demonstrate its usefulness and application.[21] In the evaluation of the resulting adaptation, Atherton notes that: 'However, there was still much to be done in terms of encouraging staff, developing skills and attitudes and increasing everyone's knowledge of the use of resources.'[22] Thus the evaluation of a library project must be concerned with what a building or adaptation achieves, as well as its satisfactory functioning and soundness.

Without using a model or framework to plan building projects, the result can be a less than satisfactory experience for the librarian (especially if, as in small-scale projects, the librarian is largely on his or her own with no specialist assistance), and can lead to unsatisfactory accommodation for the library.

Renovation of existing space

From her experience of renovating a youth services department, Winifred Kurtz suggests that when making a major change to a department the following points need to be taken into account:

1 Make an objective assessment of the current facility and determine its advantages and disadvantages.
2 Have definite goals in mind
   (a) plan thoroughly and carefully
   (b) get professional advice if possible
   (c) think things through
3 Assess what has been accomplished
   (a) were goals achieved?
   (b) have future needs been considered?
   (c) has space allotted for redesign been checked?

These comments on a renovation project helpfully underline the continuing significance of the pre-planning, planning and evaluation stages to all building projects. Kurtz ends by writing: 'Most importantly, keep a sense of humor. Without that you do yourself a disservice as well as your co-workers.'[23]

Temporary accommodation

Unless a new, free-standing library is to be built exactly on the site of the old one, the question of finding temporary accommodation for the library service does not arise. However, the complete remodelling of a school library or public library premises for children and young people may require a move to a temporary location or a constant reorganization of space and services to allow for building work to proceed and the library to remain open. In either case the librarian will have to give some thought to the impact of the temporary move or space reorganization on library services: how this will be dealt with and, where a temporary location is likely to be of some duration, how the temporary space can be best utilized. Both of the above situations, but particularly the latter, will mean that an extra move of library materials, furniture, etc will have to be planned. Particularly important of the planning steps noted by Atherton, and of that for the renovation of existing space, will be that of fully identifying the constraints posed by the temporary location, such as the amount of available space and floor loading.

If remodelling, refurbishment or relocation of a school library starts and finishes within a holiday period, a temporary library location may not be necessary. However, it will be necessary to plan to pack, label and store the library's collection of material until the work is completed. It is helpful to have the most used material, reference works perhaps, easily accessible and retrievable in case building work is not finished on time.

Road vehicles

A new mobile library vehicle is a somewhat different situation to a new building in that the librarian will play a more active role as a 'designer' as well as planner, specifying to the coachbuilder which standard vehicle chassis is to be used and the layout that will be required in a vehicle of specified dimensions. In his standard work, *The design and construction of mobile libraries*,[24] Ronald Pybus outlines a planning and design process for a 'standard' mobile library that reflects the stages described in the earlier part of this chapter, and which he sees as also appropriate for other specialist vehicles, such as a schools library service mobile.

While rightly concerned with involving staff in the pre-planning of the vehicle, there is perhaps insufficient emphasis by Pybus on studying and information-gathering about the communities to be served. The availability of such details might assist in making initial decisions about the role the vehicle is to serve and where it is to operate, the type of vehicle required (standard vehicle or trailer, for example), and its size. It might be argued that such pre-planning is even more important for specialized vehicles for service to schools, children and young people.

During the planning stage, the matters just noted will be finally determined, as well as such questions as the materials, services and facilities to be offered on the vehicle. These will be described in the written specification for the vehicle, which can also specify, for example, which heating and shelving systems are to be installed.

After the specification has gone out to tender and a coachbuilder selected, Pybus suggests that a number of visits be made during construction and these may be stated in the specification. These visits might occur: on completion of the basic structure; prior to the installation of shelves; and at the time of delivery. He suggests that other inspections might be made, for example, halfway through the construction stage; when shelving, counter and outer skin have been fitted, and prior to the final painting.

Pybus rightly emphasizes the process of staff familiarization with the vehicle, following its acceptance from the coachbuilder, and the use of the warranty period for correcting vehicle faults, but nothing is said about evaluating the vehicle in use, in the ways suggested earlier in this chapter. This seems particularly important for such a vehicle, given its relatively short life-span of ten years (compared with that for a building), and therefore its replacement in the foreseeable future.

Selection and ordering of library materials, furniture and equipment

At some point in the above process, probably while construction or remodelling is under way, it will be necessary to:

(a) select books and other library materials and, in a situation where no library has existed before, find a place where they can be received, processed and catalogued

(b) select, order and arrange for the installation of shelving, furniture and equipment, including automated equipment.

Such requirements will have been recognized, detailed and budgeted for at the planning stage. Consequently, at the same time as design and construction work is proceeding, and in order that items will be available at the occupancy stage, and the opening of the library will not be unnecessarily delayed, the librarian should set in motion the selection and purchasing of library materials, shelving, furniture and equipment. As with construction of the building itself, library shelving and other furniture and equipment suppliers may be asked to tender for the supply of such items, following the drawing up of a detailed specification.

In dealing with library shelving and furniture suppliers timing is of crucial importance. Dependent upon how this task is to be precisely handled by school or public library, it should allow time for a layout plan to be completed and agreed, a quotation to be prepared, financial approval of the order (if necessary), and manufacturing and installation. To help manage this process, it is helpful to get the supplier to quote an actual delivery date based on an assumed date when the order would be placed. Librarians without significant purchasing experience can usefully acquaint themselves with the basics of commercial practice, in particular that orders placed and accepted, even verbally, are binding on both parties.

References

1   The planning and design process is described from a public library viewpoint very fully in Holt, R. M., *Planning library buildings and facilities from concept to completion*, Metuchen, NJ, Scarecrow Press, 1989; from a school library viewpoint in Anderson, P. A., *Planning school library media facilities*, Hamden, Conn., Library Professional Publications, 1990. The architect's approach is detailed in Konya, A., *Libraries: a briefing and design guide*, London, Architectural Press, 1986.

2   Chase, B., 'Drawing strength: skillful design . . . and a little trickery', *School library journal*, **36** (2), 1990, 25.

3   Griffith, R. L., 'Doing your homework', *Illinois libraries*, **60** (10), 1978, 863.

4   A dated but still useful overview is, Spyers-Duran, P., *Moving library materials*, Chicago, American Library Association, 1965. A more recent work is, McDonald, A., *Moving your library*, London, Aslib, 1994.

5   A checklist for a grand opening ceremony is given in, Wozny, J., *Checklists for public library managers*, Metuchen, NJ, Scarecrow Press, 1989, 180–2. This includes such matters as budget, guest selection, outside publicity, platform requirements and special signage.

6   For a description and discussion of post-occupancy evaluation see Lushington, N. and Kusack, J. M., *The design and evaluation of public library buildings*, Hamden, Conn., Library Professional Publications, 1991, 115–204.

7   Meadows, A. J., *Performance assessment in public libraries*, Branch and Mobile Group of the Library Association, 1990, 7.

8   Rotherham, N. et al., *"If you can't measure it, you can't manage it": performance indicators for secondary schools*, Hertfordshire Library Service, 1991, 2.

9   Devon Education and Devon Libraries, *Resources for learning: a handbook for the evaluation of secondary school library resource provision and use*, Exeter, Devon County Council, 1990.

10 Idem, 6–7.

11 Rotherham, op. cit., 6.

12 Illinois Association for Media in Education and International Association of School Librarianship, *Indicators of quality for school library/media programs*, international edn., Illinois, IAME and IASL, 1985.

13 Idem, 8.

14 Office of Arts and Libraries, *Keys to success: performance indicators in public libraries*, London, HMSO, 1990, 13–5, 70, 73–4.

15 Idem, 70, 73–4.

16 Walter, V. A., *Output measures for public library service to children: a manual of standardized procedures*, Chicago, American Library Association, 1992, 25–34.

17 Willett, H. G., 'Looking at environments for children in public libraries', *North Carolina libraries*, **49** (2), 1991, 150–5.

18 Idem, 154–5.

19 Atherton, B., *Adapting spaces for resource-based learning*, London, Council for Educational Technology, 1980, 27–59

20 Idem, 32–6.

21 Idem, 73–91.

22 Idem, 91.

23 Kurtz, W. M., 'Changes, changes', *Illinois libraries*, **70** (1), 1988, 21.

24 Pybus, R. L., *The design and construction of mobile libraries*, 2nd edn., [London], Branch and Mobile Libraries Group of the Library Association, 1990.

4 PLANNING THE SPACE RESOURCE

Two planning situations

The role of the school or children's librarian in planning the space resource will depend precisely on what is being planned. There are two likely situations. The first is where a new public library or school building is being planned, as outlined in the previous chapter, and to which the school or children's librarian will be a *contributor* to the overall scheme. The second situation is where the intended work (whether new or remodelling) is solely concerned with the school or children's library or department, and in this situation the librarian is more *centrally* involved.

There is common planning and design ground in both situations, but, in the second, the responsibility and leadership role of the librarian is likely to be greater. As indicated in the previous chapter, much of the success of a building project turns on the pre-planning and planning stages. In addition to these matters, the ability of the school or children's librarian to create and respond to opportunities for change, and the ability to work with others, particularly as part of a team, are important.

Opportunities for change

While opportunities for new accommodation can often seem unlikely, they can occur with little warning and with pressure to proceed quickly, and so the school or children's librarian should be prepared for such an event by regularly gathering and maintaining information that can be utilized at the pre-planning stage. Systematic attention to space management, including the use of performance measures and indicators, and regular reports to a supervising librarian or head teacher, should mean that much useful information will be built-up for when such situations occur. However, in circumstances where it is appropriate to do so, for example, a proposed remodelling of the library, there is no reason why the librarian should not endeavour to initiate the whole process, particularly where the conditions seem auspicious or need is particularly pressing. By showing both enterprise and preparedness (knowing what is needed in a new or improved library and demonstrating the ability to articulate that in space terms), the school or children's librarian has a better chance of getting what is required and avoids being in the position of merely responding to the initiative and plans of others. Julie Todaro puts the ball right in the librarian's court, when she writes: 'As fads, tastes, staff, library goals, and library priorities change, children's facilities must be restructured to fit these new situations, and it is the children's librarian's responsibility to effect such changes.'[1]

The pre-planning stage

As indicated in the previous chapter, a number of matters are likely to be of concern at this first stage, but of major importance for the school and children's librarian is the question of demonstrating and assessing need – not only to plan to meet it but in order to gain support for the project. This assessment must not only be made in respect of the known local situation but in the context of the wider external environment. As Mary Anderson has written: 'Since facilities are designed around services, and services are designed around patron needs, an understanding of the changing nature of our society and the resulting needs of children in that society is essential for any involved in planning library facilities for children.'[2]

Such changes include:

(a) the size of the child and school population
(b) the number of single parent families
(c) working mothers
(d) dependence of many children on adults to get to the library
(e) that children and young people are increasingly visually oriented
(f) unemployment amongst young people
(g) the scale of paperback publishing
(h) information technology – its current use and future potential
(i) current position and proposed legal changes affecting children and young people – their welfare and education, for example.

For librarians who work with children and young people the local significance and implications of such changes will need consideration. For the school librarian, understanding the changing nature of education and its implications for learning resources and services, and thus the physical requirements of the school library resource centre, will be of particular significance.

Assessing need

This process can be seen as consisting of three components, and, where appropriate, information will be sought from the library's records, user surveys, the use of market-research techniques, as well as internal documents (such as statistical returns), or publicly available ones – census information, for example. Consultation with potential users of a library service in a school or for children and young people, as part of the pre-planning process is discussed in the following chapter. Of equal importance will be the availability of such documents as a mission statement and a strategic plan for the school or the public library service. In assessing need the librarian is not only concerned with the present but with the likely future or projected needs of the community to be served. Writing about the public library building, Anne Fleet, comments that: 'Every head of department must assess how much space is required now, and how much will be required as the community changes.'[3]

(a) Profiling the community to be served

This consists of gathering information from a variety of sources, as indicated above, about the potential user groups (for example, children of various ages, teachers, parents), set in the context of the school or local community and its future development. The answers to specific questions posed during the community profile will be reflected later in the planned library building. For as Arlene Kaspik has written about public libraries:

> Communities differ greatly as do individuals. Problems and concerns of a large suburban community with a great number of young families will differ greatly from those of a small suburban community with a large number of retired single persons. The needs of a large urban library are tremendously different from a small rural one. Yet many of the same questions can be addressed by librarians in each of the settings and used as tools for planning the library that can best meet the needs of the community they serve.[4]

Questions about young people in the local community might relate to:

(a) The local development plan.
Is a new housing estate planned in the catchment area of the proposed public library building?

(b) Population.
What are and will be the numbers of children and young people in different age and ethnic groups? For example: 'In Birmingham the twelve to nineteen population was expected to rise from approximately 100,000 in 1991 to 133,000 in 2001.'[5]

(c) Employment of young people in the community.
What is the nature of local employment? What is the level of unemployment?

(d) Education.
What schools are located in the community and what kind of library provision do they have?

(e) Recreational facilities.
What is provided by way of youth centres and other facilities?

(f) Social and other services.
What community agencies and groups, other than the library, offer services to children and young people?

(g) Transport. How will children and young people come to the library – on foot, by bicycle, with parents, as part of a group or class?

Philip Marshall explains that the service philosophy section of the Library Association's guidelines for public library service to children and young people addresses three key questions, one of which is establishing 'the characteristics of children as a client group and as individuals that affect service provision'. Amongst the 14 issues that should be addressed to facilitate these 3 key issues is the recommendation that the "study of the community is essential to establish the particular local profile of children, families, schools and other agencies'.[6]

Unless each planning situation is viewed afresh, there is a danger of basing the library building, and what is to be provided in it on tradition, the preferences of the librarian and others, and, for example, as regards teenagers, upon our guesses about the types of services . . . wanted. We are also very aware that these guesses were largely based upon stereotypes, issues that had hit the news and on our own memories. Our provision did not really acknowledge the fact that the teenage years see huge changes in a young person's life and attitudes.[7]

Or as Ruth Griffith writing about children's libraries puts it: 'Are these the services we should be providing, given the community we serve, or are they the convenient ones, the ones we have always provided?'

It may be felt that such a community profile is unnecessary to the pre-planning stage of a school library as the community is relatively small in number compared to the wider community and the librarian is fully aware of what is taking place within it. Nevertheless, this is a dangerous assumption to make, for without a structured collection of information about the school community, information may well be overlooked and its implications ignored in the planning of the school library. A list of similar headings to that for children and young people in the community can be compiled and similar questions asked. Examples[8] from Barbara Atherton include:

(a) School population.
   'Is the school roll likely to alter significantly within the foreseeable future?'
(b) Government/local education authority/school policies.
   'Is there a possibility of an amalgamation between two or more schools? Are there . . . reports, policies or proposals currently under discussion which could affect the role and requirements of the school?'
(c) Curriculum.
   'What changes are likely to occur in curriculum content or methods which will affect resource use?'

Other headings might relate to the size, study methods and information needs of particular school groups such as the sixth form, the professional development of teachers, and the plans for information technology within the school.

As is apparent from these sample questions, such a profile should not just be concerned with the present situation but with the likely future developments within the school or public library community being served. From such a profile it should be possible to discern the particular community's library and information needs – for a school population or young people (and those associated with them as parents, teachers and carers) in a given community – within a given planning time-scale. The nature of those library and information needs will determine the services – information skills teaching, loan of book and non-book materials, careers information, project collections, electronic information provision, etc. – to be provided in a school or for children and young people and these will dictate the range and amount of space needed.

(b) Profiling the present library service
To carry out this task, information is documented by the school or children's librarian about, for example, the present stated purpose of the school library or children's

department, the services that are offered, the current level of use of those services, peak periods of use, the library's collections (and their annual growth), numbers of staff, and the library accommodation. This information provides the basis for future projections of growth and use and demonstrates how the current premises handicap necessary present and potential future library development. Given the purpose of the profile, particular attention will be paid, therefore, to documenting the present drawbacks (and any advantages, such as a good location) of the present library premises, and the amount of space available. Details of drawbacks might be categorized under such headings as:

(a) Insufficient space – for staff, children or pupils, materials and equipment.

(b) New services and facilities – the inability to provide for needed developments and improvements.

(c) Comfort and convenience – the absence of an acceptable library environment for both people and library materials, and an unhelpful and time-consuming space arrangement.

(d) Economy of operation and maintenance – both may be excessively costly in terms of staff, time and money.

(e) Alteration and extension – because of its structure and location, the present library may be difficult to alter and/or extend.

(f) Dispersed accommodation – the library service may be unhelpfully dispersed over a number of rooms, floors or buildings.

(c) An outline of the requirements for new or improved library accommodation

From an analysis and comparison of the information provided by the two profiles, the school or children's librarian should be in a position to determine who is to be served and in what ways, and the general nature and requirements of the new or improved accommodation. This necessarily involves some preliminary rethinking of such matters as the library or department's purpose, services and operational methods. In particular, how, in a public library, the services to children and young people will fit in with the concept of the library service as a whole or, in a school, how the library resource centre might serve its learning and teaching needs, and integrate with or relate to those responsible for computing, audiovisual facilities or the school archives.

At this point, the school or children's librarian may, in addition, be able to:

(a) indicate the approximate size of the total library space needed – by reference to appropriate standards, for example

(b) give an estimate of cost

(c) provide a recommendation, where there is a potential choice of solution (new, replanned and/or extended premises), and advise on the location for the library, where appropriate.

Assuming that approval is given for the go-ahead of the project by the responsible local or school authority, the librarian can move to the next stage in the process.

The planning stage

With the information and understanding obtained from the pre-planning stage, the librarian is in a position to write the architect's brief for the library. In American terminology this is known as the building program and, for a school library, the educational specification. This is a document that is likely to go through a number of drafts and will benefit from the input of others, such as users and library staff, preferably in a structured way. The brief for a school or children's library or department is unlikely to be a large document, and in many circumstances will be part of that for a building of which it is to form part. In the latter situation, the consultant librarian, Robert Rohlf, emphasizes the basic responsibility of the children's librarian to write that part of the brief that relates to the children's area in connection with other people.[9] And Arlene Kaspik writes that: 'A building program involves a great deal of analyzing, estimating, conversing, debating, conferring, writing and rewriting . . . It's exhilarating and it's exhausting.'[10]

As well as a source of information for the architect, the good brief will also be a source of inspiration for the architect's concept for the library. Rohlf summarizes the brief as 'a written statement of the objectives, policies and goals of the library; a description of the physical areas and space needs for the achievement of these goals and objectives, and the relationship of these space needs to each other; the nature and amount of furniture and equipment needed for these spaces; and whatever limitations must be considered.'[11]

In outline a brief might consist of the following main elements:

(a) The community to be served.
(b) The purpose of the library – mission, goals and objectives; there's an opportunity here to finalize a rethink of the library's purpose.
(c) The services and facilities – what they are to be and how they will be provided.
(d) Operational methods – manual and/or automated.
(e) The particular qualities expected of the accommodation, flexibility, accessibility, barrier free, comfort, for example.[12]
(f) A detailed description of individual, named elements (rooms, spaces or areas) of the library, indicating their size, the function of each space; their relationship with other spaces; occupancy (people, library materials, furniture and equipment); special requirements (lighting, power, communications, finishes, etc.). For a large library such space by space detail may not all be required until a secondary briefing stage, as it overburdens the architect with information.
(g) Furniture and equipment requirements.
(h) Constraints of money, time and site.

In addition to the text, the librarian can provide:

(a) Diagrams – that help clarify the preferred space relationships of different library areas, rooms and spaces, and illustrate traffic flow patterns (users, staff and materials) through the library.

(b) Tables – such as statistics relating to collection size and library use.

(c) Charts – of the staff organization, for example.

Writing the brief can be assisted by reference to the example provided by existing briefing documents, whether of actual libraries or the textbook model variety.[13] Kaspik warns that: 'Some of the most critical problems are philosophical ones tackled at the very beginning of a building program.'[14] For children and young people this means:

(a) articulating the philosophy of the service

(b) how this philosophy will integrate with the mission and broader service concept of the library as a whole

(c) the interrelationships with other library departments and how this will be translated into a library building.

Where a children's area is part of a larger public library building, Holt suggests the following headings[15] for that part of the brief:

(a) Brief description of major functions provided; age group to be served; philosophical background.

(b) Basic relationship to other parts of the library such as the issue desk, young adults area, adult section, etc.

(c) Atmosphere.

(d) Provision and location.

(e) Relationship of staff enquiries desk to collections, seating, etc.

(f) Descriptions of the print and non-print collections to be housed.

(g) Description of how information technology will be used.

(h) Number and type of seating to be provided.

(i) Description and quantification of other equipment.

(j) Description of library activities and space required.

(k) Description of display and exhibition requirements.

(l) Toilet and other adjacent facilities.

(m) Office and workroom requirements.

For schools, Claire Sandler provides a checklist of the topics that need to be considered when planning a library media centre for the next century.[16] The main headings are:

(a) Educational objectives – current and anticipated changes.

(b) Student population – current and future.

(c) Curricular and library media programmes.

(d) Collection of material – existing and future projections of the variety and mix of formats.

(e) Behaviour and activities – study, browsing, viewing, etc.; group study; recreational uses; media-production formats.

(f) Facilities specifications – ventilation, lighting, temperature and humidity, acoustics, security, power, telecommunications, space considerations for different areas of the centre.

(g) Access – catalogue, browsing, storage, shelving, traffic patterns, barrier free

(h) Overall environment – aesthetics, comfort, efficiency, safety, visibility for supervision.

Sandler endorses the points made earlier in this chapter, when she writes: 'A vibrant 21st century library media center will result from good designs; good designs must depend on good information; good information comes from asking the right questions and seeking the answers in the right places.'[17]

These examples of outlines or checklists for a library brief or specification illustrate that such a document needs to be much more than a 'naming of parts' if it is to respond to the unique requirements of a given school or to children and young people in the local community.

Road vehicles

Ronald Pybus provides a sample specification for a 'standard' mobile library vehicle,[18] and the headings given below formed the framework for the specification for a small single-decker family bookbus:

(a) Purpose of the vehicle – for example, 'To provide an informal service to children (pre-school–11 years) at schools, playgroups and selected street stops within the Borough'.
(b) Chassis – the type of chassis chosen.
(c) General – body design, insulation, reinforcement, compliance with regulations for construction, use and lighting.
(d) Size of vehicle – height, width and length.
(e) Roof – provision of natural light.
(f) Doors – operation, size, etc.
(g) Window – in rear (size and fitments).
(h) Seats – adjustability required to allow service from a seated position behind the counter flap.
(i) General interior – wall and plinth covering; kicking strips.
(j) Floor – choice of floor covering.
(k) Shelving – requirements at nearside, rear and offside.
(l) Counter – size, location, and storage provision.
(m) Health and safety – fire extinguisher, first-aid kit.
(n) Electrical – battery, heater, lighting, fan.
(o) Livery – exterior colours and interior paintwork.
(p) Logo – library service name and logo.

The specification may be accompanied by sketch plans, probably not to scale, drawn by the librarian, and indicating the required interior layout of the vehicle and the design of the counter.[19]

Checklists

Work with both the pre-planning and planning stages can be made that much easier by reference to appropriate standards (discussed in Chapter 6), and the use of checklists.

The American publication, *Checklist of library building design considerations*, serves the dual purpose of a tool for 'evaluating existing library space as part of a library's "Needs Assessment Process," "and as" a guide . . . to make sure that all needed spaces and functions are included in the library design'.[20] As it is an adaptable publication, designed to cover all kinds of library, its sections cover such topics as, the interior, seating, non-public areas, and communication equipment. Usefully, however, sections are specifically devoted to children's facilities, and to those for young adults. While not claiming to be exhaustive, each checklist section poses questions to be answered by the librarian, whether reviewing the present accommodation or planning new premises.

Checklists for public library managers includes checklists for a library community survey (or profile); library signage (or guiding), and handicapped accessibility.[21] The latter is given some consideration in the above mentioned *Checklist of library building design considerations*.

Checklists for public library managers also includes a building programme checklist (that summarizes the steps discussed in this and the preceding chapter) that could be possibly adapted to suit planning the school library or public library provision for children and young people.

References

1 Todaro, J. B., 'Changing children's environments', *Illinois libraries*, **60** (10), 1978, 904.

2 Anderson, M. J., 'Service for the eighties: trends in society today which will affect public library service to children tomorrow', *Illinois libraries*, **60** (10), 1978, 850.

3 Fleet, A., *Children's libraries*, London, André Deutsch, 1973, 26.

4 Kaspik, A. M., 'Planning a new youth services department or beauty's more than skin deep', *Illinois libraries*, **70** (1) 1988, 24.

5 Saunders, L., 'Teenagers and library services', *Youth library review*, (16), 1993, 15.

6 Marshall, P., 'Children and young people: guidelines for public library services', *International review of children's literature and librarianship*, **6** (3), 1991, 204–5.

7 Saunders, 15.

8 Atherton, B., *Adapting spaces for resource-based learning*, London, Council for Educational Technology, 1980, 42, 34.

9 Rohlf, R. H., 'Best laid plans: a consultant's constructive advice', *School library journal*, **36** (2), 1990, 30.

10 Kaspik, op. cit., 22.

11 Rohlf, op. cit., 30.

12 A list of what might be described as qualitative guidelines is given in American Association of School Librarians and Association for Educational Communications and Technology, *Information power: guidelines for school library media programs*, Chicago, American Library Association, 1988, 99–100.

13 An outline building programme is given in Holt, R. M., *Planning library*

buildings and facilities from concept to completion, Metuchen, NJ, Scarecrow Press, 1989, 219–25. Five case-study examples of briefs are given in, Anderson, P.H., *Planning school library media facilities*, Hamden, Conn., Library Professional Publications, 1990, 95–179.

14 Kaspik, op. cit., 22.

15 Holt, op. cit., 220–1. This section also includes a consideration of the area for young adults.

16 Sandler, C., 'Planning library media centers for the twenty-first century', *Media spectrum*, **18** (1), 1991, 9–10.

17 Idem, 9.

18 Pybus, R. L., *The design and construction of mobile libraries*, 2nd edn., [London], Branch and Mobile Libraries Group of the Library Association, 1990, 76–84.

19 Extracted from a specification for a family bookbus by Cynon Valley Borough Council; sent to the author in January 1994.

20 Sannwald, W. W., *Checklist of library building design considerations*, Chicago, American Library Association, 1991, v.

21 Wozny, J., *Checklists for public library managers*, Metuchen, NJ, Scarecrow Press, 1989, 189–93, 136–46, 140–6.

5 COMMITTEES AND TEAMS

This chapter looks at the planning mechanisms required to bring about the process leading to the successful provision of library space, whether new or remodelled for pupils, children and young people, described in the previous two chapters, and in particular how they as users might be involved. Such mechanisms usually mean that in schools the responsibility for creating a library building might be given to a committee, reporting to the school's governors, for example. Day-to-day development of a large public library project, of which the children's department is part, however, may fall to teams formed especially to carry out such a task. Through the chief librarian or library director the work and decisions of such teams will gain approval by reports back to the local authority committee responsible for the public library service and ultimately the council itself. Common to both committee and teams should be the involvement of the school or children's librarian.

Schools

Discussing the refurbishment of the library at John Cleveland College, Hinckley, an upper school for 14–18 year-olds, Peter Kingham points out that, while schools want a resource centre 'that helps students learn and encourages them to be responsible for their own learning,' these requirements get overlooked. The tendency is to 'go straight to a firm specializing in library design . . . allowing little scope for discussion and involvement [within the school]'.[1] As noted earlier, there is temptation for librarians and others to look for a design solution to issues and problems that have not been thoroughly discussed. A committee or team approach to the planning and design of a library provides opportunities for such discussion and the involvement of all who have an interest in the library.

In the planning and designing of either a school or public library children's department, however, there can be too little or regrettably no involvement by staff and others, as described below. On the other hand, some kinds of involvement may be counter-productive where individuals are only concerned with maintaining the status quo or just wish the library to acquire more space.

Planning committee

Where the intended building work for the school library, whether new or remodelled, is only of a minor nature it may be conducted without any real formal administrative or controlling structure, with discussion taking place as necessary between school librarian, head teacher, architect and/or schools library service (if appropriate), and supplier (or suppliers) of shelving, furniture and equipment. However, for a significant project, a planning committee can be advisable, as suggested above, that would approve the brief, the architect's plans and budget changes, and monitor progress, leaving principally the librarian (or designated project librarian) and architect to forward the project. In a school, such a planning committee might include representatives of the governing body, school management, parents, teachers, pupils, the schools library service, as well as those with more direct responsibility for the library accommodation, such as the librarian and architect. George Buchanan, an American architect, writes that working on three libraries has reinforced his conviction about engaging the client and users in the design process, and that: 'In the hands of a talented architect and a committed client, the new facility need not resemble a camel (that is a horse designed by committee).'[2]

As indicated earlier, such elaborate arrangements may not seem necessary for all building projects, but it is important that discussion and involvement are not confined to the principal players, such as the head teacher, school librarian, architect and the shelving, equipment and furniture supplier. Even the librarian may be ignored in the planning process, however it is handled. For as Buchanan has remarked: 'the architect sometimes has trouble gaining access to the actual users. The client, whether the school head or a building committee, may be reluctant to open up the design process to librarians and staff and give up control, particularly when faced with tight budgets and/or schedules.'[3] Such a situation is not peculiarly American and may not be confined to school library situations.

Involving the school librarian

Earlier chapters have made clear the role of the librarian as a planner and his or her contribution to the planning and design process. Where a new school is to be built to include a library, it is essential that a librarian be appointed early on to agree its role, to be informed of the subjects that will be covered and other curricular needs and to be allowed to participate in the planning and design of the school and in particular the library along the lines suggested in this book. If a library is to be provided for the first time in a school, or the current accommodation is to be remodelled, then it is equally vital that a librarian be employed in good time in the first case and in the latter case be thoroughly involved in the planning and design process. The consultative and participative process proposed in this chapter is more easily facilitated where the librarian has appropriate professional status and recognition within a school.

In primary schools, or those secondary schools whose size does not justify a qualified librarian, then the head teacher or teacher/librarian will usually assume responsibility for the planning and design of the library. In both instances they should be prepared to make use of the advisory facilities of the schools library service, as indicated below, or a consultant and/or shelving and furniture supplier, as described later in this chapter.

It is quite clear from experience that the librarian and, where appropriate, his or her staff, should have both responsibility and involvement in a building project and that this should not be token participation or consultation.

Schools Library Service

In many ways the role of a schools library service, acting in its advisory capacity to a school over its library accommodation, is as a library buildings consultant. It will advise the school on space needs, the layout of the library and the acquisition and supply of appropriate shelving, furniture and equipment, often making use of the services provided by commercial firms described later in this chapter to assist with and carry out this work. Regrettably, such advisory work on the space planning of the library will usually occur after the structure and general arrangement of a school and its library has been planned and built, rather than at the preferred earlier stage. The schools library service can often also advise on the choice of an automated library management system and other information technology where this is being considered for a new or refurbished library.

Involving library users

Formal participation of library users (at the planning and design stages, for example) may be difficult although not impossible for the public library, but is, perhaps, more easily attained in a school environment by both pupils and teaching staff. Once again, the USA seems to lead the way by providing examples of situations where students in schools are seen 'as partners in library design'.[4] Robert Brown, a Boston architect, is of the view that: 'Students bring uninhibited, fresh outlook to design considerations . . . their ideas are rarely restricted by codes or cost . . . Inevitably, they innocently challenge some of the intellectual baggage that many architects and library design consultants carry with them.'[5]

He goes on to make the interesting point that, although majority users of school and public libraries, children and young people are not often involved in the process of a library's creation. Brown notes that, when consulting students, they usually want what librarians and others want by way of library spaces but there is a difference of emphasis and intention. Student comments cover such topics as:

1　The library as an easy place to get around and find what is wanted.
2　The library as a meeting place.
3　Provision for a variety of activities from study to conversation within a single library area to include
　(a)　student lounge area and casual seating
　(b)　separate quiet areas for individual work
　(c)　group study spaces
　(d)　areas for viewing and listening
　(e)　class instruction
4　Each age group needs its own space.
5　An open environment not a maze of rooms and hallways.
6　Better access to information technology and other information sources.
7　Big and small spaces, their architectural style, quality and character.

8   Lighting and colour – poor lighting adversely affects student library use; colour energizes the library and defines space for different age groups.

9   Study seating preferences – lounge, carrel and study seating to suit different needs.

Brown records that students are aware of their surroundings, use places they like, avoid those they do not and want to make a contribution to the design of the places they use and that: 'The challenge lies in giving students a way to express themselves through the planning and construction process.'[6]

In a school, Kingham suggests, like Brown, that ownership is very important and, for the refurbishment project at John Cleveland College mentioned earlier, separate library development groups for staff and students were created:

> thus providing the necessary input for the changes that we were about to make ... Having listened to all views and taken them into account, someone has to come up with a list of proposals. In our case, we discussed: I listened, noted views and then drew up a list of proposals to present to our meetings.[7]

Public libraries: children's libraries
Library team

Where a large multi-departmental public library is to be built, the children's librarian is part of the library staff building team chaired by the chief librarian or the senior librarian given responsibility for the project. The children's librarian's task is to make known the needs of that particular department and contribute a significant input to the brief and, in that connection, he or she should actively canvass the views of all departmental library staff of the children's library about the proposed accommodation in which they will work. Later, opportunities should be provided at appropriate points for departmental staff to meet, to read documentation, to see plans, and comment on proposed purchases of furniture and equipment. Robert Rohlf suggests that a building project's success depends upon teamwork and communication. This means that, in developing the brief, the children's librarian should be in a position to comment on sections of the brief for other parts of the building and that staff working in other library departments should be able to make comments on the proposals for the children's area.[8]

Design team

Once a brief for a public library has been written and an architect appointed, if the local authority is not to use its own architect, a design team will be set up to see the project to completion. The design team's membership will vary as different stages of the public library project are reached, and could include for a large project the architect, who will lead the team, chief librarian (or a building project librarian), library buildings consultant, other specialist consultants (for heating and ventilation, shelving and furniture, for example), an interior designer, and various local authority officers (from planning, financial and legal departments, for example). Only a small number of such individuals will be actively involved at any one time for, as Godfrey Thompson writes:

Despite what may appear to be a proliferation of experts forming a large and unwieldy team it must be made clear that for the great part of the time it is the architect who alone, or with one or two colleagues, works to produce the proposals . . . He will call the librarian and other members of the team to join him when he has questions to ask or proposals to discuss. The team exists but it is not in session continuously, or indeed often.[9]

Architect

The architect has a number of roles that make him a key figure once engaged for the project. These are:

(a) to advise on planning and design options within the available finance
(b) to design a building that fits its purpose, is pleasurable to use and soundly constructed
(c) to manage the building process, including paperwork and costs,
(d) to coordinate the team of specialists involved, and possibly coordinate the purchase of all equipment.

The architect will, therefore, usually chair the design team which facilitates communication between all the various parties involved in planning and design. It is important, however, that decisions reached within the design team meetings are fully documented and minutes of meetings produced recording what was decided. It is crucial that all instructions relayed to individuals are given in writing.

During the design stage it will be necessary for all concerned to consider the architect's drawings against what has been asked for in the brief. The children's librarian (or the librarian in a school) should have the responsibility for examining that department for 'function, traffic patterns, work flow, accessibility, and logical arrangements, as well as flexibility'.[10] Discussion resulting in agreed changes to drawings should be properly noted and dated.

Library buildings consultant

While there are many reasons for employing a library buildings consultant, who is usually a librarian with experience of library building projects, it may be thought to be particularly important where both librarian and architect are inexperienced in the planning and design of libraries. The practice is very common in North America and elsewhere but less prevalent, however, in the UK. This is perhaps to be regretted, as the experience, knowledge and objectivity of the consultant, his or her ability to save time, take on time-consuming work connected with the project, possibly save money through suitable suggestions and, where appropriate, mediate over disagreements with the various parties involved, make his or her fee well worthwhile. Two common tasks asked of a consultant are assistance in writing the brief and reviewing the architect's plans. However, if necessary, a consultant may be employed to assist with work on all stages of a project from assessing need to evaluating the finished accommodation. Such a consultant is unlikely to have a detailed knowledge of work with children and young people and other additional specialist sources of advice and guidance, such as staff in other libraries and library school teaching staff, may need to be tapped.

Suppliers of shelving and furniture

A number of suppliers of library shelving and furniture also offer a design service which is free of charge and this can be particularly useful in situations where the school or children's librarian does not have the services of an architect or where the latter is willing to leave the interior layout to such a company. Some suppliers advertise their use of computer-aided design in preparing shelving and furniture layouts and the librarian can see the proposed arrangement, therefore, in three dimensions, as well as in plan, before such items are put in place in the library. A number of suppliers have developed, or are agents for, shelving systems and furniture developed especially for the school or children's library market and their services and products will be particularly helpful in the design of such libraries.

While library suppliers would prefer a commitment to their products, their design services are often freely available without it. Such companies are very experienced, but in certain circumstances there is a danger, as indicated earlier, that they do the librarian's planning (in every sense of the word) and therefore the opportunities for a fundamental rethink of the library, its purposes and services, may not be fully taken – the supplier's emphasis perhaps being on maximizing floor space and ensuring the layout results in good traffic flows. Some suppliers manufacture their own shelving and furniture, whilst others source their products from a number of British and European companies. As well as creating a workable layout and supplying the necessary shelving and furniture, such firms will also arrange for its installation if required. The earlier a commitment can be made to a major supplier of shelving and furniture, the sooner they can be drawn fully into the design process.

Library users

As already demonstrated for schools, user input is important in the planning and design of a library and, as noted in the previous chapter, the pre-planning stage can provide an opportunity for contributions from users and potential users of public library children's services through user surveys and market research, even if involvement at later stages is difficult. However, there is little published evidence of public consultation taking place in public library communities in the UK, let alone with the children in those communities, although teenagers have been the subject of a few surveys in recent years.[11] However, Birmingham's ongoing consultation with users over the proposed Centre for the Child, to be located in its central library, is described in Chapter 12.

In the USA, Denver Public Library's plans for improvements to its library system, included the ambition to 'create the finest children's library in the country' and, as its customers, children were to be actively canvassed for their views and opinions.[12] The belief was held that children 'can play a role in the design of their spaces and improvement of services to them'; the usual practice is for adults to decide what children need and will respond to favourably. Prior to what was to be a market-research exercise, the library staff involved attended a design conference that included questions of child advocacy. The conference supported the staff's earlier observations, that: 'Children need to be able to manipulate their surroundings; they want to learn by doing. They love hidden, private places, bright colors, respect from adults, and environments that can change. Fun is an important word in all of their experiences.'[13]

Through partnership with private industry, market research to ascertain qualitative information was carried out using professionally led focus groups of children (ages 6–7 and 9–10) and parents.[14] By way of preparation, the market researchers and library staff involved decided on the particular matters to be considered in the groups: children's interaction with library staff; their views on current and future provision, and design issues. The children's comments and ideas, elicited in a comfortable and relaxed setting, included: walls to write on; privacy; soft, comfortable, fun seating; group spaces; the separation of older children from younger ones; computer games; and other more colourful and imaginative ideas, such as a treehouse and a room built like a castle. It was recognized that, when these views were communicated to the architect, compromise and money would constrain what finally could be achieved in the children's room. However, Denver Public library is committed: 'to provide a library environment that is designed for children and respects their need for information, comfort and a bit of frivolity'.[15] There is always the danger in such consultation exercises, however, that expectations are raised and the resulting compromises disappoint those users concerned and this point perhaps needs to be explained to those children, young adults and parents that might be involved.

Sacramento Public Library conducted a marketing study on children's services in 1985–6 for the major extension to its central library. The history of library service to children in the central library had never been a strong one and ceased altogether in the early 1980s. A study was required, therefore, to ascertain the present extent of need for services and materials. This study confirmed that there were a limited number of children in the catchment area, that many were from non-English speaking families, and that a space for children would need to be accessible for those occasions when families from beyond the immediate area could visit.[16] This information thus provided the stimulus to include a space that would attract children and their carers in the new building.

An earlier example of consultation with children took place in four Chicago public libraries in 1978.[17] Forty of them, aged between 7 and 13, were asked to respond to 14 questions related to library design and gave useful but rather ordinary replies. For example, the needs were expressed for:

(a) a non-distractive, functional environment
(b) areas that encourage quiet study
(c) signs, posters and clocks to be placed at a lower level
(d) the elimination of high shelves
(e) the opportunity to use the adult library
(f) a concern for cleanliness, comfort and safety.

The author of this exercise commented that the children's responses were 'practical and reflect traditional library design and organization.' The children did not ask for piped in rock music, all were hostile to the idea of an integrated adult and children's collection, and a majority placed the catalogue over a listening centre or paperbacks racks when asked to choose two out of a list of four items considered basic library equipment. Nor were they especially favourable towards bicycle racks, bulletin boards, fish tanks and plants. The children's responses were not 'outlandish' nor particularly creative suggestions and seemed to reflect what they knew or thought was the right reply. It also illustrates, perhaps, the significance of the more creative techniques used in the Denver approach.

Project management

Once a building project has begun, its management will be under the control and supervision of the architect, or contractor in a 'design and build' arrangement, where design and construction are carried out by the same firm. In either situation, those concerned will employ well-tried project management methods to bring the building to completion. As indicated in the previous chapter, the librarian has a number of tasks to carry out and bring to fruition by the time the library is ready to be occupied and made operationally ready for its staff and first users. These tasks relate to the selection, delivery (and eventual installation) of shelving, furniture and equipment, including automated systems, and moving in the collection, and possibly some furniture, from the old library to the new building, as well as perhaps acquiring substantial collections of new library materials. In addition there will probably be the need to employ, redirect and train library staff for the new accommodation.

The planning, control and coordination of these tasks creates a sizeable project alongside that of the planning, design and construction of the building itself, and demands the utilization of particular project management skills and techniques. Surya Lovejoy, in his readable, practical book *A systematic approach to getting results*, advocates preparing a proper project plan which 'will enable you to see exactly what has to happen when, and will identify potential problems, conflicts and emergencies before they arise'.[18]

For a small, straightforward project, detailed diary entries or a simple chart may suffice, but more demanding and complex situations might encourage the librarian to utilize Gantt charts or network analysis. Both latter techniques require the project manager to identify all the steps and sub-steps that go to make up the various components of the project, to allocate periods of time to them, and arrange the steps in a suitable sequence. This sequencing takes into account that some steps or activities can be done simultaneously while others cannot start until another step has been completed. In the Gantt chart the various steps, tasks or actions are listed vertically on the left of the chart and time is registered horizontally. Milestone symbols along the way can be used to indicate significant stages of the project – when a particular step and its sub-steps have been completed, for example – and the Gantt chart marked in such a way as to indicate the point reached (or as importantly, not reached) for particular steps at a given time.

Network analysis involves creating a network for a project and its component parts that demonstrates more clearly than a Gantt chart the interrelationships of all the tasks involved and identifies the critical path through the project; it is known as critical path analysis. This path is the longest route through the network of activities where, if the allocated time is changed for any of its component steps, the timing of the project as a whole will be affected.[19]

As with many tasks today, PC-based project management software is available (for example, Project Manager for Windows or Instaplan) which will automatically calculate the time needed to complete the project, show the critical path, and the slack time on the remaining paths, once the basic information about tasks, their duration and sequencing, have been entered. It also creates and permits the printing out of Gantt charts and critical path networks. The usual advantages of a computerized approach are to be found with such software: the ability to deal with project changes easily and quickly and generate new charts, as well as other features, such as handling all resources – time, staff and money – and providing reporting facilities. Such capabilities could be important for those who feel they would be an advantage. However, Lovejoy warns against such computerized methods, saying that 'such systems are superficially attractive, and can be extremely useful at the project *planning* stage, they are not, in my view, suitable for the project *management* process'.[20] Both school and children's librarians should consider the use of manual or automated project management techniques, simple or complex, where appropriate to the task in hand.

A planning and design summary

Lynda Fowler has drawn up a list of ten helpful pointers[21] for planning media centres that usefully summarizes major themes of this and the previous two chapters and these are given in an edited and abbreviated form below:

1 Research and study the literature.
2 Write a concise, thorough educational specification (brief).
3 Let the architect design.
4 Identify the roles of all persons involved in the building process; establish working relationships.
5 Know the building project and other deadlines, e.g. for obtaining furniture, ordering equipment, and when changes can no longer be made without major financial implications.
6 Understand the budget – know the amount available for furniture, equipment, automation, etc.
7 Examine the blueprints and drawings carefully.
8 Complete a walk through of all media centre services and activities on the blueprints.
9 Be diplomatic, be willing and prepared to negotiate.
10 Plan to spend a considerable amount of time with the building process.

Many other matters might be added to such a list, such as 'evaluate what is achieved', but it is worth emphasizing once more that the school or children's librarian must see the occasion for new or improved library accommodation as an opportunity to determine afresh the library and information needs of the community to be served and thus to rethink the mission, aims and objectives of the library service to be offered.

References

1 Kingham, P., 'Something for nothing: every school's dream', *School librarian*, **41** (3), 1993, 98.

2 Buchanan, G., 'By design: it's all in the details', *School library journal*, **36** (2), 1990, 27.

3 Idem, 25.

4 Brown, R. A., 'Students as partners in library design', *School library journal*, **38** (2), 1992, 31–4.

5 Idem, 31.

6 Idem, 34.

7 Kingham, op. cit., 98.

8 Rohlf, R. H., 'Best laid plans: a consultant's constructive advice', *School library journal*, **36** (2), 1990, 30.

9 Thompson, G., *Planning and design of library buildings*, 3rd edn., London, Buttterworth, 1989, 25.

10 Rogers, N. I., 'Getting involved; where do you fit in?', *Illinois libraries*, **60** (10), 1978, 856.

11 For example, Love, L., 'Teenagers and library use in Waltham Forest', *Library Association record*, **89** (2), 1987, 81–2.

12 Sandlian, P. and Walters, S., 'A room of their own: planning the new Denver children's library', *School library journal*, **37** (2), 1991, 26–9.

13 Idem, 27.

14 The steps for setting up focus groups are described in an insert in idem, 28.

15 Idem, 29.

16 Chekon, T. and Miles, M., 'The kid's place: Sacramento PL's space for children', *School library journal*, **39** (2) 1993, 21.

17 Huntoon, E., 'Their turn – kids speak out on library facilities', *Illinois libraries*, **60** (10), 1978, 876–80. It includes the list of questions asked in an appendix to the article.

18 Lovejoy, S., *A systematic approach to getting results*, Aldershot, Gower, 1993, xviii.

19 For fuller details of Gantt charts and network analysis *see* Lockyer, K. G., *Critical path analysis and other project network techniques*, 4th edn., London, Pitman, 1984.

20 Lovejoy, op. cit., 12–3.

21 Fowler, L.B., 'Facilities design: what I learned along the way', *North Carolina libraries*, **49** (3), 1991, 140.

6 STANDARDS AND GUIDELINES

Standards exist for many types of library in many countries and may be formulated by professional associations (both national and international), government departments and bodies, regional and local public library and school authorities, and national libraries. Typically, standards address such matters as the purpose of the library type, finance, services, staff, collections and accommodation, and appropriate quantitative guidance given. Clearly such guidance will have implications for the space requirements of the library. However, as F. N. Withers has stated, 'qualitative standards must come first, for without a clear understanding of what these are, no proper attempt can be made to express in quantitative terms what library materials, human resources, accommodation and equipment and above all funds, are necessary'.[1]

In recent years some dissatisfaction has been voiced over the quantitative element of standards because they are often cited as (and thus encourage) minimum provision and do not relate to the specific needs of a given community; the basis of such calculations is not explained, and, as far as buildings are concerned, they may be incomplete – new formats, atypical library activities may not be catered for in terms of their space needs.

For these and other reasons, there is a tendency for 'standards' to be replaced by 'guidelines', emphasizing principles and concepts, and for quantitative guidance (how much, how many) to be either limited or omitted altogether. This can pose particular difficulties for anyone involved in planning a library building as: 'The problems involved in working out quantitative standards cannot . . . be ignored. They have to be faced every time a new library is built or existing library extended or reorganized . . . Moreover . . . For both planning and evaluation purposes are essential.'[2]

Determining space needs

Early on, the librarian has to be in a position to estimate the total library space required, preferably based on a sum of that estimated to be required by individual departments, rooms, parts or areas, and consequently turns to standards for guidance. In some instances, however, the overall space allocation for a particular library type may be specified in a standards document (by a government department, for example) based on a given school or child population, and the librarian's task is to utilize that predetermined space quota through effective allocation and organization.

Some standards may include an element for non-assignable space (or balance area) in their proposals, or advise that a percentage be added to the net space requirement to give the gross space figure. Users of quantitative space standards must therefore be clear what a given allocation represents.

In the UK, as elsewhere in the world, some library and school authorities may have their own regional, state, or local guidelines and standards which librarians will have to observe, and some examples are noted later in this chapter. In considering and discussing the documents noted below, the emphasis is on their use for calculating the overall space requirements of the school or children's library, the requirements for individual areas and activities are dealt with in Chapter 8. Many of the other important matters noted in the guideline statements discussed below are referred to elsewhere in this book and, in every instance, in this chapter and in others, readers are encouraged to look at the original publications.

Schools
International guidelines

Published in 1990 by IFLA, Frances Carroll's *Guidelines for school libraries* includes a chapter on facilities, which it calls the school library media centre.[3] The chapter looks at many aspects of such a centre: its planning, location and access; the provision of adequate space; types of activity and accommodation, and furniture and equipment. Some criteria for the selection of equipment is given and guidance provided on such matters as heating, ventilation, lighting, appearance and electrical outlets.

The document makes a number of helpful recommendations of a quantitative nature, for example, seating at tables (at 3.72 m² or 40 ft² per user) in the reading room should be provided for 10% of the school population; that about '10% of the seating of the reading room should be in a browsing or recreational area'. A table of *minimum* space for school library media centres serving three sizes of population is given.[4] For a school serving:

1 1–250 students, a total library area of 159.2 m² (1,700 ft²) – basic reading, viewing and listening area of 93 m² (1,000 ft²)
2 251–500 students, a total library area of 463.34 m² (4,981 ft²) – basic reading, viewing and listening area of 186 m² (2,000 ft²)
3 501 students and above, a total library area of 574.99 m² (6,181 ft²) – basic reading, viewing and listening area of 279 m² (3,000 ft²).

As the above figures indicate, the basic library area for reading, viewing and listening is based on 93 m² (1,000 ft²) per 250 students. The table in the guidelines also shows space allocations for other parts of the library (workroom, production and storage areas, for example), indicating how the overall size noted above is computed. The smallest school library is limited to three such additional elements, the two larger sizes to seven.

United Kingdom guidelines

Department of Education and Science (DES)

The 1984 Library and Information Services Council's working party report, *School libraries: the foundations of the curriculum*, includes six paragraphs on housing and access to the school library. It regrets the fact 'that the DES has failed to give clear guidelines on the size, location and furnishing of school libraries to guide local authority architects', and urges adoption of the Library Association's recommendations or the production of DES ones.[5] It goes on to say that the DES's *Area guidelines for secondary schools* (1983) gives only an unsupported, arbitrary and, in some respects, inadequate figure for the space needs of school libraries.

This 'inadequate' figure is 0.2 m² per pupil and worked examples in the guidelines show the likely size of library for secondary school populations of different sizes and types[6]:

1   600 pupils (age 11–16), 120 m²
2   1,000 pupils (900 age 11–16 + 100 in sixth form), 200 m² + sixth form study/social area, 75 m²
3   1,650 pupils (1,500 age 11–16 + 150 in sixth form), 300 m² + sixth form study/social area, 151 m².
4   500 pupils (sixth-form college, age 16–19), 250 m² + study/social area 150 m².

The area guidelines do not match what the Library Association recommendations, described below, except in the last example, but that is considerably less than IFLA guidelines. However, such comparisons, both here and in other parts of this chapter, should be treated with caution, as like may not always be compared exactly with like.

For those concerned with sixth-form colleges, the DES's *Area guidelines for sixth form, tertiary and NAFE colleges*, recognizes the library as 'The single most important provision for the work and study time of students', and suggests space allowances related to student FTE numbers as indicated in the following three examples. For FTEs of 250, 1,000 and 3,000, total spaces of 183 m², 483 m² and 1,243 m² are listed respectively. Each total space is made up of three main areas for: bookstacks; support (counter, catalogue, office, workroom, etc.), and readers (private study, browsing and periodicals). The guidelines also recommend the provision of further study spaces around the college to cater for those with a high proportion of private study time; an allowance of 0.17 m² is suggested for each student in this category. A worked example in the guidelines for a sixth-form college of 500 students suggests a net area for the library of 293 m² and a balance area of 73 m² (gross area 366 m²) plus further private study areas with a gross area of 106 m². A bookshop is seen as part of the college's administration space provision.[7]

Non-advanced further education colleges for the many 16-year-olds who see it as an alternative to the sixth form, are discussed in the publication, *Accommodation for the 16–19 age group: NAFE: designing for change*. This is largely a case study of one college with due consideration being given to the location and space for the library.[8]

City technology colleges (CTCs) and their libraries are described in the publication, *Educational design initiatives in city technology colleges*. Figures given there for six CTCs indicate library sizes of between 210 m² and 320 m² for student populations of 900 to 1,250. The figure of 320 m² is the exception (and is not in the school with the most students); the average for the other five CTCs is 219 m².[9]

Professional and other associations

The School Library Association's *School libraries: steps in the right direction. Guidelines for a school library resource centre*[10] offers limited advice on the question of accommodation. It makes a series of helpful but brief points about access, size, atmosphere, shelving and storage, the use of audiovisual materials and reprographics, issue/enquiry desk, catalogue, security and office space. However, no quantitative guidance is given; this is provided in a later School Library Association guidelines publication, *Designing and planning a secondary school library resource centre*.[11] This states that:

> The size of the school library resource centre will relate to the school's overall accommodation. One-tenth of the pupils of the school . . . need to be catered for at one time. Additional library space in other parts of the school should be considered . . . It is therefore recommended that a formula of 10 per cent of the minimum teaching area be applied. This is the minimum space in which it is possible to carry out the functions of the school's library and information service . . .'[12]

Some examples are given in this publication of the required library accommodation at 10% of the minimum teaching accommodation: 480 pupils (age 9–13), 600 pupils (age 11–16), 1,500 pupils (age 12–18) require 144 m², 257 m², and 593 m² respectively. These recommended minimum figures are substantially better than those that might be based on the DES's area guidelines and, except for the first example, in excess of what the IFLA guidelines suggest for the main reading, viewing and listening area of the school library resource centre.

Learning resources in schools: Library Association guidelines for school libraries,[14] published in 1992, considers a variety of topics including those relating to the provision of accommodation. These include:

(a) Function and use – the comment is made that the school library is not the only place where books and other materials will be found.

(b) Siting – easily accessible from as many teaching spaces as possible.

(c) Amount of space required – promulgates the formula of 10% of the minimum teaching area allowed by the DES, subsequently adopted in the School Library Association's *Designing and planning a secondary school library resource centre*, as described above. A table of library space recommendations for primary school populations of 240– 320 pupils (e.g. 240 pupils age 5–7 and 320 pupils age 8–12, 57 m² and 85 m², respectively) and secondary school populations of 480–1,500 is provided, the latter listed in the SLA's secondary school library resource centre publication. Schools with fewer than 240 pupils should be treated as if they had 240 pupils. Large schools in separate buildings are likely to need additional library areas based on the number of pupils in the separate buildings.

(d) Allocation of space – the range of spaces needed are given, with an indication of extra spaces needed for middle and secondary schools, e.g. general work-room and planning and preparation unit, respectively, but guidance on the quantitative allocation of space is not provided.

(e) Relationships – provides advice on the arrangement of library spaces with the emphasis on ease of supervision.

(f) Furniture and equipment – shelving, guiding, counter, seating, trolleys, etc., are all briefly considered.

The final sections of the guidelines chapter on space advise on: additional space requirements; locker facilities and security; administrative accommodation for secondary and other schools (indicating workroom sizes), and includes a basic equipment checklist for the library resource centre. Chapter 5 of the guidelines is devoted to the Schools Library Service but no recommendations about its space requirements are made. However, some useful guidance is given in that respect in the Library Association's earlier document, *Library resource provision in schools*.[15]

Northern Ireland, Scotland and Wales

The Department of Education, Northern Ireland minimum standards for post-primary schools provide for a basic library/resource space allocation of 110 m² with additional areas, such as a group activities room and store/workroom bringing it up to a total of 255 m². Additional space may be permitted by the department for schools with over 750 pupils. Seating is calculated on the basis of 1 per 15 pupils.[16] The Scottish Library Association recommended in 1985 that 350 m² be allocated for the secondary school resource centre, to include separate rooms for tutorial and audiovisual work, and 100 m2 for a primary school library resource centre.[17] No indication is given as to how this space should be allocated amongst the requirements listed for the two sizes of library.

The Library and Information Services Council (Wales) 1990 report recommended that libraries in secondary schools should try to reach at least the DES guidelines of 20 m² per 100 pupils, as 75% of schools were found to have floor space below the guidelines.[18]

Local guidelines

A number of sets of local guidelines for school libraries have been issued in the UK by public library or education authorities. Bradford Education Library Service's *The effective junior and middle school library* consists of guidance on their planning, policy and management, that covers accommodation, although no quantitative standards are proposed for the latter.[19] *Learning resources in secondary schools* from Cambridgeshire Education Service sets out guidelines for good practice including accommodation. It states that the minimum space required 'to meet these guidelines will vary depending on the size of the school and the seating to be provided'. The minimum floor areas for under 1,000, 1,000–1,500 and over 1,500 students, are given as 250 m², 300 m², and 350 m², respectively.[20] These figures are a little more generous than the DES allocations for 1,000 and 1,500 students but still someway off those for IFLA. Other quantitative guidance is provided for office/workroom, equipment storage and maintenance, and the design and production of materials. Somerset's *Briefing notes on central library/resource centres in schools* treats both primary and secondary schools in the same document and, because of its date, uses the earlier version of the Library Association guidelines formula based on 8% of the minimum teaching accommodation for calculating the size of the library, although it is noted that secondary school provision may have to be based on the more modest DES proposal of 0.2 m² per pupil.[21]

North American guidelines

Standards for school libraries in the United States date back to the 1920s; particularly important and influential was the 1969 publication *Standards for school media programs*,[22] which recognized the equal importance of print and non-print materials; 'emphasized the changing role of the school media specialist in working with teachers and students', and their role in assisting students to acquire 'competence in listening, viewing, and reading skills'.[23] Six years later saw the publication of *Media programs: district and school*, which considered the role of the district programme (Schools Library Service) in the support of the individual school and how the media library resource centre changed to being 'an integral part of the total instructional program of the school'.[24]

This work is now replaced by *Information power: guidelines for school media programs*, published in 1988.[25] The new title, and ongoing joint authorship (the American Association of School Librarians with the Association for Educational Communications and Technology), acknowledges the continuing changes that have taken place in schools as 'the proliferation of information resources and the development of new technologies have broadened and redefined the mission of the school library media program and the role of the library media specialist'.[26] *Information power*, which looks to provide a basis for meeting 'the needs of students in the twenty-first century', naturally reflects the America school system but, as with its predecessor publications, it is likely to be an influential document beyond the USA. The school library media centre is much more than the UK school library resource centre, including, as it can, a computer learning laboratory, TV and audio studios and telecommunications distribution area, for example. The Introduction to Information power states that: 'Quantitative recommendations are made only when professional consensus and research provide a solid basis of support, such as in the areas of personnel and facilities.'[27]

The chapter on facilities covers the planning process, functions and space, design and relationships, spaces and arrangements, equipment and furnishings, and district library media facilities. There is a useful summary of main points called 'Guidelines for facilities'; however, quantitative guidelines are now relegated to an appendix. This is prefaced by the statement: 'The space recommendations below have allowed for flexibility to reflect differences in educational programs and in the size of the school. Each library media center should be planned in conjunction with the total educational requirements of the school.'[28]

Unlike the IFLA and UK guidelines, no overall figures for the size of the school library media centre are given. The appendix, 'Library media facilities guidelines', lists and describes areas and functions that might be part of the media centre, and indicates relationships and other considerations that relate to them. Space allocations for each area are given for schools with 500 or 1,000 students. Because of this level of detail, the list provides a useful model for a schedule of accommodation to form part of an architect's brief. A crucial factor in determining the size of the library media centre, as for school libraries elsewhere, is the percentage of the student body which is required to be seated in the library at any one time.

Canada's standards date from the late 1970s and are in the process of being updated. Entitled, *Resource services for Canadian schools*, it includes a discussion of facilities for the individual school and the district learning resource centre.[29]

A number of provinces in Canada and states in the USA have also produced their own local standards, for example Nova Scotia and Saskatchewan;[30] Ohio and Maryland,[31] that usually include a section on facilities. That for Maryland[32] recommends the following space allocations for the school library media centre:

1   Up to 600 pupils, 5,650 ft² (525 m²) – space for reading, viewing, listening, etc., 3,000 ft² (279 m²)
2   600–900 pupils, 8,100 ft² (752 m²) – space for reading, viewing, listening, etc, 4,500 ft² (418 m²)
2   900–1,200 pupils, 11,100 ft² (1,031 m²) – space for reading, viewing, listening, etc., 6,000 ft² (557 m²).

Children and young people
International guidelines

IFLA has produced two publications of interest to those planning facilities for children and young people. The first of these is *Guidelines for public libraries* (1986),[33] and the second, *Guidelines for children's services.*[34] The former gives some guidance on planning public library service points including facilities for children and young people. Its section in the guidelines on layout and planning includes a discussion of the appropriateness of the separation of adult and children's facilities in large, small and medium-sized libraries, and provision for teenagers, commenting in the latter case that it is probably not desirable to provide a separate department. Other than this, little guidance is offered, and no quantitative space recommendations, as it is considered that in the present state of library development they were not likely to be relevant. However, an appendix to the 1986 guidelines quotes the quantitative space recommendations from the previous edition, *Standards for public libraries* (1973), which includes those areas in public library buildings for children.[35]

These quantitative standards provide space guidance on children's lending and activity areas, but none, for example, on separate study space, computer facilities or the housing of non-book formats. The following figures[37] are offered for lending services – 16 m² (172 ft²) for every 1000 volumes on the open shelves, assuming shelf units of four shelves. This will allow for circulation space, staff counters, catalogues, etc. It will lead to the following likely provision for lending purposes:

(a) population of 10,000, 75–100 m² (807–1,076 ft²)

(b) population of between 10,000 and 20,000, 100–200 m² (1,076–2,152 ft²)

(c) children's activities

    (i) children as an audience, 1.5 m² (16 ft²) per place

    (ii) various creative activities, 3 m² (32 ft²) per place.

Public library space guidance in the 1973 standards, on provision for an exhibition area, storage of reserve stock, and staff workrooms and offices, for example, might also prove useful in certain circumstances in planning the children's library. The appendix to the 1986 guidelines notes that these 1973 figures are unrevised and usually intended to be minima; readers are referred to the original publications for fuller details. This statement is not quite accurate as the space required for 1,000 children's books has been increased from 15 m² (161 ft²) to 16 m² (172 ft²) in the appendix to the guidelines of 1986.

The more recent *Guidelines for children's services* is seen as supplementing IFLA's *Guidelines for public libraries*, and includes a section on facilities that covers such topics as service points, qualities required of such service points, types of area for public, technical and administrative services, and furniture and equipment, but offers no guidance on the calculation of space requirements.[37]

United Kingdom guidelines

Standards of public library service in England and Wales (Bourdillon Report), published in 1962, is still the major national source of guidance available on public library size. When published it generally endorsed the IFLA public library standards of the time, with which the Library Association's recommendations coincided,[39] and commented that provision should be made for young people on a basis of 1,000–1,500 ft² (93–140 m²) in large- and medium-sized libraries with additional study space where necessary. The allocation on which these calculations for the children's department were based was that of 50 ft² (4.6 m²) per 1,000 population for a medium-sized library.[40] No attention was given in the Bourdillon standards to libraries for populations below 10,000. *Public library service points* (1971) considered 'it desirable to provide an area of at least 2,000 sq ft in any library open for 30 hours a week or more, though not necessarily in an urban in-filling service point'. This area (500 sq ft per 1,000 for a population of 4,000) 'will provide adequately for the larger shelf stock . . . the provision of display and exhibition facilities which can help the public library play a vigorous part in the life of small communities'.[41] No mention is made as to how much of this space should be for children, however.

As demonstrated above, later IFLA space standards are bookstock rather than population based, although bookstock is based on population size. IFLA recommend that one-third of total stock (at two to three volumes per inhabitant) be provided for children up to 14 years old where they constitute 25–30% of the population; greater provision will be needed where it is more than 30%.[42]

The position on the availability of up-to-date quantitative space guidance was not really improved by the publication in 1991 of *Children and young people: Library Association guidelines for public library services*, which includes a section on planning and design.[43] This document covers a variety of topics of interest, including the arguments for and against separate or shared provision, siting, the range of areas and facilities that might be required, guidance on the layout and design of children's libraries (including comments on furniture), and the need to coordinate the planning and design of the adult department with that for children. Only one space calculation is given (that for housing 1,000 volumes), taken from the IFLA *Standards for public libraries* rather than the later IFLA *Guidelines for public libraries*, thus quoting 15 m² rather than 16 m².

Given the age of the Bourdillon standards, those of IFLA are seen as generally more relevant by British librarians today and may be adopted by particular public library systems, possibly in an amended way (that is, two-thirds IFLA standards), to suit local circumstances. The tables of space allocations provided for each building described in *Public library buildings 1975–1983* and its companion volume *Library buildings 1984–1989*, give a picture of the amount of space that has been allocated for particular populations, bookstocks, and local circumstances to children and young people in Britain's public library buildings of recent years.[44]

North American guidelines

The American Library Association issued *Standards for children's services in public libraries* in 1964 and surprisingly no more recent document has appeared. In spite of its title, it offered no quantitative space guidance in its very short final section on physical facilities.[45] In its latter section the standards devotes three paragraphs to: the requirement to have a separately allocated space for children; space to serve efficiently the various activities of children's services, and furniture and equipment to meet the needs of children, seen as being from infancy to about 13.

An example of local standards is the more recent *Standards for youth services in public libraries of the New York State*, which considers children and young adult work separately in the one document.[46] In both cases there is a short section on physical facilities, that for children reminiscent of the American Library Association's 1964 standards, but no quantitative guidance offered in either instance or elsewhere in the document. Some useful points made for children include:

1   The area for children should be an integral part of the entire library.
2   Wheelchair access and safe restrooms.
3   Ample seating, audiovisual capabilities, and an adequate supply of protected electrical outlets are essential.

For young adults, questions of location, quality of the allotted space, access to staff, furniture and equipment, and access to bulletin board space and computers are briefly considered.[47]

Under the heading of 'Service to the community', the point is made in the standards that: 'Community needs should provide the basis for planning library service to children.'[48] Interestingly, an appendix on competencies for librarians serving youth, states that the librarian will be able to 'Develop physical facilities which contribute to the achievement of youth services program goals; Create an environment which attracts and invites young people to use the collection; [and] Involve young adults, and children, as appropriate, in planning and implementing services to their age group.'[49] Other states, such as Florida (1985), Massachusetts (1987) and North Carolina (1988) have issued standards or guideline documents that include some consideration of physical facilities.

Anne Gagnon's pamphlet, *Guidelines for children's services*, the first in a series produced under the auspices of the Canadian Association of Children' Librarians, and which contains a short section on facilities, is intended as a guide to action, rather than 'quantitative standards for measuring your library service' in small- and medium-sized public libraries. The brief comments, later listed in the document as a checklist, cover many of the matters dealt with in later chapters of this book, such as location, signs, size of furniture, study area, meeting room, and safety precautions and ends with the thought that: 'Library facilities are initially judged on their visual impact.'

European guidelines

France

La bibliothèque dans la ville (*The library in the town*), published in association with France's Ministry of Culture, Office for Books and Reading, is a handbook for planning public library buildings that incorporates 20 recent case studies of such libraries. Its contents include tables of space allocations for central libraries and branches in France based on population ranges, annual acquisitions and the number of staff for each. Five elements for the children's area are noted in each such library's 'programme': lending, reference, periodicals, story hour and activities room. Four space allocations are indicated in each table as the reference collection and periodicals are seen as one area. Provision for adults and adolescents is combined and takes up the largest amount of space in each programme.

These tables are followed by a list[51] (*Surface des différentes aires d'activité*) showing how calculations can be made for the children's section:

1   Lending collection, 1.45 m² for 100 volumes – based on a stated number of books per metre, number of shelves per bay and spacing of shelving. The calculation allows for issue desk, seats (2.5 per 1,000 volumes) some tables, etc.
2   Reference collection, 0.90 m² for 100 volumes, determined in the same way as the lending area, and 2.5 m² per seat.
3   Periodicals, 38 m² per 100, determined in the same manner as for the lending and reference areas, and 1 seat for 10 periodicals.
4   Story hour, 1.10 m² per seat.
5   Activities area, 2 m² per seat.

The figure for the lending area is similar to the 1973 IFLA figure when made up to 1,000 volumes, those for activities, including storytelling, somewhat lower; extensive provision of periodicals in children's libraries – 8 to 30, depending on size – is not something that receives special attention in other documents.

Sweden

Unlike other Scandinavian countries, there are no laws regulating public library work in Sweden and this perhaps explains the absence of standards. *Folkbibliotekslokaler* (Public library buildings), published in 1981, therefore, helpfully provides guidance on space for libraries serving populations of 15,000, 25,000 and 50,000, at 2,045 m^2, 2,955 m^2 and 5,180 m^2 respectively.[52] The table of space allocations for departments and areas within each size of library, includes figures for the children's library, which consists of five main elements: young children's section; section for older children (8–12 years old); information area (information desk, catalogue, etc.), meeting room (which can be integrated with a group listening room for children, the latter otherwise listed with the music library spaces) and storage. For the three above-mentioned sizes of library, figures of 245 m^2, 315 m^2, and 405 m^2 are quoted for the children's library, although it is pointed out for the table as a whole that the figures are not recommendations but examples, taking into account significant activities, the size of a library's collection and the number of staff employed.

New Zealand guidelines

Standards for public library service in New Zealand provides an example of the adoption, incorporation and extension of IFLA's standards for public library buildings into a national standards document,[53] as well as making use of the Library Association of Australia's *Interim minimum standards for public libraries* (1972) in their formulation. Using the 1973 figure of 15 m^2 (rather than 16 m^2), for every 1,000 volumes on the open shelves, it provides a table of space requirements for children's lending and study areas related to a range of populations (3,000–150,000). Given for each population figure is: total bookstock, books on shelves (the basis of the main space calculation) and the number of study places. The latter is calculated on the basis of one per 3,000 population, with a minimum of two, requiring 2 m^2 each. Thus for a population of 50,000 a total lending and study area for children would come to 484 m^2, that is, 450 m^2 for the on shelves bookstock (30,000 items) and 34 m^2 for 17 seats. The figure includes circulation space, issue and return desks, catalogue and informal seating.

Space sizes for types of children's activity in groups of 20 to 60 in number are also tabulated, and are based on the allocations recommended by IFLA, but with the addition of a standard of four places per 1.5 m^2 for story hour type activities. A table is also given by population size for the 'transitional services' space requirements for young adults, noted as ranging from a few bays of shelving in a small library to a special area in larger ones. For populations of 15,000, 50,000 and 100,000, 8 m^2, 25 m^2, and 50 m^2 are respectively are recommended. As with IFLA standards, other more general guidance on workrooms and offices etc., is provided in the document and this can be usefully employed in calculating space requirements for other aspects of library service to children and young people.

Unlike the position with schools in the UK, or state public libraries in the USA, there is little evidence of the preparation by UK public library systems of local standards or guidelines to direct policy and practice, including that related to children and young people and their accommodation. The changing political and financial climate would seem to encourage their formulation, however.

Guidelines for road vehicles

There are no guidelines for special vehicles to serve children and young people, but IFLA's *Mobile library guidelines*,[54] published in 1991 for the IFLA Round Table on Mobile Libraries, recognizes the existence of such vehicles and notes that they are a reflection of the degree of sophistication of the total library service.[55] However, bearing in mind Ronald Pybus's comment about the applicability of principles in planning specialist vehicles, it is thought worthwhile to provide an outline of these guidelines insofar as they relate to the vehicle itself.

The relevant sections of *Mobile libraries guidelines* concern finance, in particular vehicle costs; vehicles (types and technical matters); furniture and equipment, and the service base. Before giving details of the first two topics (the last two will be dealt with in later chapters), it is worth drawing attention to the guidelines' advice that they should be adapted to local conditions and environments as these vary from country to country.

The section on finance recommends that all vehicles should be purpose-built and provides a method for calculating the replacement costs of a mobile library over ten years (using an annuity), which for a mobile library costing 100,000 units (sterling, dollars, marks, francs, etc.) would be 259,374 units, assuming an annual inflation rate of 10%. 'At an assumed annual interest rate of 10 per cent, with no tax liabilities, the annual contribution required of the authority for the replacement fund would be 16,275 units.'[56] This section also draws attention to ways of compiling the annual operational budget for the mobile library and states the need to take into account the 'Specific budgetary items which are distinctive to mobile library operations . . .', for example vehicle maintenance and repair, stopping place repair and the vehicle replacement fund.[57]

The section on vehicles restricts itself to three types: van, bus and semi-trailer or articulated type, and, while noting the wide range of sizes, states that neither the interior height nor the interior width should be less than 2 metres (6.5 feet). The following overall lengths are suggested for the three types of vehicle:

(a) Van type – overall length about 7 m (23 ft) carrying 1,500 to 2,000 volumes.
(b) Bus type – overall length about 10 m (33 ft) carrying 3,000 to 4,000 volumes.
(c) Semi–trailer – overall length may be in excess of 15 m (50 ft), carrying around 5,000 volumes.

A survey of 1985 showed that very few vehicles in use in England and Wales approached 15 metres in length and none were in excess of it.[58] The rest of this section of the guidelines deals with technical recommendations with regard to the engine, chassis, brakes, mirrors, interior finish, safety features, etc.[59]

References

1 Withers, F. N., *Standards for library service: an international survey*, Paris, Unesco, 1974, 16.

2 Idem, 17.

3 Carroll, F. L., *Guidelines for school libraries*, The Hague, International Federation of Library Associations, 1990, 23–31.

4 Idem, 34.

5 Library and Information Services Council, *School libraries: the foundations of the curriculum*, London, HMSO, 1984, 14–15.

6 Department of Education and Science. Architects and Building Group, *Area guidelines for secondary schools*, London, Department of Education and Science, 1983, 5, 14–8.

7 Department of Education and Science. Architects and Building Group, *Area guidelines for sixth form, tertiary and NAFE colleges*, London, Department of Education and Science, 1983, 3, 11.

8 Department of Education and Science. Architects and Building Group, *Accommodation for the 16–19 age group: NAFE: designing for change*, London, Department of Education and Science, 1980.

9 Department of Education and Science, *Educational design initiatives in city technology colleges*, London, HMSO, 1991, 57.

10 School Library Association, *School libraries: steps in the right direction. Guidelines for a school library resource centre*, Swindon, School Library Association, 1989, 3–4.

11 Charlton, L., *Designing and planning a secondary school library resource centre*, [Swindon], School Library Association, 1992.

12 Idem, 6.

13 Idem, 7.

14 Kinnell, M. (ed.), *Learning resources in schools: Library Association guidelines for school libraries*, London, Library Association, 1992, 26–36.

15 Library Association, *Library resource provision in schools: guidelines and recommendations*, reprinted with supplement, London, Library Association, 1977, 41–2.

16 Department of Education circular 1982/87 Northern Ireland.

17 Scottish Library Association, *The school library resource service and the curriculum 'before five' to 'sixteen plus'*, Motherwell, Scottish Library Association, 1985, 58–59, Appendix IV.

18 Library and Information Services Council(Wales), *Report of a working group on libraries in maintained secondary schools in Wales*, Cardiff, Library and Information Services Council (Wales), 1990, 2, 9.

19 Bradford Education Library Service, *The effective junior and middle school library*, Bradford, Bradford Metropolitan Council, 1990.

20 Cambridgeshire County Council Education Service, *Learning resources in secondary schools: guidelines for good practice*, Cambridge, CCCES, 1988, 27.

21 Somerset County Council Library Service, *Briefing notes on central*

library/resource centres in schools, Bridgwater, School Library Service Resource Centre, 1988, para. 3 in both sections.

22 American Association of School Librarians and the Department of Audiovisual Instruction of the National Education Association, *Library standards for school media programs*, Chicago, American Library Association, 1969.

23 Idem, vi.

24 American Association of School Librarians and the Association for Educational Communications and Technology, *Media programs: district and school*, American Library Association, 1975.

25 American Association of School Librarians and the Association for Educational Communications and Technology, *Information power: guidelines for school library media programs*, Chicago, American Library Association, 1988.

26 Idem, ix.

27 Idem, x.

28 Idem, 131.

29 Branscombe, F. R. and Newsom, H. E. (eds.), *Resource services for Candian schools*, Toronto, McGraw–Hill Ryerson, 1977.

30 Sernich, G., *Learning resource centres in Saskatchewan: a guide for development*, Regina, Saskatchewan Education, 1988; Nova Scotia School Library Association of the Nova Scotia Teachers Union, *Nova Scotia school libraries: standards and practices*, Nova Scotia, Nova Scotia School Library Association of the Nova Scotia Teachers Union, 1987.

31 Ohio Department of Education, *Quality library services K-12*, Colombus, Ohio, Ohio Department of Education, 1986; Maryland State Board of Education, *Standards for school library media programs in Maryland*, Baltimore, Md, Maryland State Board of Education, 1987.

32 Maryland State Board of Education, op. cit., 21.

33 International Federation of Library Associations, Section of Public Libraries, *Guidelines for public libraries*, Munich, Saur, 1986.

34 Fasick, A. M. (ed.), *Guidelines for children's services*, The Hague, International Federation of Library Associations, 1991.

35 International Federation of Library Associations, Section of Public Libraries, *Standards for public libraries*, Munich, Verlag Dokumentation, 1973, 47–9.

36 International Federation of Library Associations, Section of Public Libraries, *Guidelines for public libraries*, 64.

37 Fasick, op. cit., 19–25.

38 For a useful summary, *see* Thompson, G., *Planning and design of library buildings*, London, Butterworth, 1989, 201–5.

39 Library Association, *Public library buildings: the way ahead*, London, Library Association, 1960.

40 Ministry of Education, *Standards of public library service in England and Wales*, London, HMSO, 1962, 120–1.

41 Department of Education and Science, *Public library service points*, London, HMSO, 1971, 11–12.

42 International Federation of Library Associations, Section of Public Libraries, *Standards for public libraries*, 24.

43 Library Association, *Children and young people: Library Association guidelines for public library services*, London, Library Association, 1991, 12–6.

44 Harrison, K. C. (ed.), *Public library buildings 1975–1983*, London, Library Services Ltd, 1987; Harrison, K. C. (ed.), *Library buildings 1984–1989*, London, Library Services Ltd, 1990.

45 American Library Association, *Standards for children's services in public libraries*, [Chicago?], American Library Association, 1964, 23–4.

46 New York Library Association, *Standards for youth services in public libraries of New York State*, New York, New York Library Association, 1984.

47 Idem, 9, 11, 15.

48 Idem, 6.

49 Idem, 24, 25, 26.

50 Gagnon, A., *Guidelines for children's services*, Ontario, Canadian Library Association, 1989, 9–10.

51 Bisbrouck, M-F., *La bibliothèque dans la ville*, Paris, Editions du Moniteur, 1984, 171–91.

52 Statens Kulturråd, Folkbibliotekslokaler en handbok, Stockholm, Statens Kulturråd, 1981, 130–1.

53 New Zealand Library Association, *Standards for public library service in New Zealand 1980, reprinted with additional policy statements 1988*, Wellington, New Zealand Library Association, 1988, 19–27.

54 Pestell, R., *Mobile library guidelines*, The Hague, International Federation of Library Associations, 1991.

55 Idem, 4.

56 Idem, 10.

57 Idem, 11–12.

58 Pybus, R. L., *Mobile libraries in England and Wales: a guide to their construction and use*, 2nd edn, St Albans, Branch and Mobile Group of the Library Association, 1985.

59 Pestell, op. cit., 13–24.

7 LOCATION OF THE LIBRARY

Generally speaking, the issue for school libraries and public library facilities for children and young people is that of location rather than siting; the relationship of the school or children's library with other school or public library departments and areas in the same building, rather than with other buildings and, in the public library case, the wider external environment. However, some school libraries may be in a separate building, independently sited to the main or other school buildings (Elgar High School, Worcester, for example) and, in some circumstances, provision for children and young people may be made in a service point separate to one offering services to adults. Located in a school, and serving both school and the local community, including children, is the dual-purpose library.

In all these cases, location or siting will be a crucial factor in determining the amount of use and thus in many ways the success of the library. Peggy Heeks, talking about the siting of public library buildings, confirms that it 'is the most important single factor in its success – more important than its size' and, that where there is a choice location should take priority over size.[1] The ease with which the library can be visited, the entrance located, and entry for all, including the disabled, are, along with generous opening times, therefore crucial.

Schools
Location and access

The school library resource centre is often seen as the hub or centre of a school and its work, and this should be reflected in its location. The Cohens put this strongly when they write: 'In some educational facilities the library is not tangential to the classrooms, it is the focal point of the entire complex, so much so that the building was designed with the library as the ideological and physical center.'[2]

In a single-storey school on a large site, the library could occupy part of a centrally placed wing. In some instances, however, as noted earlier, the library may constitute an entirely separate building but the accessibility of its location with regards to the rest of the school buildings is vitally important.[3] Anthony Thompson also suggests that: 'If a [school] library is an independent building, access by some form of covered way, . . . should be considered; and a lobby or vestibule large enough to hang coats is needed, as well as lavatories.'[4] Millfield School Library and Resource Centre, Somerset (1980) is a separate building located next to the main entrance to the school and it was hoped it would come to symbolize the school's aspirations. Although not on a covered way, it does provide toilets and bags/cloakroom facilities for pupils. The library lies to the edge of the campus with some school buildings close by but others not so close.[5]

On urban sites, where there is less space, and multi-storied school buildings are likely, the School Library Association recommends a ground floor location with vehicular access;[6] this allows for the delivery of books and other materials. If access is required after school hours (including Saturdays), for school and/or community use, this will further influence decisions about a ground floor location and possibly an after-hours entrance. If the library is not located on the ground floor, it should be located all on a single floor and not higher than the first floor of the building. The resource centre at Bacon's City Technology College, Rotherhithe, with its semi-circular glass-fronted feature, is located on the first floor and is accessible (and visible) by stairs from the converging wings of the college building. Leigh City Technology College, Dartford, also has its library on the first floor of its main block.

Colin Ray notes that the school library 'must be where everyone can visit it easily and conveniently'.[7] This reaffirms the idea that it should occupy a central location – the heart of the school. However, where a central location is perhaps impossible because of a school plan solution dictated by the site, or the need for after school hours access, for example, Ellsworth and Wagener recommend compromise, such as a location 'along the edge of the center – on the periphery of the building, . . . rather than deep inside it'.[8]

Where a 'central' location is not possible, then it is suggested that the library should be closest to those who can be expected to make most use of it. However, whatever its location, the school library should not be used as a classroom, as a 'dump' for unsupervised students, nor seen as a sixth-form private study areas to the regular exclusion of younger pupils.

Speaking of American students, the architect, Robert Brown, indicates that, while 'the drop-in library, along a main path where students feel they can stop at any time to study or socialize' (the library at the 'centre' approach), is commonly supported, a minority voice would like the library to be separate, remote – the 'place to go for a different feeling' or 'to get away'.[9] One understands this view without necessarily agreeing with it; most of these minority requirements could be met in a well-designed, user-orientated accessibly placed library with adequate space.

The visible library

Whatever its site or location, students need to be reminded of the presence and position of the library by adequate directional signs within the school and an external location sign and, if possible, by a glimpse of the interior as they pass by it. A wooden door marked 'library' or 'resource centre' in small letters is no way to demonstrate its location nor to signify its importance to staff and students. As Frances Carroll has written: 'A desirable location affirms the philosophy that materials of the school library media center have a centrality to learning and learning to society.'[10] At the Royal Grammar School, High Wycombe, the school's main entrance provides a good view into the library which is opposite it and, because of its height (it is in a converted hall), there is a view down into the library from a first floor corridor glazed partition. At Standish Community High School, Wigan, (Figure 7.1), a glass fronted information technology room adjacent to the inviting entrance advertises the library resource centre's presence more forcibly to students passing by.

Relocation

Opportunities may arise to improve on the location of the library within the school building, and Leonore Charlton offers the following advice[11]:

(a) Examine all areas of the school.
(b) Consider the possibility of exchanging present location for one more centrally located.
(c) Alternatively, knock through into an adjacent room to create extra space. Create arches if walls cannot be removed. This gives some privacy and divides areas while still allowing supervision.
(d) An open area is more flexible than a number of small rooms.

The questions of location and expansion are considered in more detail below.

Primary and middle schools

Bradford Education Library Service recommend that ideally the library should be centralized in one place with easy and open access to all but that in practical terms it may have to be located in a number of different places to ensure such ready access.[12]

Fig. 7.1 *Standish Community High School, Wigan – entrance to library resource centre with information technology room to left of entrance*

Somerset Library Service offer some additional points to those considered in this chapter and suggest[13]:

(a) That the library be overseeable from as many teaching spaces as possible

(b) It is preferable that pupils do not have to leave the building to visit the library, especially in primary schools.

(c) That ideally the library should not be part of a larger area used for other functions. If such a space is not available, the implications of the other users (e.g. noise) should be taken into account, and the library element of shared space clearly identified and defined.

(d) It may be desirable to locate reprographic and other resource-creating facilities adjacent to the library.

(e) Consideration should be given to the relative location of any other resource areas (e.g. audiovisual materials, computer area) not allowed for in the library.

Secondary schools

Somerset Library Service offer some additional points to those considered in this chapter and suggest that[14]:

(a) If not located at the geographic centre, then a position where there is already a high pupil traffic (e.g. near the main entrance).

(b) Consideration should be given to the relative location of any other resource collections (e.g. careers information, sixth-form study space) where not allowed for in the library resource centre.

At Winstanley Sixth Form College, Wigan, the careers service is adjacent to the library entrance and some careers material is housed in the library.

Factors affecting location

As indicated above, many factors may affect the siting or location of a school library, including a resistance to building on a 'sensitive' site in an old school, but the following are particularly important.

Access

It has been recommended that the school library 'should be on a thoroughfare; but it should not <u>be</u> a thoroughfare'. However, an informal reading area for younger children might be created out of a corridor through which they pass.[15] As the examples below indicate, many library/resource areas in primary and middle schools may be part of commonly owned circulation/teaching space. Where the school library is not placed centrally, then, as indicated earlier, a location, such as close to the school entrance, that staff and students regularly pass for other reasons might be considered. Other important factors affecting location include the library's relationship to the staff room and other resources, including information technology facilities, as at the Study Centre, Petersfield School, Hampshire.

Disabled access

A Department of Education and Science publication provides guidance (minimum requirements) on making educational buildings, both new and old, accessible to disabled people, including their arrival, departure, parking, approach and entrance, and means of escape. It noted that, where disabled pupils are present in larger numbers, provision will need to be greater than the suggested minimum.[16]

For schools, good accessibility will depend upon the relationship of the library to the rest of the school building or buildings. For the public library service point for children, its siting in relation to the rest of the community will be important, including the question of accessibility on foot, bicycle, car or public transport. Access to the public library building for the disabled child and young person is equally as important as in schools. Selwyn Goldsmith considers the needs of both the wheelchair and ambulant disabled in *Designing for the disabled*, both generally and in terms of specific building types, such as schools and libraries. He notes in the latter case that at least one entrance, preferably the main one, should be accessible to chairbound people.[17] At the Wiend Centre for children, which includes an exhibition hall, there is disabled access to all floors and toilet facilities.

Expansion

Consideration should be given to the future expansion possibilities for the library of the chosen location. With future needs and growth in mind, the library could adjoin a classroom or other easily altered and incorporated space for possible future expansion. The placement of stairs, lifts, and rooms with plumbing that is not easily altered, will possibly constrain expansion opportunities and should be taken into account when considering the library's proposed location and future space needs. The location of the library at the end or at the side of a building may allow for a future built extension, as well as (or instead of) taking over adjacent classrooms or other space. Diagrams in such publications as *The school library* and *School media centres* give some helpful illustrations of the possible location of the school library in relation to both access and expansion.[18]

Noise

In order to avoid disturbance from noise 'the library must be carefully located in relation to the areas for music, physical education and workshop activity'.[19] Also noise from the playground must be taken into account. However, the question of noise is probably less important than accessibility.

Decentralization

The School Library Association states that: 'The establishment of several independent "libraries" in various parts of the premises without a dominant central unit must at all costs be avoided: the functions of a school library and resource centre cannot be fulfilled under such conditions.'[20] However, the association recognizes that in a large secondary school separate provision (junior and senior) may be provided and in different blocks, but states a preference for adjacent and communicating libraries.[21]

Careful integration, however, would seem a much better solution. However, if access to library resources is to be encouraged in a large school, such physical separation may be necessary.

Modern primary schools are likely to have a central library resource, which might occupy quite a small area, easily accessible from adjacent activities areas, and with small classroom libraries associated with other teaching and learning resources.

As noted in *Information power*; 'Convenience and high usage may dictate that certain resources be housed closer to the point of use, such as in subject resource centres.'[22] Such dispersed resources should, however, be available to the whole school; central automated resource control identifies their location.

Some examples of location

Schools of thought: Hampshire architecture 1974–1991, describes with plans the building output of Hampshire County Architects Department, and in particular its many schools, mainly infant, primary and middle schools.[23] Distinctive architecture and a careful consideration of site have led to a number of much appreciated schools of which resource and library areas form part.

Generally speaking the library and associated resource areas are close to the entrance and staff room (sometimes adjacent) and form part of the shared/circulation area. The library and resource areas may not be strongly defined, or conversely well defined but open to circulation space and possibly visible over a low internal wall. At Queen's Inclosure First School (Figure 7.2) the library is located in a pod that is open to the circulation space. Depending on the school plan the library will tend to be located centrally or towards one end of the school, as at Hatch Warren Junior School, Basingstoke (Figure 7.3)

A more recent Hampshire school, Woodlea Primary School (Figure 7.4) has the library and information space at the centre of the building, but the school is seen as outward looking as it is intended 'to encourage children to make use of the landscape as a learning resource [and this] is reflected in the numerous entrances and exits from the building'.[24] This means the library is less busy than its hub position would suggest although not all classrooms are yet in place.

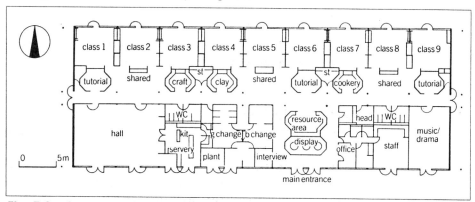

Fig. 7.2 *Queen's Inclosure First School, Cowplain (1988)*
(Reproduced through the courtesy of the Architects Dept., Hampshire CC)

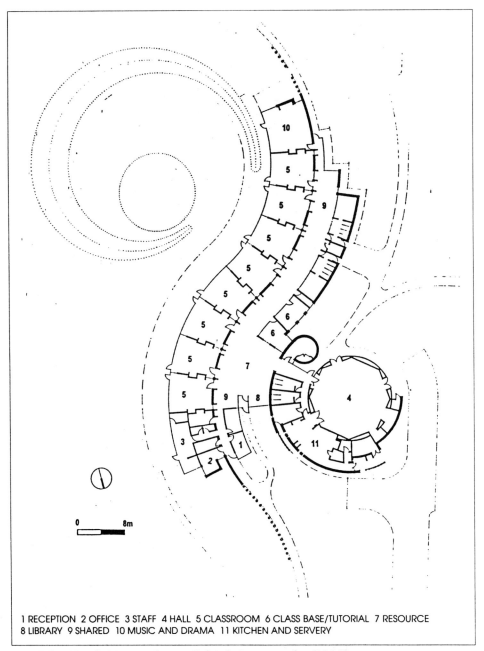

1 RECEPTION 2 OFFICE 3 STAFF 4 HALL 5 CLASSROOM 6 CLASS BASE/TUTORIAL 7 RESOURCE
8 LIBRARY 9 SHARED 10 MUSIC AND DRAMA 11 KITCHEN AND SERVERY

Fig. 7.3 *Hatch Warren Junior School, Basingstoke (1990)*
(Reproduced through the courtesy of the Architects Dept., Hampshire CC)

Nelson Mandela Community Primary School has its library close to the entrance, adjacent to the assembly hall, and open to a central 'street' that is wide enough to function as a teaching space.[25]

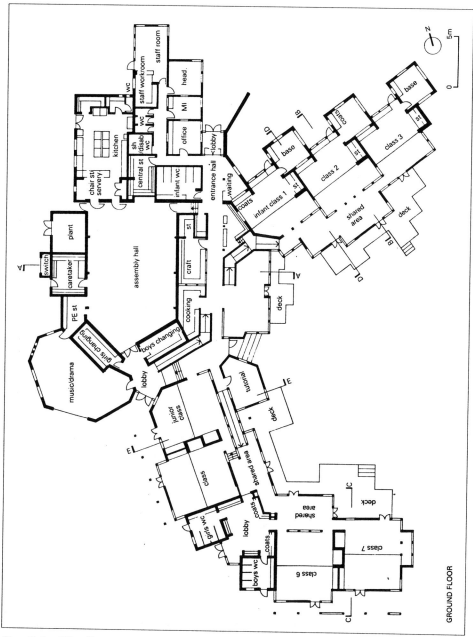

Fig. 7.4 *Woodlea Primary School (1992)*
(Reproduced through the courtesy of the Architects Dept., Hampshire CC)

Swanlea Secondary School, Whitechapel (Figure 7.5) is the first new London secondary school for ten years and claims to incorporate the design implications of the National Curriculum. It is planned round a series of courtyards and a central mall connects all the ground floor areas. The library is on the ground floor at the beginning of the mall facing the school entrance. To one side and accessible through the library

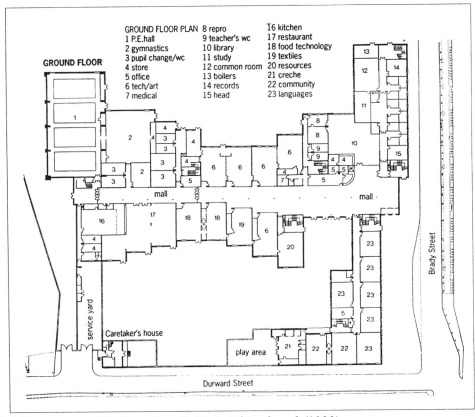

Fig. 7.5 *Swanlea Secondary School, Whitechapel (1993)*
(Reproduced through the courtesy of the Percy Thomas Partnership)

is the media resources workshop dealing with reprographics, off-air recordings, etc., and to the rear a study area for teacher's professional development which is adjacent to the staff common room.[26] An article in the *Architects' journal* briefly outlines the participatory process for the design of Tanbridge Comprehensive School, West Sussex, with its philosophy of a 'school-as a-village'. The library is shown in the middle of a run of classroom clusters to one side of an entrance, with the staff room on the opposite side of the entrance.[27]

As regards the location of city technology colleges, the DES states that: 'It is important for the library to occupy a central space in the college, so that it can be easily reached from all parts. All curriculum areas require access to library material at some stage. Ideally it should be visually linked to the main circulation or reception area.'[28] Djanogly City Technology College, Nottingham (1989), has its library centrally placed, near the school reception area, and adjacent to a quiet central courtyard. Figure 7.6 shows the position at Emmanuel College of Technology, Tyneside (1990).

Dual-purpose libraries

While many advantages can be advanced for dual-purpose libraries, the greatest criticism can be of their siting for access by the local community. In small com-

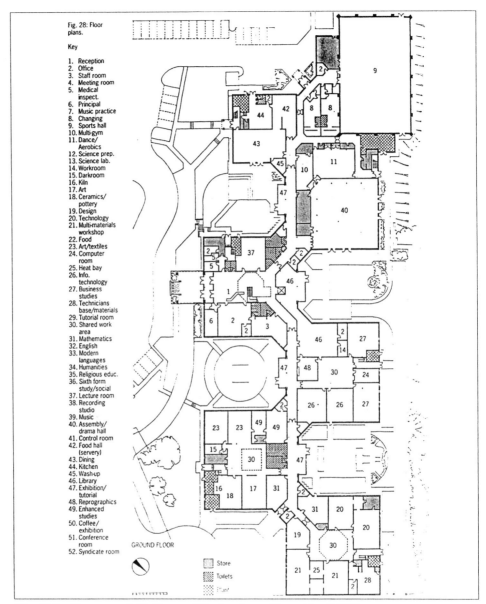

Fig. 28: Floor plans.

Key

1. Reception
2. Office
3. Staff room
4. Meeting room
5. Medical inspect.
6. Principal
7. Music practice
8. Changing
9. Sports hall
10. Multi-gym
11. Dance/ Aerobics
12. Science prep.
13. Science lab.
14. Workroom
15. Darkroom
16. Kiln
17. Art
18. Ceramics/ pottery
19. Design
20. Technology
21. Multi-materials workshop
22. Food
23. Art/textiles
24. Computer room
25. Heat bay
26. Info. technology
27. Business studies
28. Technicians base/materials
29. Tutorial room
30. Shared work area
31. Mathematics
32. English
33. Modern languages
34. Humanities
35. Religious educ.
36. Sixth form study/social
37. Lecture room
38. Recording studio
39. Music
40. Assembly/ drama hall
41. Control room
42. Food hall (servery)
43. Dining
44. Kitchen
45. Wash-up
46. Library
47. Exhibition/ tutorial
48. Reprographics
49. Enhanced studies
50. Coffee/ exhibition
51. Conference room
52. Syndicate room

GROUND FLOOR

Store
Toilets
Plant

Fig. 7.6 *Emmanuel College of Technology, Tyneside (1990)*
(Crown copyright. Reproduced with the permission of the Controller of HMSO)

munities the school may be sited centrally, in larger communities schools may not be in the centre of town and thus they may be rather far away for the elderly, the disabled, and mothers with young children to easily visit. Access for students, school staff and the general public, usually means two separate entrances and a location of the library within the school that may favour one group over the other.

Writing in 1977, Arthur Jones summarized the problems associated with the siting of dual-purpose libraries.

If public use is not to be inhibited it is important that there should be direct access to the library from the street, and that this should be close to shops or some other focus of pedestrian movement. Secondary schools are seldom situated in shopping centres; however, if the community use of a school is developed on a large scale the school itself might provide such as focus. An educational complex is likely at least to have ample space for car parking, especially in the evening, and in some communities this is a consideration which compensates for the distance from shops and other amenities. Primary schools for younger children are more centrally placed in the communities they serve, and may thus be particularly suitable as bases for dual purpose libraries.[29]

One example of a successful dual-purpose library is the Top Valley Joint Library (Nottingham), reopened in relocated, converted premises within Top Valley Comprehensive School in 1984 (Figure 7.7). Its librarian claimed that its success, demonstrated by its use, 'has been achieved through the careful thought given to the siting, design and staffing of the library'.

The community served by the library consists of two large housing estates on the edge of Nottingham, each with their own row of shops, neither of which are in a central position for the whole area. The school, however, is so sited that none of the houses on the two estates are over a mile away.

Within the school, the library's original location (on the first floor) was not a good one, but the new location, on the ground floor, opposite the main entrance is much more accessible. The library's public entrance faces the road, encouraging community access; the school entrance is at the end of a ground floor corridor leading to all parts of this relatively compact school.

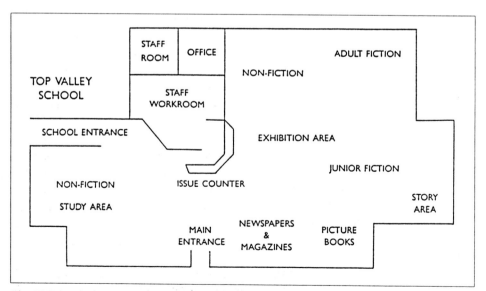

Fig. 7.7 *Top Valley Joint Library, Nottinghamshire (1984)*
(Reproduced through the courtesy of Notts Leisure Services)

Schools Library Service

The location of the schools library service depends on local circumstance but should ensure adequate space. It is preferably housed in a library headquarters, central or district library because of the availability of centralized services and facilities to support its activities.[31] Hertfordshire have recently occupied a converted secondary school building (1,730 m²) on an out-of-town site that houses the county's central libraries support services. The site also houses the schools library service (1250 m²), as well as some other local authority sections.

Public libraries

Geography and population considerations, along with the priorities and objectives of a local authority, will determine the number, size and siting of its public library service points, which may be part of a leisure or civic complex, sited in association with other community facilities, or in a shopping centre. However, it is unlikely that the children's librarian will be involved in any major way in the choice of site for a public library building. Nevertheless, it is vital to ensure that community factors about children and young people (for example population distribution, the location of schools and youth centres, accessibility and traffic problems) have been taken into account in its choice, and that potential problems for children will be minimized. These matters are particularly important in the siting of separate library buildings, or space in a non-library building for children and young people. Most younger children are dependent on parents or carers for library visits and questions of parking, pram, pushchair and buggy space need to be considered.

Barrier free access

Helen Lewins and Frances Renwick, looking at barriers to library access for pre-school children, suggest, after illustrating the various hazards for mother and toddler, that the ideal for wheeled access is: 'wide, automatically opening doors; no steps or staircases either at the entrance or inside; no security barriers to be negotiated; no split level design which would necessitate parking the pushchair and carrying the child(ren).'[32] The authors emphasize that security barriers and doors should be wide enough to accommodate a double pushchair or buggy. As regards mobile and container libraries, they comment that: 'The universal barrier ... was a set of three or more steps at the entrance. Doors, while not wide enough to accommodate double buggies, seemed to present less of a problem than might be expected.'[33]

The access needs of the disabled child have already been mentioned and Margaret Marshall makes a number of points appropriate to their entering the library. These include: reserved parking space close to the building for vehicles carrying children; ramps *and* steps with handrails; lifts with adequate space; wide, preferably automatic, doors; non-slip flooring; good lighting and interior circulation space.[34]

Entrances

While sometimes found in older library buildings, it is not usual to provide a separate children's entrance in public libraries today, as adults and children are often served by a common issue counter. However, it is possible to find libraries where children have a choice of entrance, including one leading directly into their department or area. For example, Birmingham Central Library (1973),[35] with a entrance down a flight of steps from the main lobby and a separate side entry; Salisbury, Wiltshire (1975), where there is direct access from a pedestrian walkway; or Newport, Isle of Wight, (1981), where the individual linked library 'blocks' (one of which is the children's library) encourage this (Figure 7.8). Aylesbury, Buckinghamshire (1987), a conversion of the former ground floor of a Woolworth store, has a main street entrance and a second one for both children and adults at the rear. The latter entrance leads to the children's library and activity area to the left of it; there is a secondary issue counter located here.

The location of the children's library

The need for supervision, the problem of noise, and a common issue desk, often mean that the children's area is located near the issue desk, and is thus usually close to the entrance area of the library, in both single and multi-storied buildings.

In a multi-storey library this can mean the ground floor or entry floor (in a shopping centre, for example, this may not necessarily be at ground floor level). Bexley (1980 and phase 2, 1989) has the children's library occupying a good proportion of the ground floor, together with some adult services, and includes stage/kinderpit, study/activities room and separate children's enquiry desk (Figure 7.9). Sometimes, because of competing demands from non-library occupants of the building, the children's department may be 'isolated' on the ground floor from all or most other public library provision, as, for example, at Croydon (1993), or Stourbridge, Dudley (1985) (Figure 7.10). These ground floor locations are of great benefit from an access point of view, however, to mothers and carers with young children.

Alternatively, however, due to lack of space on the entry floor (a small city-centre site may determine this), the children's library may be placed at first floor level (Petersfield, Hampshire, 1981; Ealing, 1984, on a mezzanine floor), in the basement floor (Newcastle-under-Lyme, Staffordshire, 1975; Chester, 1984), or lower ground

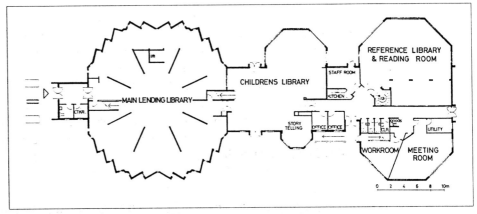

Fig. 7.8 *Newport Library, Isle of Wight CC (1981)*
(Reproduced with the permission of Library Services Ltd)

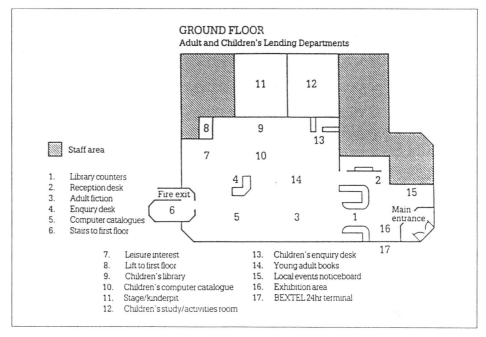

Fig. 7.9 *Bexley Central Library (1980, 1989)*
(Reproduced with the permission of Library Services Ltd)

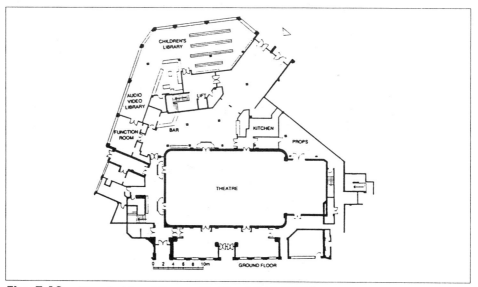

Fig. 7.10 *Stourbridge Library, Dudley MBC (1985)*
(Reproduced with the permission of Library Services Ltd)

floor level (Portsmouth, Hampshire, 1976; Sevenoaks, Kent, 1986, Figure 7.11). The argument being that children (but not perhaps the youngest) can manage stairs more easily than many adults, although a lift should be provided, as is the case, for example, both at Chester (Figure 7.12) and Ealing, if the needs of the disabled and parents with young children are to be considered as well. Basement or lower ground floor locations for children's areas require particular attention over their design if charges that children are getting second-best as regards location are not to be levelled at those responsible for the planning and design of the library. A sloping site may allow for some windows, for example.

Relationship to adult library

Where the adult and children's libraries are on the same floor, whether in single or multi-storied buildings, two main approaches are noticeable as regards their treatment.

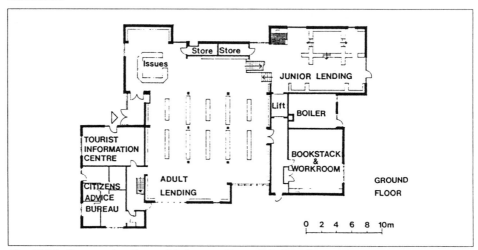

Fig. 7.11 *Sevenoaks Central Library, Kent CC (1986)*
(Reproduced with the permission of Library Services Ltd)

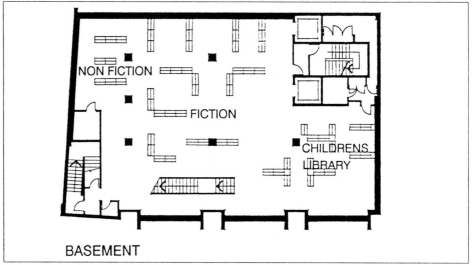

Fig. 7.12 *Chester Library, Cheshire CC (1984)*
(Reproduced with the permission of Library Services Ltd)

Open-plan layout

As a major, yet usually smaller element of an open-plan library compared with the adult section, the children's area is often placed to the left, right or behind a common issue desk for children and adults. Some examples of these locations, seen from the library entrance, are:

(a) left of issue desk – Chorley, Lancashire (1986); Coventry (1986); Ince, Wigan (1985)

(b) right of issue desk – Burntwood, Staffordshire (1987, Figure 7.13); Telford, Shropshire (1988); Woodsend, Trafford (1990)

(c) rear of issue desk – Keith, Moray (1987); Greasby, Wirral (1986, Figure 7.14).

Where the issue desk is in the body of the library, rather that at its entrance, this location can be used to both link and yet separate, to a greater or lesser degree, the adult and children's areas. In such cases the children's area may lie to the front of the issue desk, as at Royston, Hertfordshire (1987), for example (Figure 7.15). In other arrangements, the children's library will often merge into the adult section. A young adults' area may be provided as a transitional area between the two, as at Bexley and Shipley, Bradford (1985) for example (Figure 7.16).

In some larger open plan libraries the children's area may be at the rear of the library, beyond the adult section. Examples of this are to be seen in some Hampshire libraries, for example, at Havant (1991), where it is close to a shared enquiry desk,

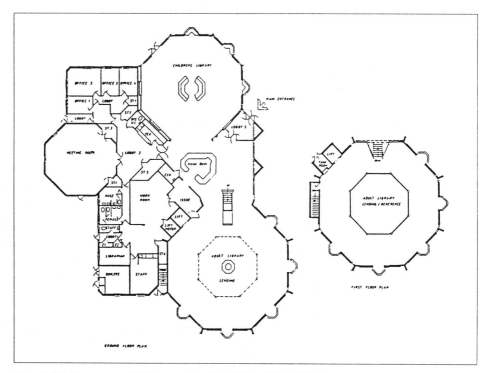

Fig. 7.13 *Burntwood Library, Staffordshire CC (1987)*
(Reproduced with the permission of Library Services Ltd)

and Portchester (1984), where it is a triangle in the corner of the building (Figure 7.17), and in Fleetwood, Lancashire (1988), where a far corner from the issue desk, beyond part of the adult lending stock, is used. This rear position means that in these libraries, unlike the earlier examples, the children's area is neither near the library

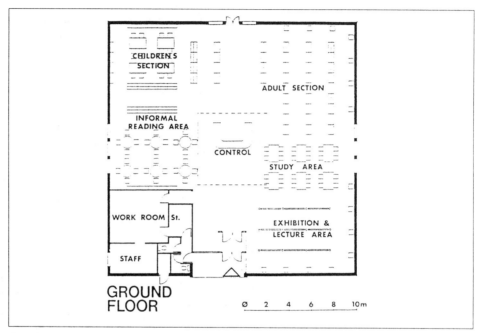

Fig. 7.14 *Greasby Library, Wirral MBC (1986)*
(Reproduced with the permission of Library Services Ltd)

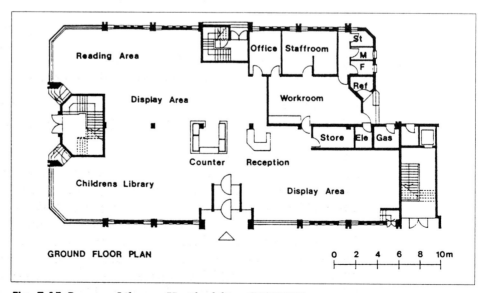

Fig. 7.15 *Royston Library, Hertfordshire CC (1987)*
(Reproduced with the permission of Library Services Ltd)

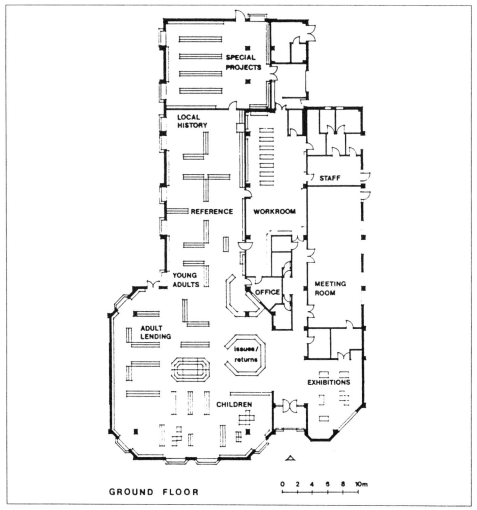

Fig. 7.16 *Shipley Library, Bradford MBC (1985)*
(Reproduced with the permission of Library Services Ltd)

entrance nor its counter. At Carlisle, Cumbria (1986), the children's area is at the far end of level one and has its own counter in operation during busy times.

As a separate department

In some libraries, the children's area may be partially enclosed or completely so as a separate room, for example Conisbrough, Doncaster (1985, Figure 7.18) and Petersfield. Or the children's area may be more closely defined than in some open plan libraries by the shape of the building (St Neots, Cambridgeshire, 1985, Figure 7.19), the arrangement of furniture, or the raising of the children's area above the main floor level, as at Woodthorpe and Reading, Berkshire (1985); the latter has a raised circular area for children. Such design approaches as this, which mark out the children's department or area more closely, could lead to a better allocation of space

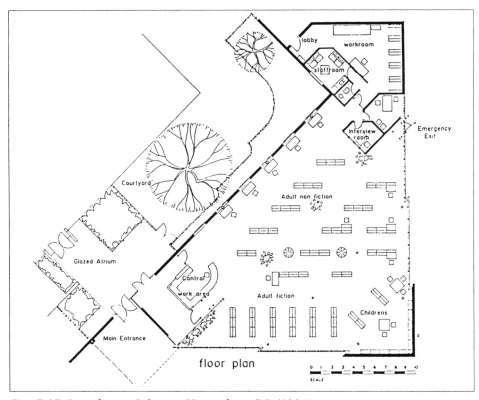

Fig. 7.17 *Portchester Library, Hampshire CC (1984)*
(Reproduced with the permission of Library Services Ltd)

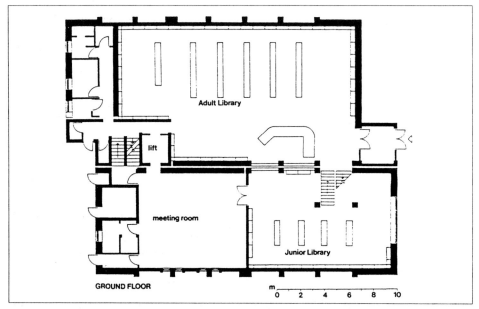

Fig. 7.18 *Conisbrough Branch Library, Doncaster MBC (1985)*
(Reproduced with the permission of Library Services Ltd)

to children within the building as a whole. The children's lending department at Beith Library, Cunninghame (1987), a converted building, is in an enclosed upper floor overlooking the adult library below and there is a separate issue desk.

Separation from the adult library is emphasized where the issue counter is located centrally but enclosed within a foyer or entrance area, which divides the library into two areas for adults and children. This was a design solution that had some popularity in the late 1950s and early 1960s and was used more recently in the L-shaped library at Newent, Gloucestershire (1987).

The children's area may be placed adjacent to a multi-purpose room that can also be used for children's activities, as at Conisbrough. During very busy times a children's library may have its own manned issue counter.

The size and variety of accommodation for children and young people in the largest libraries may suggest a separate, enclosed department, rather than an open-plan arrangement, especially if it is occupying a major part of a building, such as at Birmingham (1973), Dundee (1978) or Croydon central libraries. In the very largest American public libraries, such as those at Dallas and Chicago (1991), it might occupy a major part of one large floor area; at Chicago it occupies 18,000 ft^2 (1,672 m^2) of the second floor.

Shop window of the library service

Given its varied and colourful nature, the children's section may be placed in an area directly behind that part of the ground floor or entry-level facade which is glass-fronted as a means of publicizing its facilities and the library generally. Some

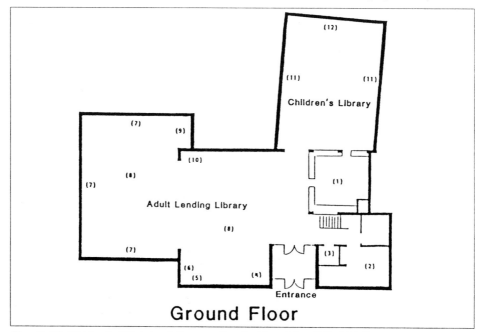

Fig. 7.19 *St Neots District Library, Cambridgeshire CC (1985)*
(Reproduced with the permission of Library Services Ltd)

examples of this approach are Edmonton Green Library (Enfield, 1991) and Hounslow Library (1988). Alternatively, windows may offer a view of the children's library to the passer-by, as at Shipley.

Location changes during planning or after

A description of the planning of Sacramento Central Library (1992) – an extension to an earlier building – indicates how various options for the location of the children's department may be examined during the design process in order to give it the required space and its own identity.[36] The children's department was to serve pre-school children up to young teenagers. Originally the children's room was to share the main floor with the business collection; hardly ideal companions. Then a second floor location with adult fiction and non-print materials, which offered opportunities for a separate activities space, was viewed quite favourably, but abandoned because it was not easily accessible to children. The department was then returned to the ground floor, sharing it with the popular library, but limiting the space available and eliminating the possibility of an activities area. Finally it was placed on a lower level with half the room open to the first floor and stairs leading up to it. This permitted integration with the main floor above, provided light from street-level windows, and resulted in more space.

The library at the Plas Coch Primary School, Clwyd, was relocated on the advice of the Schools Library Service to a different, and more attractive atrium space, from that originally proposed by the school's architect and provided in the finished building.

Separate buildings for children's libraries

Public libraries at some distance from the majority of children, dangerous roads, and other factors, such as a lack of space in an existing building, may assist in the decision to set up separate children's libraries. One of the separate children's libraries in Barcelona, Biblioteca Infantil i Juvenil Lola Anglada, a semi-circular building, is located in a small, urban, park-like square. The latter seems easily accessible, and contains play equipment for young children, thus bringing together two elements of provision for them in the one place.

The Wiend Children's Library in the Wiend Centre (Wigan, 1987), replaced a former separate children's library which became increasingly isolated by new housing and road construction and was demolished following a compulsory purchase order. The new Wiend Children's Library is near a shopping centre, set back from the busiest streets but with parking facilities only for staff. The building's distinctive architecture and its site on a slope at the top of a hill, gives it prominence locally.

The three-storey Cheltenham Library (phase one, 1988) is, at 715 m², about one-fifth of what is proposed when the building is completed. At present, the building houses a children's library on the ground floor, a music and picture library on the first floor, and the Young Arts Centre and meeting room on the second floor. Of its site, it has been reported that: 'Though the library is tucked away behind the old building which is itself 200 yards from the main shopping area, this is offset by the public being long accustomed to using the area for cultural purposes; attempts to find better sites in any case were not successful.'[37] The entrance hall doors have been found too heavy for children and are due for replacement; 'all the more necessary in the long run when the entrance will cease to be the main entrance and be used principally for the children's library'.[38] There is a seemingly poorly placed lift in phase 1, which takes a wheelchair and attendant, but this is destined to be a service lift when a new main entrance and lift are in place at a later phase. A later phase, and indeed current usage, mean that the building is not, and will not in the future be, totally devoted to children.

The Children's Library of the American Memorial Library, Berlin (1957), which is built on the south-east corner of the main building, provides an interesting example of a considerable degree of separateness within a building. There is separate access for children at the rear of the main building and an interior link for both staff and children. However, no separate provision for goods deliveries to the children's library was made.[39]

Young adults service points

The variety of provision for teenagers ranges from separate buildings, separate rooms, to separate areas of various sizes within open-plan libraries, usually placed between the adult and children's library. The latter is probably a fairly common solution, as at Bexley Central Library, noted earlier, and Havant, which has sequences for 'teen read' and the 14–19 age group. Other libraries may locate the teenage section:

(a) in the adult library, as, for example, at Waterthorpe Library, and at St Neots District Library, where it is housed close to videos, records, cassettes and CDs
(b) in the children's area, as at Croydon or Whifflet, Monklands (1986)
(c) at the rear of the library, as at East Kilbride Central Library (1989), where the young adults section is housed beyond the adult lending collections and alongside the reference area; young people have to pass through the audio library in order to reach it.

The Library Association's Community Services Group in Scotland, in its 1985 publication, *Library service to teenagers*, however, recommends the independent teenage library as the best solution, or where this is not feasible, a separate room for their sole use.[40] The publication notes that: 'Setting up an independent teenage library enables us at one stroke to provide the teenager with the kind of library he wants and yet protect the regular users of the existing service from unwarranted noise and interference.'[41] Where a separate room is currently provided, this is sometimes located next to the audiovisual area of the library and may be on the ground floor, as at the Marcus Garvey Library (Haringey, 1991). The smaller Woodsend Library has an enclosed space for teenagers to the rear of the library, adjacent to both adult and children's sections. An American publication, *Standards for young adult services*, emphasizes, for practical and psychological reasons, that the 'young adult area should not segregate teenagers from the rest of the library' and that they should be housed within or adjacent to the adult area, and encouraged to use the whole library. A location near the staffed area is recommended 'to allow for assistance and supervision without making the section appear to be under observation.'[42]

These American standards seem to confirm the usual well-intentioned, but unproved professional philosophy towards teenagers in public library service points and tends, therefore, to conflict with the recommendation for independent accommodation made above. The examples of Waterthorpe Library (Figure 7.20) and Petersburn Community Library (described in Chapter 12), show how both integrated and separate facilities for young people can be provided in the same building. Waterthorpe has its 'Artspace' below the library, accessible both from it and from the outside. This accommodates, amongst other things, a main room for 160 (with stage, sound and lights systems), a recording studio and the use of musical instruments, and a bookstore.[43]

The Bradford experience with Xchange, its teenage library, seems to indicate that young people are prepared to travel to suitable facilities, as a quarter of its users travelled into Bradford to use it, but most were within easy walking distance.[44]

Mobile Libraries

As regards access to mobile libraries, Pybus provides a great deal of detail about the entrance and makes the following main points[45]:

1   It should be wide enough to permit easy access but not too wide as to lose shelving.

2   Usually air-operated doors are fitted with manual override for emergencies;

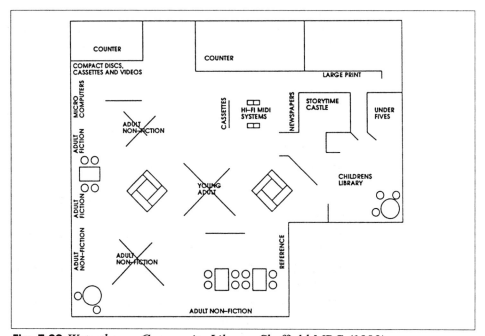

Fig. 7.20 *Waterthorpe Community Library, Sheffield MBC (1989)*
(Reproduced with the permission of Library Services Ltd)

the latter should be out of children's reach.

3 Design of the door needs careful consideration but whatever is chosen it needs to be fitted with sensors (in case anything is trapped between the doors) and a buzzer to prevent moving off with an open door.

4 Steps need to be fitted with automatic, flush-mounted light.

5 Design of steps into the vehicle needs careful consideration.

6 Lift access for the disabled; the combined step/lift is preferred.

7 Stairwell protection on both sides.

8 Door and step operation should be controlled from the counter area.

A similar range of guidance is given in IFLA's *Mobile library guidelines*,[46] although there is some difference of opinion with Pybus over the height of the riser of each step. Pybus quotes between 200 mm and 270 mm, and the IFLA guidelines 178 mm (7 inches) to a maximum of 200 mm (8 inches); the guidelines also suggest a minimum step width (presumably depth) of 254 mm (10 inches).[47] Other than the statement that 'Entrances should have handrails fitted to both sides of the stairwell to facilitate entrance by the disabled, elderly and young people'[48] in the IFLA guidelines, neither publication give children or young people special consideration in discussing this part of the vehicle.

References

1 Heeks, P., *Administration of children's libraries*, London, Library Association, 1967, 19–20.

2 Cohen, A. and Cohen, E., 'Remodeling the library', *School library journal*, **24** (2), 1978, 30.

3 Thompson, A., *Library buildings of Britain and Europe*, London, Butterworths, 1963, 214–23. Provides detailed descriptions, including siting, of three quality school library buildings from the early part of this century with formal layout plans.

4 Idem, 214.

5 Allies, B., 'Library and resource centre, Millfield School, Street, Somerset', *Architects' journal*, **173** (17), 1981, 791–806.

6 School Library Association, *School libraries: steps in the right direction. Guidelines for a school library resource centre*, Swindon, School Library Association, 1989, 3.

7 Ray, C., *Running a school library: a handbook for teacher-librarians*, London, MacMillan, 1990, 8.

8 Ellsworth, R. E. and Wagener, H. D., *The school library*, New York, Educational Facilities Laboratories, 1963, 84.

9 Brown, R. A., 'Students as partners in library design, *School library journal*, **38** (2), 1992, 33.

10 Carroll, F., *Guidelines for school libraries*, The Hague, International Federation of Library Associations, 1990, 23.

11 Charlton, L., *Designing and planning a secondary school library resource centre*, [Swindon], School Library Association, 1992, 6.

12 Bradford Education Library Service, *The effective junior and middle school library*, Bradford, Bradford Metropolitan Council, 1990, 2.

13 Somerset County Council Library Service, *Briefing notes on central library/resource centres in schools*, Bridgwater, School Library Service Resource Centre, 1988, paras 2.1, 2.3–2.4, 2.6 in primary school section.

14 Idem, paras 2.1, 2.6 in secondary school section.

15 School Library Association, *School libraries: their planning and equipment*, London, School Library Association, 1972, 6.

16 Department of Education and Science, *Access for disabled people to educational buildings*, 2nd edn., London, Department of Education and Science, 1984, 1.

17 Goldsmith, S., *Designing for the disabled*, 3rd edn., London, RIBA, 1984, 374–8, 391–2.

18 Ellsworth and Wagener, op. cit., 84–90; Ontario Department of Education, *School media centres*, Ontario, Ontario Department of Education, 1972, 6–11.

19 School Library Association, *School libraries: their planning and equipment*, 6.

20 Idem, 1972, 7.

21 Idem, 1972, 6–7.

22 American Association of School Librarians and the Association for Educational Communications and Technology, *Information power; guidelines for school library media programs*, Chicago, American Library Association, 1988, 72.

23 Weston, R., *Schools of thought: Hampshire architecture 1974–1991,* Winchester, Hampshire County Architects Department, 1991.

24 Owens, R., 'Clear–sited design', *Architects' journal*, **195** (22), 1992, 30.

25 Owen, R., 'Sparkbrook surprise: Nelson Mandela School', *Architects' journal*, **191** (14), 1990, 35–41, 46–9.

26 'Benefits beyond the curriculum', *Architects'journal*, 20 October 1993, 37–42.

27 Weston, R., 'A schooling in community values', *Architects'journal*, 2 September 1992, 22–5.

28 Department of Education and Science, *Educational design initiatives in city technology colleges*, London, HMSO, 1991, 66.

29 Jones, A.C., 'Dual purpose libraries: some experiences in England', *School librarian*, **25** (4), 1977, 314.

30 Shaw, M. 'Top Valley: a joint-use success story', *School librarian*, **38** (2), 1990, 51.

31 Library Association, *Library resource provision in schools: guidelines and recommendations*, London, Library Association, 1977, 41. The suggestion that the school library service could beneficially be housed in a teachers' centre seems no longer appropriate.

32 Lewins, H. and Renwick, F., 'Barriers to access: libraries and the pre-school child in one English county', *International review of children's literature and librarianship*, **4** (2), 1989, 87.

33 Idem, 88.

34 Marshall, M., *Libraries and the handicapped child*, London, André Deutsch, 1981, 160–4.

35 The children's library was destroyed by fire in 1991 and it is hoped to reopen it in a new location within the central library in the near future as the Centre for the Child, as described in Chapter 12.

36 Chekon, T. and Miles, M., 'The kid's place: Sacramento PL's space for children', *School library journal*, **39** (2), 1993, 21–2.

37 Harrison, K. C. (ed.), *Library buildings 1984–1989*, London, Library Services, 1990, 165.

38 Idem, 165.

39 The library is described in Thompson, 223–4.

40 Library Association, Community Services Group in Scotland, Teenager Sub-Committee, *Library service to teenagers*, [Glasgow], Library Association Community Services Group in Scotland, 1985, para. g.

41 Idem, para. a.

42 New York State Library Association, *Standards for youth services in public libraries of New York State*, New York, New York Library Association, 1984, 11.

43 Harrison, op. cit., 274.

44 Nicholson, J. and Pain-Lewis, H., 'The teenage library in Bradford: an evaluation of Xchange', *Journal of librarianship*, **20** (3), 1988, 210.

45 Pybus, R.L., *The design and construction of mobile libraries*, 2nd edn., [London], Branch and Mobile Libraries Group of the Library Association, 1990, 38–40.

46 Pestell, R., *Mobile library guidelines*, The Hague, International Federation of Library Associations, 1991, 18–19.

47 Pybus, op. cit., 39; Pestell, op. cit., 18.

48 Pestell, op. cit., 18.

8 THE RANGE OF ACCOMMODATION

The range of accommodation provided in the school or children's library in order to offer certain services and facilities will be determined by the aims of the library (reflecting the goals of the school or public library service), user needs and the activities associated with them. As indicated in Chapter 3, the listing and detailed description of the library's various components will appear in the architect's brief. The following sections consider the possible roles of libraries in schools and those for children and young people, some of the particular needs and activities of the user groups they serve, and the range of accommodation that might be provided to meet those roles, needs and activities. Such details are not comprehensive nor are they meant to be prescriptive.

School library resource centre
Roles and responsibilities

Within the overall purpose of facilitating learning and teaching, the role of the school library is spelt out in *Learning resources in schools*, and the main points[1] are:

1 To provide a comprehensive source of learning materials to satisfy curricula, cultural and other needs.
2 To organize learning and teaching materials and provide a centralized information system concerning them.
3 To liaise with outside agencies and information sources.
4 To acquire and inform all staff about materials to meet their professional needs.
5 To help teachers achieve their learning objectives.
6 To develop the school library resource centre as a focus for a school's information skills curriculum.

However, while the school library may be designated a learning resource centre, the precise interpretation of that role, in terms of the points noted above, may vary from school to school but will need spelling out in the architect's brief, as this will have a considerable impact on the amount and variety of space that will be required. Major features of such a role are, commonly: provision for pupil-centred learning through reading, listening, viewing and computing; an information skills pro-gramme; an off-air recordings facility; materials for the professional needs and development of teaching staff; the design and production of teaching materials, and reprographic and related facilities for pupils. Other associated resource centre duties could include responsibility for: textbooks and non-book formats; careers and higher education material; language laboratories; the provision, storage and maintenance of audiovisual and computer hardware used in areas outside the library. In some long-established schools, the library may house its archives.

In the American publication, *Information power*, the role of the school library is encapsulated in the mission statement: 'to ensure that students and staff are effective users of ideas and information'.[2] This mission is seen as being achieved through seven objectives[3]:

1 To provide intellectual access to information.
2 To provide physical access to information [within and without the school].
3 To provide learning experiences that encourage users to become discriminating consumers and skilled creators of information.
4 To provide leadership, instruction and consulting assistance in the use of instructional and information technology.
5 To provide resources and activities that contribute to lifelong learning.
6 To provide a facility that functions as the information centre of the school.
7 To provide resources and learning activities . . . supporting the concept that intellectual freedom and access to information are a prerequisite to effective and responsible citizenship in a democracy.

These objectives or roles are somewhat more encompassing than those from the UK and specifically mention the need to provide a facility that functions as the information centre of the school. To fulfil the library's mission and its objectives, *Information power*, lists five challenges that face the library, such as:

(a) to ensure equity and freedom of access to information and ideas, unimpeded by social, cultural, economic, geographic, or technologic constraints
(b) to participate in networks that enhance access to resources located outside the school.[4]

Carroll suggests importantly that, amongst other things, 'The role of the school library media center is best expressed as: . . . A partnership between the teaching staff and the school library media specialists for the benefit of students' learning.'[5]

User groups

Pupils

Library provision will be required for classes and groups of pupils, as well as for the needs of individuals for borrowing materials and private study; especially sixth-form students in the latter case. The activities of classes or groups, involved in information skills tuition, for example, should not interfere, however, with that of individuals. Children's activities will be concerned with information gathering for school subjects from periodicals, videos, reference works, or databases, or other formats, as well as reading, listening and viewing, sometimes for hobby and recreational purposes, and possibly at or from other locations in the school. Involvement in media production of one kind or another, such as audio-cassettes or developing film, or the need to prepare, present and reproduce school work, may also need to be taken into account in providing certain types of facilities. Where appropriate, consideration will need to be given to the requirements of children with special educational or other needs, such as the physically or visually impaired.

Teachers, other members of staff, etc

Where a full learning resource-centre approach is taken, then this will include production and reprographic facilities (that can be shared with pupils), to assist teachers in their work, as well as a collection of professional materials. The information needs of other members of the school staff, such as administrative personnel, technicians, etc., in relation to their school duties and responsibilities should not be overlooked. Consideration could also be given as to how the library can assist appropriately with the information needs of school governors and parents; it may provide a meeting place for the latter (and other groups) if the library space is adequate and flexible.

Range of accommodation

A school library resource centre might, therefore, consist of some or all of the following, depending upon its role, on the age group served, size of the school population, the attention to non-book material, responsibility for media and computer facilities, and so on.

(a) Main area providing seating (both formal and informal) for browsing, reading, study, listening, viewing and computing, and the display of library materials.

With possibly:

(b) Separate browsing and reading area for newspapers and periodicals.
(c) Separate reference area.
(d) Issue counter area.
(e) Catalogues and indexes area.
(f) Advice and information desk.
(g Librarian's office.
(h) Workroom for staff.
(i) Areas for class and group work.
(j) Information skills room.
(k) Audiovisual room.
(l) Computer room.
(m) Exhibition and display area.
(n) Limited access storage for library materials and equipment.
(o) Secure bag and coat storage area.
(p) Reprographic, photographic and preparation room(s).
(q) Television studio.
(r) Audio studio.

A list of library areas is given in *Designing and planning a secondary school library resource centre*, which does not include, for example, the studio facilities noted above.[6] This is also true of *Learning resources in schools*, where the minimum provision for all types of school is given plus an indication of the additional facilities required for middle and secondary schools.[7] The Millfield School, Somerset (1981) provides an interesting example of a UK school with a wide range of accommodation, where, in addition to the library hall, a bookshop, viewing room, and TV studio and associated areas were provided (Figure 8.1).

Both IFLA's *Guidelines for school libraries* and *Information power* suggest space allocations for many of the areas listed above and for others (a multi-purpose room and group study rooms, for example), the latter publication in respect of school populations of 500 and 1,000 students,[8] and these are summarized in Table 8.1. Similar figures are not given in *Learning resources in schools*, as it is felt that: 'It would not be appropriate to lay down precise amounts of space for each individual item listed [in paragraphs 2.12–2.14], since schools' needs will vary and the school library resource centre must be seen in the context of the whole school.'[9] However, as regards the library staff workroom, it suggests an area of not less than 20 m² for a secondary school and not less than 12 m² for middle, special and primary schools. Leonore Charlton suggests that if the design and production of materials is the school's main reprographic centre, a minimum area of 14-16 m² is required in addition to that recommended for the school library as a whole.[10] The latter figure is also repeated in Cambridgeshire's *Provision of learning resources in secondary schools*, which also recommends minimum areas for: an office for a resources coordinator (7 m²); a workroom, to include closed access storage (14 m²); equipment storage and maintenance (about 18 m²).[11] The difficulties posed, however, by a lack of detailed quantitative space provision guidance have been discussed in Chapter 6.

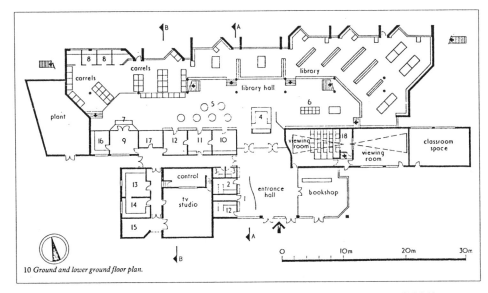

10 Ground and lower ground floor plan.

Fig. 8.1 *Millfield School Library and Resource Centre, Somerset (1981)*
(Reproduced through the courtesy of Jeremy and Caroline Gould, architects)

Table 8.1
Recommendations for space allocations in the school library resource centre

(a)	Main area for reading, browsing, etc	3.72 m² (40 ft²) per user
	seating at tables	10% of school population
	individualized study area	1.11 m² (12 ft²) – 2.32 m² (25 ft²)
	browser seating	10% of the seating in the main area
(b)	Production area and staff work space	3 m² (32.3 ft²) per user
	minimum area	83.7 m² (900 ft²)
	booths for previewing, recording, etc	4.65 m² (50 ft²) each
	office space for technician	13.94 m² (150 ft²)
(c)	Non-professional staff	
	workroom	10-12 m² (108–129.5 ft²) per staff member
		minimum size 37.2 m² (400 ft²)
(d)	Limited access storage rooms	55.79 m² (600 ft²) each
(e)	Offices	14 m² (151.1 ft²) each
(f)	Multi-purpose room	40 m² (431 ft²)
(g)	Group conference (study) rooms	14 m² (151.1 ft²)
	minimum of 2	

1   Extracted from, Carroll, F. L., *Guidelines for school libraries*, The Hague, International Federation of Library Associations, 1990, 25–7.

	500 students		1,000 students	
	Space allocation			
	m²	ft²	m²	ft²
(a) Entrance/circulation	23.22–46.45	250–500	55.74–74.32	600–800
(b) Main area for reading, browsing, etc.		25–75% as required		

25% of the area available for student seating @ 3.72 m² (40 ft²) per student

In some schools 1/3 to 3/4 of the student population may need to be accommodated

Carrels require 1.48m² (16 ft²) to accommodate a computer and printer

	500 students		1,000 students	
	Space allocation			
	m²	ft²	m²	ft²
(c) Small group areas for listening and viewing	13.93 each	150 each	13.93 each	150 each
(d) Equipment storage and distribution	37.16–55.74	400–600	46.45–74.32	500–800
(e) Maintenance repair	13.93–27.87	150–300	13.93–27.87	150–300
(f) Media production laboratory	46.45–65.03	500–700	65.03–83.61	700–900
(g) Darkroom	13.93–27.87	150–300	13.93–27.87	150–300
(h) Conference areas (2–4 areas)	13.93 each	150 each	13.93 each	150 each
(i) Multipurpose room	65.03–83.61	700–900	83.61–111.48	900–1,200
(j) Work area	18.58–37.16	200–400	27.87–46.45	300–500
(k) Periodical storage	23.22–37.16	250–400	37.16–55.74	400–600
(l) Teacher/professional area	46.45–55.74	500–600	55.74–74.32	600–800
(m) Computer learning laboratory	55.74–74.32	600–800	74.32–92.9	800–1,000
(n) Stacks	37.16 minimum	400 minimum	37.16–55.74	400–600
(o) Television studio	148.64	1,600	148.64	1,600
(p) Audio studio	13.93 minimum	150 minimum	13.93 minimum	150 minimum
(q) Telecommunications distribution	74.32 minimum	800 minimum	74.32 minimum	800 minimum

* In the original publication space allocations are given in square feet.

2   Extracted from, American Association of School Librarians and Association for Educational Communications and Technology, *Information power*, Chicago, American Library Association and AECT, 1988, 131–9.

Main library area

Space will be required for the storage and display of books, periodicals and newspapers, vertical file materials, maps and charts, audiovisual, CD-ROMs, and other non-print materials, and the equipment that might be required in connection with the use of some of them, such as, microform readers and computer terminals. Other equipment includes items such as photocopiers. Special pupil-orientated collections related to careers and higher education and, for teachers, a teaching collection, might also need housing.

A variety of seating provision will be needed at tables, in carrels, in casual seating, and at benches and workstations for computer use. The seating at tables may be arranged in such a way that a class, or possibly classes, may be accommodated in the library area. The two secondary school plans given in *Designing and planning a secondary school library resource centre*, provide useful examples of this potential.[12]

In a number of instances all features of the school library may be contained in one room, the counter acting as the only work area for the staff. In other instances, as described below, there may be additional accommodation for library staff and pupils.

Other library areas

A variety of areas and rooms will be needed by users for such purposes as private study, reference, browsing, seminar, class or group work, computer use, and viewing and listening. In secondary schools with a sixth form, it is not unusual to find a room, area or gallery, set aside for sixth-form study. Library computing facilities may be housed separately or be part of the main library area. In some primary schools an area for informal library use and for storytelling might be provided.

Staff accommodation

In addition to the issue desk, which will often also serve as enquiry point, office, workroom and specialized accommodation will be needed for library, technical staff and users. This might include areas for such activities as teachers' preparation, reprographics, film and video production, audio recording, and equipment inspection and repair.

Catalogue etc.

Other areas will house the library's catalogue, exhibition and display facilities, and storage for lesser or seasonally used materials.

Case studies

Case studies of school libraries, described in Chapter 12, provide examples of the range of accommodation to be found in three UK schools. See also the library provision and layout for Djanogly CTC in Figure 8.2.

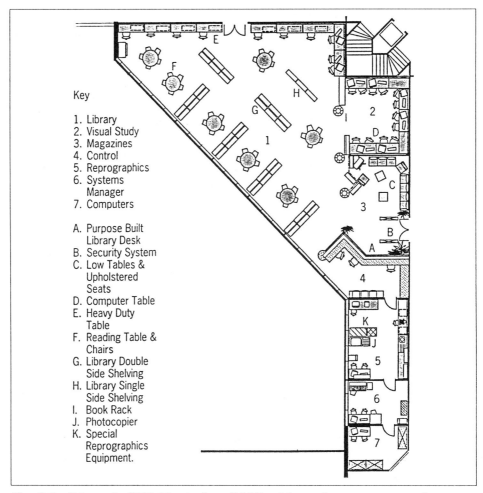

Fig. 8.2 *Djanogly CTC, Nottingham(1989) – library layout, reprographics area and computer rooms*

(Crown Copyright. Reproduced with the permission of the Controller of HMSO)

Describing library spaces

Administering the school library media center identifies five major groups of function that should generally be part of a plan for any school library media centre, reflecting much of what has been said above, and these are:

1   Reading, listening, viewing and computing areas.
2   Space for distributing, organizing, accessing and storing collections.
3   Area for producing instructional material.
4   Maintaining and repairing equipment area.
5   Providing computer services areas.

The author comments on other spaces within these larger areas, such as seminar rooms, and storage areas, and considers questions of size, furniture and environmental matters.[13]

111

It is impossible to provide detailed descriptions of all possible school library spaces in this book but, in preparing the brief for the architect, it is important to have a framework for the consistent and helpful description of individual library spaces and such a framework is proposed by Leland Park using the following headings[14]:

(a) Type of space (i.e. the name of the space).
(b) Function: a simple explanation of what will go one in this area.
(c) Location: its location in relation to other areas.
(d) Special requirements, e.g. wiring.
(e) Occupancy: number of reader spaces to be provided in this area.
(f) Shelving: number of volumes for which shelving should be provided.
(g) Total space: number of square feet/metres required for the area.
(h) Furniture and equipment: list what will be provided by way of chairs and tables, computers, etc.
(i) Comments: e.g. an explanation of the way the total space was calculated; quality of furnishings required; shelving to be wall mounted.

Examples of descriptions of individual library spaces that cover many of the requirement noted above are given in *Information power*, and in *Designing and renovating school library media centers*.[15] The latter publication notes a list of 18 activities, such as students and teachers browsing through computer databases or creating visuals in the production area, and lists 13 spaces in a facilities list to cover these activities. The descriptions of the spaces, such as the main entrance, and those for circulation and display, or large group instruction, follow some of the requirements noted above, although omitting square footage as this varies from one situation to another.

Lushington and Mills provide a list of 16 named areas for a school library media centre, in their now somewhat dated but still useful book, followed by descriptions of each area. These provide further examples of the need to describe fully, the use, occupancy and content of areas such as, an office and administrative area, a reading and listening area, and an equipment inspection and repair area; an indication of the likely size of the space needed is also given.[16] These examples are, of course, presented from an American viewpoint but no similar published descriptions exist for British school libraries, although *Learning resources in schools* gives a little guidance for some areas, such as those for seating and work spaces and administrative accommodation, as does Leonore Charlton.[17]

Schools Library Service

Learning resources in schools sets out the aims of the Schools Library Service as:[18]

(a) Services to schools, e.g. loans, bibliographical information, exhibition collection of recommended materials.
(b) Professional support to schools, e.g. advice on the management, organization and development of learning resources within schools, including recruitment, staff development, and performance measurement.
(c) Professional support to local education authorities, e.g. establishing a school

library resource centre policy for an authority; liaison with the public library and other local authority services, museums, arts, archives, on provision for schools.

The Scottish Library Association has briefly spelt out the role of the regional library resource service, as it is known in Scotland, particularly its importance in setting standards for the management of resources. It has also provided details of the range of accommodation required for such a regional service, and the following points are based on its suggestions.[19]

User groups

The centre's staff will need satisfactory facilities for its wide range of functions, for example, the despatch of resources, and bibliographical, training and technical services. Visitors will include librarians, teachers and pupils, who will be reviewing resources, visiting exhibitions or taking part in in-service meetings.

Range of accommodation

Storage and display
Various library resource areas will be required for the storage and display of loan, reference, project, exhibition, purchase and special collections.

Rooms
In addition to an exhibition hall and conference room, rooms and working space will be needed for working parties, selection meetings, in-service training, and reviewing film, video and computer software.

Staff accommodation
Alongside the usual offices and workrooms, required for the reception, unpacking, cataloguing, processing and despatch of library resources, areas will be needed for audiovisual and computer technicians, and a graphic artist. Staff room, tea room and cloakroom facilities for staff and visitors will complete the facility.

Vehicles
The earlier Library Association publication, *Library resource provision in schools*, also describes the space needs of the schools library service, much along the lines noted above. However, it also includes the requirement for loading bays and garaging (including packing and despatch areas) at 50 m² per van.[20]

Space recommendations
The same publication offers other space guidance: viewing and listening facilities, 9 m²; offices for senior staff, 15 m² each; work and storage space for general assistants 1.8 m² per assistant, and a meeting room, accommodating at least 30 people, 50 m² minimum.[21]

District library media facilities (USA)

District library media facilities is the name given in the USA to those facilities that support local schools in the district and enhance and augment local schools resource centre work. Functions of these district or regional level facilities include: processing of all materials; equipment repair and maintenance; printing and graphic services; film and video collections; television distribution; media production, and the examination of materials, including computer software.[22] These functions go well beyond that which is currently provided by schools library services in the UK and provide a useful developmental model for consideration. Details of the accommodation required to carry out these functions are given in *Information power* and include a professional library and teacher centre, equipment services area, and a production area, both electronic and other.[23]

Public libraries
Role of lthe ibrary service to children and young people

The nature of the accommodation provided for young people will be determined by the roles chosen for the library service and how these are interpreted, and whether different age groups, such as teenagers, are to be separately served. While public libraries acknowledge the major roles of education, information, recreation and culture (and possibly a welfare role), it could be argued that children's provision serves predominantly recreational and information purposes and that the educational role is largely a passive one.

Depending upon circumstances, public libraries, in less developed countries, for example, may decide generally to place an emphasis on the educational rather than the leisure role of the children's library. Elsewhere, others may make a deliberate policy decision to see the educational role as their primary service philosophy. Tempe Public Library in Arizona has made such a decision and places the emphasis on the book, reading and study. As its library director writes: 'You won't find a jungle gym, beanbag chair or a merry-go-round. This is not a gymnasium; it is not a social welfare agency; it is not a video arcade. It is a library.'[24] To reinforce this philosophy one entire wing of the building, known as the student centre, caters solely for the needs of students and stays open well beyond the rest of the library. While providing mainly for individual quiet study, there are also four group study rooms. The children's room is totally dedicated to the book and has been criticized for being too much like a library; the library director suggests that this means the project was a success: 'We make no apologies that our building exudes the feeling of a traditional and basic educational mission.'[25] Compare this approach with Dallas's provision noted below and the acknowledgement that: 'Fun was the key word during planning and design.'[26]

The Library Association guidelines, *Children and young people*, offer a rationale as a foundation for children's public library service 'which is both customer-focused and customer-led'.[27] Its first paragraph states: 'All that follows is based on the premise that consideration of the child is what must inform and determine the nature of library services to children.' The guidelines see that 'whilst the service's natural impetus is to create and retain library users, it has a wider role in the promotion of reading, which it shares with schools, bookshops and other agencies.'

However, although facilities may be generally offered in line with this 'natural impetus', the provision of community and other information to children, particularly to the older child, has received very little attention in UK public libraries. Elizabeth Maxwell draws attention to 'a public information for children' project at Roskilde Public Library in 1987.[29] An information stand was erected in the children's library and was made up of notice boards, tilted shelves and video showing facilities. Information informed children of events, news, after-school jobs and facilities for children; a directory for children was compiled by the library staff. The varied roles that can be played by a large modern children's library (including that of information provision), both towards children and parents, is illustrated by Birmingham's Centre for the Child, described in Chapter 12.

User groups

The task of the public library is usually seen as to make both formal and informal provision for local young people of all age groups from pre-school children to teenagers. To relate that provision to other library services, and to facilitate visits by family, school and other groups, as well as the individual.

In offering a range of public library accommodation for children there is always the danger of under provision, particularly in large public libraries where children are thought not to be a likely significant user group. A classic example of this is the Dallas Central Library (1981/2). Billed at 650,000 ft² (60,385 m²) as the century's largest central library building, it provided 3,000 ft² (278.7 m²) for children 'hidden away in a remote corner of the Humanities Division'. Patrick O'Brien has recounted the story of how the space for children was increased to 11,000 ft² (1,021.9 m²), relocated and improved to create the Children's Center.[30]

Children

The library should meet the needs of children and young people for reading, browsing, lending, reference, information-seeking, library instruction, discussion, and study, particularly with regards to homework and school projects. The latter becomes especially important in the absence of adequate school libraries locally. Consideration should also be given to providing opportunities for listening, viewing and computer use. It is usual to meet children's needs for using their imagination and creativity through story hours, competitions, puppet shows, play, theatre, craft, club and other such activities. It is likely that individual use of the library will differ in and out of term time and during the day and after school.

Pre-school children

Very young children, usually accompanied by a parent or older child, will use the library in a very different way to older children. An atmosphere conducive to play, reading aloud, storytimes and other activities (such as art and crafts), and noise, will often be provided. Provision of library materials can be quite varied, to include

115

picture and other books, toys, games, sound recordings, videos, jigsaw puzzles, comics, colouring sheets, and finger and nursery rhymes to use in the library, to loan or keep. In this way the library can 'assist the child's intellectual development', much of which 'takes place in the pre-school years'.[31]

Teenagers or young adults

The Americans, Nolan Lushington and James Kusack, state that:

> The primary purpose of the young adult area is to serve the recreational and personal development needs of adolescents. Their informational needs will be met primarily from the adult non-fiction and general reference collections. The young adult area for youth up to eighteen years of age, still in school or not, serves as a bridge between the children's room and the adult areas.[32]

Lushington's earlier book, with co-author architect, Willis Mills, noted the young adult's desire for music, paperbacks, conversation and social communication, and the inappropriateness of what library materials (recorded music, for example) may often be offered them.[33] They commented that: 'It is exceedingly difficult for librarians to keep pace with the changing sophisticated tastes of young people and almost impossible to provide satisfactory services to them without their continual input.'[34]

While teenagers use libraries for recreational, informational and educational purposes, and may make use of a wider range of media, from video games to books, than others, their attitude to formal library provision is very much related to their age and development. However, a late 1980s survey of teenagers and their use of libraries in the London Borough of Waltham Forest, showed that, while requesting magazines, music, computer software, videos, improved display, guiding and arrangement of stock, and various facilities, such as refreshments, teenagers also asked for more books and demonstrated a demand for a place to study in. Overall the survey provided the information for improved provision but demonstrated that the then library service, for those 11–16-year-olds who were using the library, was of a reasonable standard. However, the needs of those who had left full-time education, especially boys were still largely uncatered for.[35]

Bradford's Xchange teenage library was set up in its central library in 1985 to overcome the observed decline in use of the library by teenagers moving from the children's to adult library, probably caused by a of lack of interest in borrowing traditional library materials, and the physical and mental barriers involved. There was also the problem of teenagers using the library as a meeting place and congregating on stairs and landings. With these points in mind, an informal teenage library was set up which was also seen as a drop-in centre. In a 1987 survey of Xchange and its use, it was suggested by respondents that it be divided into two rooms – one in which music was played and one where there was quiet and teenagers could study if necessary. While highlighting Xchange's success, it demonstrates the potential danger of providing everything within it rather than encouraging use of central library adult services. The point is made that 'Xchange is part of a library service' and that it has a responsibility to ensure that 'once teenagers become members they use Xchange as a bridge not a stop-gap'.[36]

Patrick Jones has identified ways in which libraries can meet the development of young adults who are gaining independence, managing excitement, searching for identity, and seeking acceptance.[37] These responses include an appropriate music collection, magazines, games, creative opportunities, the library as a positive and relevant experience, and a space that clearly belongs to young people, not just a collection of books. How well this last response can be met by public libraries is discussed later in this chapter.

Other groups

Parents, local teachers, day care personnel (for example, childminders, workers in nurseries and playgroups) may also be served by the children's library service through various educational programmes and information services (books and magazines on child welfare, and community information on health, welfare and other topics), and the loan of materials, such as toys, games, books and project collections. Such services for parents and others help them to supplement their own resources for assisting the intellectual development of children. Materials for parents on childcare etc., would benefit from being located or duplicated in the children's library where they are more likely to be used.

Outreach

Members of all the above groups, both children and parents may have difficulty in reaching a static public library service point or might not be well provided for at such a service point – the under-5s or teenagers, for example. There are also those who may not see themselves as library users, whether as individuals or in groups, and some form of outreach service and promotional activity is needed to encourage them. In all of these cases, library service direct from a mobile library vehicle will help meet such people's needs and a number of such services are described below.

Range of accommodation

The range of accommodation provided for children and young people varies between central, district and branch libraries of various sizes. In small libraries there may be just one well-defined part of the accommodation for children with a limited variety of features. In larger libraries, such as Hounslow Library, two or more different spaces may be provided for different age groups and their associated activities (Figures 8.3 and 8.4). In some libraries a feature may be made of the entry to the children's area; walking through a dragon's mouth, for instance, at Heidelberg Public Library (1990) in Germany. The Library Association's guidelines, covering the 0–16 age group, suggest that, in addition to the basic provision (an area to accommodate children's lending and reference stock), larger libraries should include, and all libraries should consider providing:

- a pre-school area
- a homework and study area
- an activities area

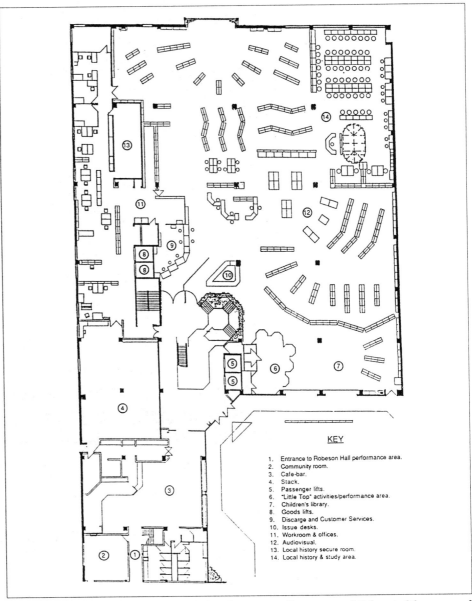

Fig. 8.3 *Hounslow Library (1988) – location of counter, children's library and activities/performance area*
(Reproduced with the permission of Library Services Ltd)

- storage for materials and audiovisual equipment
- a parent's collection
- toilet and washing facilities
- baby feeding and changing facilities.[38]

No mention is made of the more varied provision that might be made for

Fig. 8.4 *Hounslow Library: part of children's library*
(Photo: Ravinder Dhaliwall)

teenagers, the space required for one or more OPACs, computer facilities provision; the emphasis in the guidelines seems to be very much on the younger age groups.

The children's library

At its simplest, the children's library will require space to shelve and display books and other materials for loan and consultation, utilizing low wall and island shelving, as well as other display furniture such as carousels. Special areas may be devoted to children's periodicals, a reference collection, and collections for pre-school children (the under-5s), and parents and carers. Walls above the shelving will usually be covered – with hessian for example – to allow them to be used for display purposes. Books and other materials for teenagers may be provided close by, plus notice board and possibly a vending machine.

The area for very young children will have picture books, displayed face-on on sloping shelves, in kinderboxes (with low tub seats) and in 'play and display' furniture, such as that in the shape of a railway engine with carriages or covered wagon, as well bath-books, jigsaws and toys. Where no separate accommodation can be provided for activities and story hours, then the provision of curtains or folding doors around the children's library, or part of it, enables the temporary creation of an enclosed space for such activities. The use of mobile shelving and kinderboxes enhances the flexibility of such an activity space.

Bigger libraries, such as Croydon Central Library, discussed in Chapter 12, offer opportunities for larger and more varied collections of materials, a wider range of facilities, and more well-defined areas for different age groups and some of these possibilities are listed below. An American example is Dallas's Children's Center, noted earlier, which caters for children through 12 years old, and includes: a storytelling area 'in a forest'; multi-purpose theatre; computer learning centre (eight PCs); pre-school area (laid out as a village); play space for arts and crafts; service desk (identified by a large 3D question mark), and computer catalogue terminals.[39]

Seating

A variety of seating will be needed in different parts of the children's library for informal reading, viewing and listening, and activities such as board and other games, and for more formal activities, such as study. If necessary, separate homework or study rooms might be considered in busy libraries, with appropriate tables and seating. Listening points should also be considered, permitting children (or groups of children) and parents to share stories or music, and facilities for viewing (of television or video cassettes) and computer use will usually be needed. Informal seating areas can be created through carpeted architectural features of the children's area, such as a kinderpit or a tier of 'steps' (Figure 8.5); they can also be used for formal storytelling occasions. A playpen for the youngest children is a helpful feature in the pre-school area.

Activity and other rooms

A suitably equipped and wired multi-purpose activities room (possibly with adjacent storage for chairs, other equipment and furniture) will permit story hours, film shows, theatrical presentations, music listening, class visits, and recreational and craft activities. In wet activity areas, equipped with cupboards and sinks, the use of taps which shut off automatically and cannot be left running should be considered. Specially designed and equipped story rooms – as found in Scandinavia and elsewhere – could be an imaginative feature of larger libraries. In a small number of UK libraries, for example, Woodsend Library, Trafford, access to a courtyard or other outdoor space, provides opportunities for storytelling and other outdoor activities in good weather.

Counter, catalogue, etc.

Depending upon the size of the library and its organization, space may be needed for a separate issue counter and enquiry desk for children, the storage of on-request library materials, to house the catalogue (increasingly an OPAC), for display, and for

Fig. 8.5 *Carpeted steps for reading and listening, Düsseldorf Central Library, Germany*
(Photo: J. Feist. Reproduced through the courtesy of EKZ GmbH)

audiovisual equipment and general storage.

Special collections housed in the children's library, for example rare children's books or a local history collection, will require individual consideration as regards storage (which may have to be secure and in the staff area) and display.

Toy provision

The display and storage of toys poses particular problems and, although adjustable library shelving can be used to store toys by size, Jill Hewitt suggests that libraries look into what toyshops do themselves by way of storage and display.[40] She goes on to argue against a separate area for the housing and lending of toys and suggests that, as a complement to books, they should be located among books, and that toys for particular age groups should be with other provision for those age groups – pre-school toys with picture books, for example. The Nottinghamshire Working Party For Toys in Libraries has suggested the range and number of toys and games that might be provided in small, medium and large libraries and the age groups that should have priority. In small libraries, it was thought that probably only 4–6 toys could be accommodated and that these should be aimed at the pre-school child.[41]

The Wirral Toy Library is in its own purpose-built accommodation and consists of a generous, flexible entrance/reception area that gives parents and children direct access to the library, nursery, parents'/volunteers' room and offices. Toilet facilities are located at the back of the building but accessible from nursery and staff room.[42]

Staff accommodation

Depending upon staff numbers and their deployment in the library as a whole, office and workroom accommodation will be needed. Workroom accommodation should include adequate shelving, cupboard storage and work surfaces (to prepare displays, for example), and, if appropriate, facilities to provide drinks and so on to parents and children at events.

Public facilities

Where possible, a place for children to hang coats and to wash hands, toilets, and baby feeding and changing facilities should be provided. Toilets designed for children should take into account such things as the height of door handles, mirrors and tap fittings, as well as locks that can be operated from both sides so that a child cannot be locked in. Baby feeding and changing facilities need to consider matters such as space for buggies and other children, privacy for nursing mothers, wall-mounted bottle warmers, ventilation and the maintenance of high standards of hygiene.

A safe space to park buggies and prams and bicycles will also be needed, although if buggies are permitted to be wheeled round the library it will be necessary to allow sufficient circulation space, bearing in mind, however, that they can be an unexpected hazard for other library users. The provision of specially designed trollies to seat young children, like those in supermarkets, might be of benefit to all concerned.

A creche is provided in some public complexes and library users may wish to consider using this. Willesden Green Library Centre (Brent, 1989), however, has a well-used creche at which children can be left for up to two hours. Local authority requirements as to numbers, toilet provision and sleeping facilities would need to be taken into account.

Young adults or teenagers

A centre for young adults, as proposed by the Americans, Lushington and Mills, would be equipped with music and video collections, paperbacks and magazines, coffee bar and a group meeting room. Examples given below show how these, and other materials and services, are provided in the all too few UK libraries which cater for teenagers in any substantial manner. Of course, whether such facilities are best provided as part of a library or in a youth centre is a matter for professional debate, although it does seem possible to marry elements of the two successfully within a library service.

Bradford's Xchange teenage library and drop-in centre was furnished to create 'an atmosphere somewhere between that of a bookshop and of a coffee shop'. The mainly paperback bookstock is arranged in genre categories and non-fiction consists of topics of interest to teenagers such as sport, pop music and hobbies. In addition there are sound recordings (rock, pop and Asian music), a wide range of magazines, information on topics of concern to teenagers, a computer, television and video, and a number of board games.[43] It would seem that by consulting teenagers before setting up Xchange, the right stock, staff attitudes, atmosphere and decoration were created that were instrumental in its success. The 1987 survey of use, with its suggestion for certain improvements and development, confirms 'again and again that Xchange is right for its members. It is a particularly good example of how the public library can have a positive, constructive and innovative role to play during adolescence'.[44]

Glasgow's small, low-tech Yoker Youth Library (90 m²), is a library service designed just for teenagers and young adults, and offers books videos, computer games cassettes and CDs for loan, and provides 38 magazines, including comics, football, pop and video titles, and two daily papers. For a variety of reasons, such as other more appropriate venues and lack of participation, extra-mural activities have been gradually wound down. A popular service – the place sounds like a disco, local involvement (users and community leaders are the managers), liaison with parents and others, and a personal touch, seem to get the best results.[45]

Renfrew Library service was aware that it was not attracting or keeping teenagers, that there was very high unemployment amongst young people in the Johnstone area, and its conventional teenage collections were of limited effect. In 1984, after funding had been obtained, the top floor of a disused Victorian school building was opened as the Johnstone Information and Leisure Library (JILL). This was an 'attempt to provide a library service for teenagers, on their terms and based primarily on their interests, outlook and life-styles'.[46] As with the other examples, JILL was noisy, provided with a variety of materials and facilities, from paperbacks to microcomputers, and was an immediate success. Because of this, larger and better premises had to be found in a former branch library close to the town centre. In the reorganized and redecorated branch library there is a separate workroom, staff room, staff area, strongroom facilities, a partitioned area for playing musical instruments such as the guitar, and an audiovisual area with security cameras. Through its facilities, advice and information services, clubs, activities and band rehearsal provision, it has become a focus for teenagers, with calls for similar libraries elsewhere in the district.

Monklands District Council's Petersburn Library and teenage drop-in centre, opened in 1992, is a very recent example of special provision for teenagers and is described in Chapter 12.

Road vehicles

All mobile library vehicles are built to be different to each other in some respects. However, certain standard features for children include kinderboxes with cushions and kneeling pads, and deeper than standard shelving to take picture books, audio and video cassettes. More daring vehicles have different coloured shelving in this section, using primary colours, and may also have a different coloured carpet. Bookbus-type vehicles dedicated to children and schools' needs are also all different in some way depending upon the needs of the particular library service and the engineering and financial constraints. The quality of the exterior artwork and signwriting on all of these vehicles, particularly those aimed primarily at children, is seen as being of vital importance to the success of the mobile library or bookbus.

The design of Coventry's new mobile, which began service in late 1990, was required to take into account a number of matters, including a consideration of the needs of mothers and young children. This resulted in a vehicle of 33 feet in length, carrying 4,500 books, paperbacks and audio items, with access for the disabled, a staff area and toilet, and a specially designed children's area. This was placed at the front of the vehicle with browser boxes, paperback spinners, different carpet tiles and a raised area. Other features included a few padded seats for children, and safety locks on the handbrakes and windows.[47]

Recent road vehicles dedicated to the service of children include those at Gloucestershire, Cynon Valley, Birmingham and Hampshire. Some serve children of all ages, others a particular group, while others may be dedicated to serving schools.

Gloucestershire's Share-a-Book children's library van, which serves children of all ages in Gloucester and Cheltenham, began service in 1983; a new vehicle was acquired in 1989. This visits schools before, during and after the school day, parking close to or inside school premises, and is used by children in class groups or with parents and siblings. There are also visits to playgroups, family centres, and opportunity groups for children with learning difficulties or disabilities. The bookstock, which has the aim of enhancing children's leisure reading rather than meeting school project requirements, is all paperback and ranges from board books and toddlers books through storybooks and information to teenage novels.

The current vehicle does not have disabled access, although all new vehicles will facilitate this. Traditional mobile shelving is fitted round the walls of the van, with some kinderbox-type storage, and shelves below the rear window with space above them for storing plastic crates containing books for younger readers. There is also shelving at each side of the counter for returned books and reference works. Dark-blue felt covers storage cupboard doors and is continued around the top of the van, above the shelves and rear windows, to provide plenty of display surfaces for posters, children's drawings and so on. The deep blue colour is picked up in the shelving uprights and dividers. Cupboards for storage are provided around the drivers cab and above the windows, and large cushions are carried for use at storytelling times. The van's basic white and blue external livery is enlivened by a colourful design of a child and dragon reading together; the dragon's fiery breath spelling out 'share a book' above them.

Cynon Valley's family bookbus (Figure 8.6) also provides an informal service to children up to the age of 11 at schools, playgroups and selected street stops within the borough. The stock is mostly paperback with a large proportion of picture books displayed on spinners, kinderbox-type fittings, as well as conventional shelving, with some facility for face-on display. Interior surfaces not used for other purposes are covered with red pinboard for display purposes. The bookbus is painted yellow with 'Readabout' lettered across the vehicle and a graphic of two children holding books underneath it.

In contrast, Birmingham's 'Words on wheels' (Figure 8.7) is specifically an under-

Fig. 8.6 *Cynon Valley's family bookbus*
(Reproduced through the courtesy of Cynon Valley Libraries)

Fig. 8.7 *Birmingham's 'Words on wheels' mobile*
(Reproduced through the courtesy of the Leisure & Community Services
Department, Birmingham City Council)

5s mobile 'designed primarily to make links with parents and carers of very young children'.[48] It visits health clinics, shopping centres, mother and toddlers groups and elsewhere to meet and talk to parents about library services. It contains an exhibition collection of best books for the under-5s, as well as displaying a wide range of information on matters like child development, health and early literacy.

The 33-feet-long vehicle has a pictorially decorated exterior and attractive interior, and carries toys, posters, mobiles, music and video facilities – not forgetting a portapotti. There is often a problem over toilet provision on mobile library vehicles unless available close to a stop.

IFLA's *Mobile library guidelines* describe the service-base requirements of the mobile library in respect of integrated garage and work areas. Recommendations include[49]:

(a) a minimum of 1.5 m (5 ft) space surrounding the vehicle to allow room for inspection and maintenance

(b) drive through garages are preferred

(c) electronically operated doors, with manual back-up system, are preferred

(d) a loading bay at least 1.5 m (5 ft) wide with a ramp of maximum gradient 12 (1 : 14) to garage floor

(e) loading bay and work access should be on one level

(f) shelving in the work area should be no more than 1.8 m (6 ft) high with a minimum gangway of 1m (3.3 ft) to allow staff easy access.

References

1 Kinnell, M. (ed.), *Learning resources in schools: Library Association guidelines for school libraries*, London, Library Association, 1992, 14–15.

2 American Association of School Librarians and Association for Educational Communications and Technology, *Information power: guidelines for school library media programs*, Chicago, American Library Association and AECT, 1988, 1.

3 Idem, 1–2.

4 Idem, 2–13.

5 Carroll, F. L., *Guidelines for school libraries*, The Hague, International Federation of Library Associations, 1990, 2.

6 Charlton, L., *Designing and planning a secondary school library resource centre*, [Swindon], School Library Association, 1992, 6–7.

7 Kinnell, op. cit., 29.

8 Carroll, op. cit., 25–7; 131–9.

9 Kinnell, op. cit., 29.

10 Charlton, op. cit., 11.

11 Cambridgeshire County Council Education Service, *Provision of learning resources in secondary schools: guidelines for good practice*, Cambridge, Cambridgeshire County Council Education Service, 28.

12 Charlton, op. cit., 18–19.

13 Morris, B. J. *et al.*, *Adminstering the school library media center*, New

Providence, NJ, Bowker, 1992, 228–33.

14 Park, L. M., 'The whys and hows of writing a library building program', *Library scene*, **5** (3), 1976, 3–4.

15 *Information power*, op. cit., 132–9; Klasing, J. P., *Designing and renovating school library media centers*, Chicago, American Library Association, 1991, 10, 12–16.

16 Lushington, N. and Mills, W. N., *Libraries designed for users*, Syracuse, NY, Gaylord, 1979, 180–8.

17 Kinnell, op. cit., 32–4; Charlton, op. cit., 9–11.

18 Kinnell, op. cit., 62–5.

19 Scottish Library Association, *The school library resource service and the curriculum* . . . , Motherwell, Scottish Library Association, 1985, 59, 76.

20 Library Association, *Library resource provision in schools: guidelines and recommendations*, London, Library Association, 1977, 42.

21 Library Association, op. cit., 42.

22 *Information power*, op. cit., 96.

23 Idem, 96–8, 100.

24 Manley, W., 'The Tempe Public Library: a model for the 1990s', *Wilson library bulletin*, **64** (4), 1989, 25.

25 Idem, 158.

26 O'Brien, P.M., 'Dazzling center opens in Dallas', *American libraries*, **20** (6), 1989, 591.

27 Marshall, P., 'Children and young people: guidelines for public library services', *International review of children's literature and librarianship*, **6** (3), 1991, 204.

28 Idem, 205.

29 Maxwell, E., 'The planning and design of children's libraries', *Library management*, **14** (7), 30.

30 O'Brien, op. cit., 591–2, 594.

31 Lewins, H. and Renwick, F., 'Barriers to access: libraries and pre–school children in one English county', *International review of children's literature and librarianship*, **4** (2), 1989, 91.

32 Lushington, N. and Kusack, J.M., *The design and evaluation of public library buildings,* Hamden, Conn., Library Professional Publications, 1991, 45.

33 Lushington and Mills, op. cit., 177–8.

34 Idem, 178.

35 Love, L., 'Teenagers and library use in Waltham Forest', *Library Association record*, **89** (2) 1987, 81–2.

36 Nicholson, J. and Pain-Lewis, H., 'The teenage library in Bradford: an evaluation of Xchange', *Journal of librarianship*, **20** (3), 1988, 216.

37 Jones, P., *Connecting young adults with libraries: a how-to-do-it manual*, New York, Neal Schuman, 1992, 19–23.

38 Library Association, *Children and young people: Library Association guidelines for public library service*, London, Library Association, 1991, 14.

39 O'Brien, op. cit., 592.

40 Hewitt, J., *Toys and games in libraries*, London, Library Association, 1981, 41.

41 Idem, 42–3.

42 Anderson, B., 'Designs on a new toy library', *Ark*, Spring 1992, 12.

43 Nicholson and Pain-Lewis, op. cit., 206.

44 Idem, 216–17.

45 'Yoker Youth Library', *Service point*, (57) 1993, 7, 9.

46 Hendry, J. D., 'JILL's pure brill', *Library Association record*, **88** (2) 1986, 78.

47 Scott, C. 'Coventry's state of the art mobile library', *Service point*, (52) 1991, 4, 6–7.

48 'Wheels around Birmingham', *Service point*, (55) 1992, 14.

49 Pestell, R., *Mobile library guidelines*, The Hague, International Federation of Library Associations, 1991, 41–2.

9

POLICY AND PRACTICAL ISSUES

In writing the brief for the architect many matters of policy as regards the new or remodelled accommodation will need to be considered that will have practical design implications. Some of these matters will be common to both school, children's and young people's libraries, others will not. While these issues are discussed in a certain amount of detail here, the references to this chapter indicate where a fuller discussion and advice on these matters are to be found. Practical points relating to furniture are considered in Chapter 10.

General
Open plan or enclosed spaces?

As noted earlier, the days are gone when library activities were divided into separate rooms. Nowadays there is a preference for a large open-plan space, containing issue desk, enquiry point (the two are often combined), catalogue, shelving, seating and so on, that allows freedom of movement. Such large, regular-shaped spaces are more flexible and provide the opportunity for future change, but they must be varied, and planned in an interesting fashion, if they are to be exciting places and, in schools, not to resemble classrooms. Nevertheless, for noise reasons, separate rooms may be provided for quiet study or library-based activities. Susan Dailey writes: 'However, "flexibility" and "openness" are not synonymous terms. While a totally open library will certainly be flexible, a flexible library does not have to be completely open . . . Without advocating a library with many small rooms, separating areas that will be noisy from those that need absolute quiet does seem logical.'[1] Unless provided in large numbers, however, there is usually no need for AV and IT technologies to be placed in separate rooms.

Multi-purpose and shared space

Where space is at a premium, the ability to utilize areas for different purposes could be important. Movable furniture (such as shelves on castors) and stackable chairs could allow part of the school or children's library to be adapted for meetings, small musical or theatrical performances, for example. A multi-purpose room in a school library could accommodate a class or group of teaching staff. Suitably equipped it could be used for the group viewing of videos or films, or, if appropriate, storytelling and other such activities. Planning for the shared use of facilities, for instance an activities/meeting room, computer room, or exhibition space, with other school or library departments, is another way of maximizing the use of all available space.

These ideas, and those concerned with open-plan space, are part of the flexible approach to library accommodation that librarians request in their brief and anticipate will be present in the space provided.

Number of entrances and exits

Primary school libraries may be in an open, accessible space with no thought given to making them secure. However, in other libraries, it is generally considered not good practice to have more than one user exit/entrance to the library, often with a security system, in order to protect the library's resources. This is more likely to be an issue in some schools where there is potential for the library to be approached by several routes within a building, than in a public library children's department, as, in the latter case, the main library entrance will usually lie beyond it. In dual-use libraries, separate entrances may be provided for pupils (from the school) and for the public (from the street) and both will need security systems if it is policy to install them. The location of entrances in all such cases should not pose a problem of supervision for the library staff. The architect will advise on what is necessary by way of emergency or fire exits and these should be equipped in such a way – with an alarm, for example – so as to not need direct supervision.

Wall and window space

Good lighting is an important feature of a well-designed library, but an excessive number of windows to provide natural light (and possibly a nice view) may not only affect the comfort of those using the library but also reduce the amount of wall space that can be used for shelving and display purposes. Where the space available for the library is less than generous, this can be a particular problem, as valuable floor space will be taken up by a greater number of freestanding bookcases and display boards. Windows above wall shelving or roof lights may be seen as possible solutions in certain situations. The location of radiators or other heating fitments can also limit the use of wall space for shelving and affect the placing of seating. Vertical rather than horizontal installation of radiators, or fewer but larger units, may help matters in some cases.

Dual-use libraries: integration or separation?

A decision is required in dual-use libraries as to what extent public library and school facilities are to be integrated or kept separate, and the extent of any separate public library children's provision. Most dual-purpose libraries in the UK, such as those in Cambridgeshire and Cheshire, seem to offer as full an integration of stock and space as is possible. However, some libraries may have an area or seating reserved for schoolchildren or divide the library into busy and quiet zones to facilitate study. Arthur Jones suggests that the main lesson to be learned from the early dual-use libraries was the provision

> of spaces which are sufficiently separated to allow them to be used simultaneously for different – and sometimes noisy – purposes without mutual disturbance . . . All

these requirements call for the provision of a suite of rooms, or at least a room of irregular shape, where space can be used flexibly according to changing patterns of need.[2]

At Top Valley Joint Library (Nottinghamshire) a study area is located close to the school entrance to the library, near the issue counter and staff workroom, and away from the children's book and story area on the other side of the library; the latter area can also be used for class visits. Non-fiction stock is integrated and most is located near that part of the library which adjoins the school. Thus: 'Through the design and arrangement of the library, the architect and the library staff have succeeded in reducing the potential for conflict of use.'[3]

Other possible arrangements include a dual-use library restricted to children, or a 'separate' children's department within such a library to be used jointly by pupils and other children.[4]

Disabled children and young people

UK legislation (Chronically Sick and Disabled Persons Act 1970) requires that all public buildings be designed to make appropriate provision for the needs of the disabled as regards access, parking and sanitary facilities, and the question of access was discussed in Chapter 7. For financial and structural reasons, providing such access may pose problems when remodelling or converting an older building. In addition, there is the difficulty that most libraries cannot be designed solely for the benefit of the physically disabled and so a reasonable compromise is required. Given various constraints, it will be necessary to decide on the extent of the compromise in respect of design aspects, such as the top shelf height and the location of bottom shelves, as well as taking into account, where appropriate, the requirements of children with other disabilities, such as visual handicaps, or special learning needs.

Whatever is done to facilitate access and use of a library building by disabled children and young people is likely to make life easier for all library users. For the physically disabled, particular attention should be paid to routes 'to bookstack areas, catalog and circulation areas, and seating spaces'.[5] Margaret Marshall and Linda Walling provide advice on the many other space and design factors, such as lighting, flooring and signposting, that need to be taken into account when creating library facilities to be used by handicapped children and students, including those with learning problems that are related to their disabilities.[6] This advice includes such points as:

(a) Carpeting can interfere with the free movement of wheelchairs, (unless it has minimum pile), and absorbs noise, thus limiting environmental clues for the blind.

(b) Blind students need braille and tactile signs and maps, along with voice announcements.

(c) Sharp edges and corners on furniture and equipment are serious hazards and must be rounded or padded.

    (d) Attention should be given to the height of desks tables, shelves, handles, equipment, etc.

    (e) The provision of toilet facilities capable of wheelchair access.

Supervision and security

The need for supervision and security in school libraries and those for children and young people, will influence such matters as the location of staff desks and counters and shelving layout, and may also require the use of a book security system, security mirrors (to check on areas that are out of sight) and closed-circuit television, to supervise an unstaffed gallery, for example.[7] In schools, especially where there is no security system, a place outside the main library area, with racking for students to leave bags and coats, might be considered necessary.

As libraries contain an increasing amount of portable audiovisual and IT equipment, prominent ownership marks and security devices to detect unauthorized taking of property should be considered. Responsibility for the security of equipment loaned from the library should also be clearly laid down.

Safety

The question of responsibility for the safety of library users has already been commented on in Chapter 1, and The Library Association has issued guidelines about the particular problem of unsupervised children in libraries. While not dealing with design issues, other than suggesting making provision in the children's section for adults supervising their children, it emphasizes the need for librarians to take 'reasonable' care of children on their premises.[8] The practical implications mean that the librarian must be aware of the potential danger to young people of, for example, glass doors, hot radiators, window seats and accessible opening windows, stair design, galleries, play furniture, and the use of electrical equipment (childproof sockets could be necessary), where these are part of the library's proposed provision and design. Choice of soft furnishings and furniture should take into account their use of fire-retardent materials and the lack of toxic fumes should a fire occur. In some circumstances, consideration may need to be given to providing fire extinguishers suitable for electrical fires as well as the more usual type. It would be useful to compile a checklist of potential hazards to be avoided and Leslie Edmonds provides such a list, which, although now dated, is a useful point of departure.[9] The checklist offers a means of evaluating existing children's departments and is one that can be adapted for new or remodelled buildings. It covers: exits, lighting, electrical matters, structure and furniture, accessibility, staff training, housekeeping and other procedures.

Concern for safety on mobile, particularly school mobile libraries is vital. As regards the latter, Pybus notes the need for[10]:

    (a) Vision around the vehicle.

    (b) Very low rear window to check for children gathering at the back of the vehicle.

    (c) Audible and visible warning devices to be activated when the vehicle is reversing.

    (d) Entrance handrails correctly positioned.

    (e) Protection from sharp edges at lower levels of the vehicle.

    (f) Control switches and buttons out of reach to children.

    (g) Security for staff's personal belongings.

Centralized or decentralized library processes?

A decision to centralize or decentralize, to a greater or lesser extent, the selection, acquisition, cataloguing and processing of library materials for constituent libraries of a school (junior and senior school, for example), or public library children's service, will have implications for the amount of staff work and storage space to be provided in each library and in a main library or headquarters accommodation.

Shelving requirements

Estimates for shelving space in a school library or public library children's department should take into account how much material it is expected will be on loan at any one time. A figure of 25% of the collection is a usual allowance, but modern collection management would aim for a higher loan percentage figure. Seasonal fluctuations would also need to be taken into consideration in any such calculation. In addition, if all the books and other materials are called in at any one time by a school library, then extra storage space will be necessary to accommodate the total stock for a limited period.

Seating

In providing seating, consideration needs to be given as to the way children interact with library materials. They often consume books on the spot, perhaps laying on the floor and adopting poses that seem uncomfortable to the adult. Nolan Lushington comments on the young child's need for private places and the ability to alter their environment. In the former case he suggest small alcoves created by low shelves that can be supervised by staff where children can settle down individually or in small groups.[11] Small alcoves or special seats for one or two children, to give a sense of personalized space can be created virtually anywhere around the walls of the library using, for example, specially designed furniture or providing seating below windows. Beanbags and other light, informal seating will allow children to move them around as they wish.

What this demonstrates is that, in addition to function and aesthetics:

There must be a very clear understanding of the behavioral expectations of students and staff . . . Layouts should encourage the behavioral patterns expected from users, both faculty and students (for this reason the planning team for a school library should include student representation). Given recent observations about behavioral understanding, it could be concluded that it ranks above the aesthetics of the media center and is as important as function in contributing to successful design.[12]

Gütersloh Stadtbibliothek, Germany, has probably one of the most varied and imaginative ranges of seating provision for children seen by the author and includes a carpeted and tiered kinderpit, hanging basket chairs and elevated, enclosed wire pods (Figure 9.1), as well as more formal seating.

A study of children and their territorial behaviour in a library setting suggests 'that freedom to move, to freely select positioning and a flexible seating arrangement seems to help children . . . to enjoy reading'.[13] Where the library environment is completely determined as regards seating, children's freedom to behave as they would wish could, therefore, be restricted.

IT and AV provision

The use of computers, telecommunications, audiovisual equipment and reprographic equipment, and multi-media production requirements, and the potential use of cable and satellite TV, and other modern developments, will make considerable demands on power and other cabling for the library. Not only must the school library, for example, be capable of external communications, for such services as online searching and the Campus 2000 viewdata system, but internal networks within a school for catalogue and other information provision, are becoming important. In planning, the librarian must take into account likely future demands for the quality of, access to and the capability of the power and other cabling to be installed.

A flexible solution to the installation of cabling should be looked for that does not pin equipment down to particular locations and can cope with increased demands.

Fig. 9.1 *Elevated enclosed seating pod, Gütersloh Library, Germany*

There are three possible solutions, or mixes thereof: perimeter, ceiling or floor cabling. Carroll suggests that wiring in floors and ceilings be installed in a grid pattern, providing outlets at regular intervals;[14] such a grid may not necessarily extend to all parts of the library. The most flexible system is probably ceiling cabling but the resulting cable poles in areas away from walls and columns are not always well designed, may be considered unsightly, and thus disliked.

The use of computers and other equipment has considerable implications for safety, ventilation, lighting, acoustics, wire management and the design of furniture. Failure to take these matters into account can lead to unsightly and uncomfortable conditions for both library users and staff, resulting in a 'physical environment [that] can affect learning, problem solving, and information handling and retrieval'.[15] The extent to which the library decides to utilize information technology in new or remodelled accommodation for its housekeeping activities, such as its issue system and catalogue, will affect such matters as the design of the issue counter, and the need to provide seating and/or standing facilities to consult online public access catalogue terminals. The latter may be grouped centrally or distributed around the library; in some buildings there could be a mix of the two.

Three published American accounts demonstrate how modern technology is affecting the school library resource centre. The first, by Bernice Lamkin, describes how 'a media center for the 21st century' was created at a Michigan central high school. Using a network system, teachers are able to have sound and video programmes set up and delivered over the system to a teaching station. It is anticipated that the system would eventually expand to allow: 'Students and staff alike . . . to call up homework assignments, advanced classes, tutorials, professional development activities and management programs from their homes as well as school.'[16]

Robert Swisher and others discuss the use of computer-based telecommunications and telefacsimile to provide information for management and services to users. It shows that telecommunications permits networking and enables libraries to share resources and decision-making, for example. It allows students, staff and administrators to have worldwide communications (through e-mail and bulletin boards), access to online databases, to interrogate remotely held CD-ROMs, and to forward interlibrary loan requests (copies may be received by fax). From the example given, it is clear that individual schools and public libraries will benefit from being part of a local regional networks, such as that which could be based on the schools library service, through which information about new books and other material could appear on bulletin board, and downloaded directly into a school's computer. Linked networks and the Integrated Services Digital Network (ISDN) that simplify the linking of personal computers to each other and to mainframes, 'could open the world of databases, electronic mail and shared resources to most personal computer users'.[17] Whether this will ultimately lead to the 'virtual library' – the library without walls – remains to be seen.

In describing her own information centre, Kim Carter comments that there is more to technology than computers and that production equipment is a key component:

Videotape recording and editing equipment, computer-based media production, interactive media, scanning, graphic design, video still photography, video microscopy, and a powerful and flexible sound production system all provide a wide range of options. These capabilities are vitally important as we work to empower students to communicate through a variety of media and modes.[18]

Library environment
Ambience

While the functional and behavioural aspects of a library's design are very important, its aesthetics and internal environment, and the ambience these create, deserve a great deal of attention. The 'feel' or 'mood' of a library will be the sum of many things (including the attitude of the staff), such as spaciousness, colour, decoration, lighting, the materials used for soft furnishings (such as curtains and blinds), equipment and furniture.[19] The overall effect should be to create a comfortable (but stimulating) and inviting atmosphere, which also appeals to the young person's imagination and age, and invites use. Peggy Abramo sees the library environment as communicating and sending out messages. She has written that:

> We want to encourage positive, growth-producing library experiences for even our youngest patrons by providing a library environment that welcomes them, makes them comfortable, meets their various information needs, tells them clearly the various activities they may do in a given space, considers that they are active learners, and stimulates them to return.[20]

The library should have its own identity, one that clearly distinguishes it from other parts of the school or public library. While deliberate choice in the areas of colour, decoration, finishes, furniture and so on will be an influence, the chosen aims of the library, resulting in particular services, such as special play or games features, or computer facilities, for example, will provide a distinctive ambience, or a contribution towards a variety of ambiences within a large children's library or department.[21]

Another way of creating a special ambience is to give the library a thematic treatment, such as animals, medieval times, or the railway. In Wuppertal, Germany, the children's library, opened in 1984, is called the 'bookship'; the idea developed from the shape of the room rented in the '*Haus der Jugend*'. This modern children's library is also in part a maritime museum, nautical terminology, therefore, is used (on signs, for example), and the interior decoration is inspired by the sea.[22] A maritime theme was also adopted for the children's department in the new Croydon Central Library described in Chapter 12.

In school libraries, it is important to try and avoid the classroom look where large numbers of seats are provided. Smaller groups of seating divided by shelving, seating in alcoves, and the judicious use of carrels can help mitigate this impression. However, it is recognized that libraries with less than their required space will need to arrange seating as economically as possible and this may not facilitate a more varied arrangement. The photographs of the new library of St Paul's School, New

Hampshire, USA, show a library of panelled walls, built-in wall shelving, fireplace, and sofas and armchairs that clearly makes a statement about its ambience.[23]

The ambience of a library for teenagers is likely to be very different to that for children and school pupils. The Yoker Youth Library is said to look more like a Virgin Store cafe, as it has made use of alternative furniture suppliers to the traditional ones, its walls are festooned with posters, and music is played.[24] The American author, Todd Strasser, makes a plea for appropriate seating, tables, library materials, display features (and noise) in a school library, if it is to appeal to teenagers. 'If a school library has one thing that attracts students, it is an environment like the one they're used to – one that respects their tastes and interests.'[25]

Colour

Strong, primary colours are usually avoided in the decoration of libraries, as such colours have the ability to excite or depress and may also become irksome and seem dated after a while. Consequently, library interiors tend to be rather unobtrusive, safe, and similar throughout, using neutral colours such as beige, light yellow, grey or off-white, or more recently soft pastel colours. It is often suggested that colour will be provided in the library by its materials and users. However, one might question whether such bland, neutral colours are always suitable in libraries for children and young people, and whether something more adventurous should not be attempted where appropriate.

Aaron and Elaine Cohen argue for the 'judicious application of primitive color', as both children and young people respond to their use, although they warn against too much colour.[26] Colours can be used to give an interior a colour accent – on a far wall or bookstack end panels, for example – or to make a space more inviting, larger, or smaller. The Cohens advise that:

- light colors, pastels and sunny yellows, make rooms seem light and airy; small rooms appear larger and low ceilings, higher;
- dark colors, dark blues, browns and even blacks, make rooms seem smaller and bring down ceilings and shorten walls;
- warm colors, reds, oranges, and bright yellows (good for windowless rooms), make rooms seem warmer, particularly those facing north, northeast, and east;
- cool colors, pale greens and blues, retreat to make rooms seem cooler, especially rooms with west and southwest exposures.[27]

As regards floor colour, they suggest a medium tone, preferably patterned carpet (to hide dirt and wear), and for the ceiling, which will diffuse and disseminate light, they suggest it be painted white in the 80–90% reflectance range.

Another writer indicates that red, orange and yellow can dominate a space and are better used as colour accents; blues and greens are suggested as main colours. Red, orange and yellow used in children's areas may also make children physically active and not as interested in borrowing books. The writer suggests that, in the library media centre: 'Warm yellows, peaches and pinks can work well for children, while young adults tend to respond better to blues and greens.'[28]

Whatever view is taken, there must be a coordinated approach to the colours used on interior finishes, furniture and equipment, soft furnishings, and floor covering, and their implications for maintenance and lighting taken into consideration.[29]

The design, colour and lettering for use on the exterior of mobile libraries is discussed by Pybus, who points out that the move to a corporate style can take decisions on these matters largely out of the hands of librarian.[30] Nevertheless some very distinctive and colourful designs have appeared on vehicles for library service children in recent years.

Decoration

As public buildings, decorative features are perhaps more likely to be found in public library children's departments than in school libraries, and a small percentage of the total budget should be set aside for them. They can include such things as works of art, murals, use of textiles, large banners, large papier-mache figures, friezes, graphics in entrance door glass, additions to shelving (such as animal cut-outs on the canopy) and furniture that caters for play and/or display of library materials, such as a Shipley's dragon. Such components can date quickly but, where appropriate, if left in place long enough, assume an historical interest and significance for later generations.

Art was the central theme of the renovation of the children's room at Kalamazoo Public Library, USA. With grants from a foundation, it was able to commission murals, soft sculptures and stained-glass windows depicting scenes from children's books for its children's room.[31] While few libraries are likely to be able to afford or find financial support for such a range of art, consideration should be given to the possibility of some form of art provision, especially where local artists can be involved. Kalamazoo's director writes that the tone and visual environment of the room has been improved and that: 'From a boring area of square footage populated by good books and good stuff, it has become an exciting room where children, adults and staff really can imagine words on the pages as pictures on the wall.'[32]

Other things that can lend interest to the library are plants, an aquarium, and a display of exhibits loaned from the local museum or art gallery, or from other departments of the library.

Display

Providing plenty of space for display in the library enables the exhibition of children's work in addition to that material shown by the library for promotion and information to young people and their parents. Display boards, both movable and wall mounted, near the entrance, and dispersed throughout the library (perhaps combined with shelving to allow for book display); one or more exhibition cases; and leaflet dispensers, and other furniture, will together provide a good basis for such work. Too much display space, however, may place a drain on the librarian's time and ingenuity and may encourage children's displayed work not to be renewed regularly to the detriment of the library's appearance. Facilities for display outside the school library or children's department might also be considered in order to publicize work with and services for pupils or children.

Guiding

Guiding is often an overlooked aspect of the library interior; an afterthought rather than a planned, integrated component. A variety of guiding and signs will be needed to provide information, direct children and young people, and indicate the location of sections of the library collection, including particular subjects. The wording of guiding should be suitable for the age group(s) served, and the use, for example, of colour-coding, pictorial book supports and pictograms and the provision of a library plan, will help users to understand the library's arrangement. An easily comprehensible layout, however, should lessen the need for too much guiding. The design of the guiding may have to fit in with the overall scheme for the school or public library building but its selection should have due regard to size, colour, placement, flexibility (to enable easy relocation after a rearrangement of the library), readability and maintenance. Whether it is easily removed or altered by children or young people is another point to be considered. While guiding can be suspended from the ceiling and placed on walls, the ability of shelving to accommodate guiding on the top or at the side of bays should be a factor in its selection. Peggy Heeks suggests that shelf guides are likely to be unnecessary in a small library where the amount of shelf space given to any one subject is very limited.[33]

Environmental comfort

If the library is to attract and retain users, then it should be a comfortable place to be all the year round. While heating, ventilation and air-conditioning (where provided) will be common to the school or public library as a whole, any particular needs of the school or children's library should not be forgotten, such as good ventilation for areas where numbers of children may be present for some time, or where reprographic or other equipment is in use. However, lighting, and acoustic treatment to combat noise, may be made much more specific to the school or children's library's needs.

The rather specialized cooling, heating and lighting requirements of mobile libraries are described by Pybus, who notes, for example, the need to give priority to heating the staff area, the ability to open windows and roof vents, and that lighting in the saloon area should be about 450 mm from the shelves.[34]

Lighting

Whereas access to natural light is a much requested quality for a library, it poses problems of fluctuation in quality, and a large number of windows may lead to unacceptable heat gain and loss, and thus discomfort for children or staff when seated in adjacent areas. The duration of that discomfort will depend on the orientation of the building; blinds, for example, will be necessary where it is a problem. Artificial light will, of course, be required and factors to consider here include: its quality and distribution; whether adjustable task lighting at study tables and carrels is to be provided; glare and shadow; maintenance, cleaning and replacement; and its aesthetic use. The proper location of computer terminals in relation to both natural and artificial light is important if they are to be comfortable in use; at right angles to sources of natural light and parallel to overhead fluorescent light fittings. Lighting standards for libraries were issued by the Chartered Institution of Building Services in 1982.[35] The standards, for example, recommend 150 lux for bookshelves, measured vertically at floor level, and 500 lux at study tables: the lux is a unit of illumination.

Acoustics

Noise from conversation, equipment and movement can be an irritating distraction for both staff and users, especially in an open-plan library. The use of carpet, acoustic tiles, acoustic panels, concern for the best spatial relationships of library areas, designated quiet or silent areas, and the layout of the library shelving, may all help to combat and control this problem. It should be recognized, however, that many young people read and study to the accompaniment of their preferred type of music and may not find noise the distraction that others do. It may also be necessary to deal with outside noise and Peggy Heeks suggests that: 'Double glazing may be advisable in a busy area to shut out traffic noise, especially in rooms where extension activities are held.'[36]

As important as it is to combat noise, it is also necessary to create the conditions where it cannot flourish. as Carol Doll writes: 'Students at tables tend to talk with one another. Table size subtly affects the number of users who sit there and so helps to control the amount of interaction.'[37] The number of tables and thus the number of students in any one area also seems to encourage noise; rearranging tables in smaller groupings, perhaps broken up by shelving might help reduce noisy conversation. Doll continues: 'it should be possible to identify ways to rearrange tables, chairs, and other movable objects within the space available to create areas for relaxation, quiet, and group work'.[38]

Floor covering

Carpet is almost universally rejected in Scandinavian libraries for health reasons, as it is said to exacerbate allergies in people. Conversely, it is almost universally accepted in the UK and the USA for its ease of maintenance, its colour and, if carpet tiles are used, the simplicity with which worn or damaged areas can be replaced. The possibility of static electricity discharge from certain types of carpet and metal finishes (handrails, for example) should be investigated. Other surfaces, such as linoleum, plastic tiles and rubberized flooring, may be utilized where wear is heavy (in entrance areas, around counters, and other major traffic routes, for example), and in activity areas where children will be using play and educational materials. Gresswell supply a 'wonder mat', which is useful for defining play and activity areas for young children. It is described as being 'a colourful shock absorbent floor covering made up of easily assembled interlocking pieces. It's virtually impossible to tear, waterproof, non-abrasive and non-toxic.' Anne Fleet suggests a number of factors that should be taken into account when deciding on floor covering for children's libraries: 'durability, maintenance, non-slip qualities, warmth, noise, design, variety and cost'.[39]

Schools
Centralization or decentralization of library services?

In *The school library*, the American writers, Ellsworth and Wagener, discuss the merits of a centralized library, which recognizes, for example, that knowledge cannot be put into separate boxes, and that it is less expensive of staff and materials. It admits that in some situations a compromise may be necessary which could result in departmental or subject branch libraries in large schools, or a library service to classrooms in smaller ones. Such classroom collections, it is suggested, might be quite generous in schools for younger pupils.[40] Some large British schools may have separate junior and senior school libraries.

Writing about British primary schools in 1986, Cecilia Gordon comments that new school plans 'are being submitted without provision for a central collection. Even the alternative, providing areas for a dispersed collection, is not adequately considered.'[41] She later suggests that, in spite of centralized resources, some schools may wish to retain a small book room for quiet reading or storytelling. Because of the possible drawbacks which are then described, this appears in reality to be an argument for more varied, integrated accommodation.[42] However, where no centralized provision has been made in a school building, and there is nowhere capable of adaptation – or teachers are not in favour of it – resources will be dispersed. Because of their less sophisticated needs, this may be seen as more acceptable for primary school pupils than older children. Nevertheless, there may well be problems of neglect and limited choice in separate classroom collections without some central organization.

The preferred situation is expressed in the Library Association's guidelines: '

> It is now generally recognized that a central organization of library and information resources is necessary in all types of school . . . Such provision does not suggest that the school library resource centre is the only place where books and other learning materials will be found . . . especially for young children.[43]

Where schools do not take the centrally organized route to school library and information services, the teaching, learning and space implications of other or additional arrangements will need to be thought through and taken into account at the planning stage.

Public libraries
Integration of children's and adult services

As discussed earlier, the relationship of the children's department to the adult area is seen as important, and in some libraries there may be shared uses of common areas. In that case the latter must be designed both from the viewpoint of the child and the adult. There is room for disagreement, however, as to how far children's facilities should be separated from those for adults. The Library Association guidelines offer arguments for both positions. Separate provision gives children their clearly identified area, facilitates activities and permits acceptable noise. In addition, staff develop good relationships with children and get to know the library materials. An open-plan arrangement facilitates family visits, eases the transition to adult reader, encourages all staff to be involved with service to children and makes the best use of space, staff and other resources.[44] It has been suggested that neither approach is ideal but that 'it is possible to overcome the disadvantages of each type by maximizing the positive features available'.[45]

However, policy decisions with regard to the integration and/or categorization of library materials, and shared use of the issue counter, for example, will have an impact on space requirements and relationships, and the layout of the library and may go someway towards overcoming the disadvantages of separate provision. Perhaps the ideal situation is one that provides clearly delineated space for children and young people of different age groups but also permits and encourages use of the library building as a whole.

Materials

The content, organization, arrangement and display of the library collection will have considerable planning implications. A decision to adopt stock categorization, or to integrate bookstock – children's non-fiction or reference works with their adult counterparts, or teenage fiction (suitably identified) with adult fiction, for example – or to display a substantial part of the bookstock face-on, as opposed to more traditional approaches, will affect spatial relationships, space requirements, library layout, and the requirements for storage and display shelving and furniture for library materials. Such alternative arrangements of the bookstock are seen as particularly helpful to teenagers, who find 'that it opens up the entire resources of the library . . . in a simple and intelligible manner and enables staff to judge community needs and demands more accurately than ever before'.[46] It has also been pointed out that, for the adolescent, 'there is no longer any danger of him being seen to be "childish" if he wants to borrow a children's book, and there is no longer any transfer problem'.[47]

Perhaps because of the less than satisfactory space allocated to children, rather than conscious attempts at collection segregation, other media are often not provided in children's libraries. This may be seen as an example of the preferential treatment that adults often get in the public library building and assumes that the availability of audiovisual materials for children and their parents and carers elsewhere in the library is well publicized. If other media are provided in the children's library, then some thought might be given as to whether the different formats should be interfiled on the shelves or not.

Combined issue counter

In small, and in many medium-sized, open-plan libraries, it is usual for there to be a single issue counter serving both adults and children and its design should try to take this into account. In libraries where children's accommodation is more separate and a separate counter is provided this must be:

(a) suitable for the issue system in use – a wire management facility will be important for automated systems
(b) convenient for small children
(c) of modular design to facilitate its relocation or rearrangement.

The plan of the library and a policy for or against greater integration of adult and children's facilities, will determine the number of counters, their size, design and location.

Administration

Administrative integration within an individual library, over such matters as the ordering and processing of new library materials, the handling of enquiries, dealing with interlibrary loans, and staffing arrangements will have space implications for children's library accommodation, particularly as regards that for staff. As noted earlier, the nature of administrative relationship with the wider library system to which an individual library belongs will also dictate whether more or less space is needed for staff within that service point.

References

1 Dailey, S., 'Establishing an atmosphere for success', *Indiana libraries*, **8** (2), 1989, 100.

2 Jones, A. C., 'Dual purpose libraries: some experience in England', *School librarian*, **25** (4), 1977, 315. A number of plans of dual-use libraries, 1962–75, are illustrated on p. 317.

3 Shaw, M., 'Top Valley: a joint-use success story', *School librarian*, **38** (2), 1990, 52.

4 For fuller details of local arrangements *see Directory of dual use libraries*, 2nd edn., Ipswich, Suffolk County Information and Library Service, [198?].

5 American Association of School Librarians and the Association of educational Communications and Technology, *Information power: guidelines for school library media programs*, Chicago, American Library Association, 1988, 90.

6 Marshall, M., *Managing library provision for handicapped children*, London, Mansell, 1991, 103–7; Walling, L. L., 'Granting each equal access', *School media quarterly*, **20** (4), 1992, 216–22.

7 Department of Education and Science, Architects and Building Branch, *Crime prevention in schools: closed circuit TV surveillance systems in educational buildings*, London, HMSO, 1991. (Building bulletin, 75). Not about libraries, but covers the planning, system design, installation, maintenance and budget for CCTV in schools.

8 Library Association, *Unsupervised children in libraries: guidance notes*, London, Library Association, 1991.

9 Edmonds, L., 'Sorry about safety?', *Illinois libraries*, **60** (10), 1978, 871–4.

10 Pybus, R. L., *The design and construction of mobile libraries*, 2nd edn., [London], Library Association, Branch and Mobile Libraries Group, 1990, 70.

11 Lushington, N., 'Designed for users', *Wilson library bulletin*, **58** (6), 1984, 424.

12 Bennett, J., 'Trends in school library media facilities, furnishings and collections', *Library trends*, **36** (2), 1987, 318.

13 Sever, I., 'Children and territory in a library setting', *Library and information science research*, **9** (2), 1987, 103.

14 Carroll, F. L., *Guidelines for school libraries*, The Hague, International Federation of Library Associations, 1990, 30.

15 Fuller information about these issues can be found in, Dyer, H. and Morris, A., *Human aspects of library automation*, Aldershot, Gower, 1990, (see esp., pp. 75–162); Robertson, M. M., 'Ergonomic considerations for the human environment: color treatment, lighting and furniture selection', *Library media quarterly*, **20** (4), 1992, 215. Legal requirements for those working with VDUs are dealt with in the Health and Safety (Display Screen Equipment) Regulations 1992.

16 Lamkin, B., 'A media center for the 21st century', *School library journal*, **33** (3), 1986, 28.

17 Swisher, R. *et al.*, 'Telecommunications for school library media centers', *School library media quarterly*, **19** (3), 1991, 158.

18 Carter, K., Images of information in a 21st century high school', *School library journal*, **40** (2), 1994, 29.

19 Dziura, W. T., 'Media center aesthetics: focus on design, color scheme and furnishings', in *Reader in children's librarianship* (ed.) J. Foster, Englewood, Colo., Information handling Services, 1978, 369–75.

20 Abramo, P., 'Communicating with environments', *Illinois libraries*, **60** (10), 1978, 875.

21 For ideas relating to this and the following paragraph, *see* Hart, T. L., *Creative ideas for library media center facilities*, Englewood, Colo., Libraries Unlimited, 1990; McCormick, E., 'Revitalising the children's area', *American libraries*, **17** (9), 1986, 712–14.

22 Nielsen, G. S., 'Bogskib ohoej!', *Bogens verden*, **68** (7), 1986, 383–4.

23 Wyatt, G. and Cassels-Brown, R., 'A new library for St Paul's School', *School library journal*, **38** (2), 1992, 35–7.

24 'Yoker Youth Library', *Service point*, (57), 1993, 7.

25 Strasser, T., 'Lending ambience to libraries', *School library journal*, **4** (10), 1988, 59.

26 Cohen, A. and Cohen, E., 'Remodeling the library', *School library journal*, **24** (6), 1978, 30.

27 Idem, 30.

28 Doll, C.A., 'School library media centers: the human environment', *School library media quarterly*, **20** (4), 1992, 226.

29 Habley, K., 'The many uses of color in the library rooms serving children', *Illinois libraries*, **60** (10), 1978, 891–8.

30 Pybus, op. cit., 55–7.

31 Amdursky, S.J., 'Re-creating the children's room: a renovation project at Kalamazoo Public Library', *School library journal*, **39** (2), 1993, 25–7.

32 Idem, 26.

33 Heeks, P., *The administration of children's libraries*, London, Library Association, 1967, 37.

34 Pybus, op. cit., 43–7.

35 Chartered Institution of Building Services, *CIBS lighting guide: libraries*, London, The Institution, 1982. See esp. Table 1.

36 Heeks, op. cit., 21.

37 Doll, op. cit., 227.

38 Idem, 227.

39 Fleet, A., *Children's libraries*, London, André Deutsch, 1973, 37.

40 Ellsworth, R. E., and Wagener, H. D., *The school library: facilities for independent study in the secondary school*, New York, Educational Facilities Laboratories, 1963, 37–43.

41 Gordon, C., *Resource organisation in primary schools*, 2nd edn., London, Council for Educational Techhnology, 1986, 24.

42 Idem, 31–2.

43 Kinnell, M. (ed.), *Learning resources in schools: Library Association guidelines for school libraries*, London, Library Association, 1992, 27.

44 Library Association, *Children and young people: Library Association guidelines for public library services*, London, Library Association, 1991, 12–13.

45 Esson, K. and Tyerman, K., *Library provision for children*, Newcastle-under-Lyme, Association of Assistant Librarians, 1991, 2.

46 Library Association, Community Services Group in Scotland, *Library services to teenagers: a report by the Teenager Sub-committee*, [Glasgow], Library Association Community Services Group in Scotland, 1985, paras. (e) and (f).

47 Barnes, M. and Ray, S., *Youth library work*, London, Bingley, 1968, 44.

10 SPATIAL RELATIONSHIPS AND THE LIBRARY LAYOUT

Design and the librarian

A principal managerial role of the librarian, in the creation of a design for a library, is as a planner – the supplier of sufficient information (in the form of the brief), to enable the architect to arrive at an appropriate design solution for the building. However, the librarian also has to take an interest in design, particularly as regards the functional suitability of what the architect might propose, in order to be able to comment as to its acceptability. And, as has been pointed out earlier, there are space planning challenges where the school or children's librarian may be without specialist help. In both these situations the librarian needs some understanding of the practice and principles that will affect the arrangement and layout of the interior space of the library, and the knowledge and confidence to use and review architectural drawings.

A knowledge of design will also help the librarian understand the requirements and importance of certain parts of the brief when it is being prepared, such as the constraints imposed by security and supervision, and provide a framework for making recommendations (about space relationships for example), in that document that will affect the organization of the library interior.

The library shape

It has been argued that the square or rectangle is the best and most flexible shape for the main part of a library.[1] Its advantages are that:

1   Rectilinear items, such as shelving, are more easily accommodated and can be arranged in either direction across the library.
2   All points are equidistant and can be viewed from the centre of the library.
3   Space is not wasted.

While a simple rectangular-shaped school library or children's department will have the above advantages, and perhaps fit more easily into its larger parent school or public library building, such shapes can be seen as rather uninteresting. A circular-, hexagonal-, octagonal- or irregular-shaped building may therefore be proposed and the latter may be dictated by the nature of the site. Such buildings, while visually attractive, are likely to be more expensive, less flexible, and may require custom-built shelving and other furniture to make the best use of wall angle and length. A library building with a high ceiling will often permit the inclusion of a gallery (open

146

or enclosed) as part of the design, where a further floor is not feasible, and this usefully provides extra square metres.

The design process

Amongst other things, the brief will have described the named library spaces, together with their sizes, that have to be accommodated in the architect's plan for the library. It will also have indicated in those descriptions the preferred relationships of the library spaces with each other. These relationships may also be expressed diagrammatically in a number of ways for the architect. An increasingly common method is the bubble diagram. With a knowledge and understanding of these relationships, the architect is able to propose how the available space, which may be on more than one floor, might be allocated to various sections, rooms or areas of the library, maintaining, as far as possible, the preferred relationships.

Space relationships

A problem for the librarian at the briefing stage, therefore, is making decisions about what are the best space relationships, so that all the library areas will be in logical and convenient relationships in the finished library for both users and staff and the movement of library materials. One way of approaching this task is to classify the various relationships of the different components of the library by degrees of preferred proximity.

In *Facilities planning*, Roger Brauer suggests five different relationships, as indicated in Table 10.1 below.[2]

Table 10.1 Space relationship codes of proximity

Code	Relationship
1	Spaces must be adjacent.
2	Adjacency is preferred, but not absolutely necessary.
3	Anywhere nearby is fine.
4	Distance is not important.
5	Spaces should be far apart or in different buildings.

Using Brauer's numerical codes, these relationships may first be charted as a matrix, in order to record in detail what is required, and then presented in the form of a bubble diagram, where each space or component of the library is represented by a circle in the diagram. As Brauer indicates, all the specified relationships cannot be incorporated into the design solution and that: 'A relationship matrix and the bubble diagram that result are merely guides.'[3] A large building project may require a number of bubble diagrams, for example to show the relationship of the library to the rest of the school and the children's department to the complete library building, or to illustrate the relationships within the departments or areas of a large school or children's library.

There are various methods of drawing bubble diagrams ranging from the simple to the more complex. In general these drawing methods allow the bubbles to give an indication of the relative sizes of the various library spaces and the required adjacency, or otherwise, by the linking, distancing or grouping of bubbles. The annotated bubble diagram method permits other requirements to be shown, such as acoustic or visual isolation.[4]

The role of the relationship matrix and the bubble diagram in helping to determine the final design solution is shown in Figure 10.1: the use of the block diagram and the floor plan, as illustrated there, is discussed in the following pages.

Limited guidance on the creation and use of the relationship matrix and the bubble diagram (or similar methods) is to be found in the library literature, but there are useful short sections in the works by the Cohens, Holt, and Thompson.[5] A number of examples of the use of bubble diagrams for designing school libraries are to be found in the case studies described in Pauline Anderson's *Planning school library media facilities*.[6]

Logicality and convenience suggest, however, that the librarian has certain underlying requirements that will assist in classifying space relationships first of all, and then be reflected in any proposed layout and arrangement of the library interior.

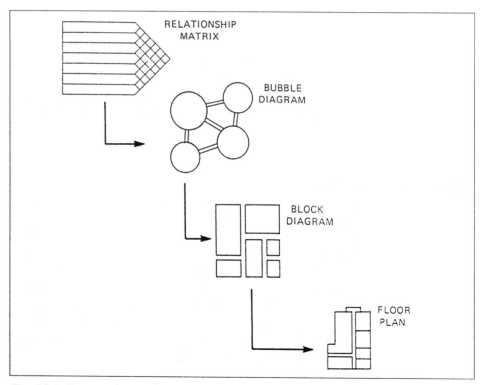

Fig. 10.1 *Space relationships to floor plan.*

(Reproduced with permission of the publisher from *Facilities planning* by Roger L. Brauer, © 1992 Amacom, a division of the American Management Association. All rights reserved)

Factors affecting spatial relationships

The following are common factors affecting decisions about spatial relationships.

1 A particular planning philosophy, for example:
  (a) that library areas for popular materials and their use will precede those housing more serious, purposive ones
  (b) that technology will command centre stage rather than printed materials[7]
  (c) that the central visual focus will be a conversation area[8]
  (d) that the issue desk will be 'viewed as a central resource rather than an entrance barrier to the library'.[9]

2 The arrangement of the library will reflect planned traffic flows of staff, users and materials through the building.

3 Noise: not only will the finishes and treatment of interior surfaces help overcome the noise problem but also the layout of the library. This means the layout following a progression from noisy to quiet (even silent) areas; planning traffic patterns that do nor disturb nor distract users, and concentrating noisy activities together, as suggested in the 'central space concept' outlined below.

4 Access to plumbing, electrical and other building services, such as a lift or book hoist.

5 Communication between staff and colleagues and with users will affect the location of offices, workrooms, service counters and desks.

6 Convenience will dictate, for example, that the information service point be located close to catalogues, indexes, databases and quick reference materials.

7 The need for supervision of users and to give assistance in their use of equipment (to interrogate CD-ROMs, for example) and machinery, such as a photocopier, can affect the arrangement of the library.

Other factors include user accessibility and questions of security and supervision.

Central space concept

The Cohens, in their book, *Designing and space planning for libraries*,[10] advance the central square concept. This square is seen as the focal point of the library and is the area opposite the main entrance, which is centrally located. Regardless of the shape of the library, this 'central square' is the space needing most control and is the area of most change in the library. From this point all user activities radiate. 'Departments that require less user interaction should be located away from the central square.'[11] The concept can be applied everywhere in a building – each floor or department can have its central square. This approach encapsulates many of the points made above about the factors affecting spatial relationships but also introduces the idea of the 'area of most change' within a library.

Allocating space

With the aid of the bubble diagram and other information in the brief, the architect can decide on the location of particular spaces within the overall floor plan, and these may be first labelled or marked out as blocks of space. Such plans are known as block diagrams and many of the items in the Bibliography to this book include floor plans that simply indicate the location of particular library rooms and areas without the detail of the layout of shelving, furniture, etc., and these represent this stage of development in the design of the interior.[12] The Cohens suggest that traffic patterns should be drawn on the block diagram and that these could also appear on the final layout.[13]

Interior layout of shelving, furniture and equipment

Once the librarian has agreed with the architect over the proposed general space disposition and relationships, as indicated on the block plans, work can proceed on making detailed decisions about the precise location and arrangement of the required shelving, furniture and equipment in each of those areas. This detail can then be used to create complete floor plans.

The layout of shelving, furniture and equipment within library areas will also be governed by some of the relationship factors indicated above – communication and supervision, for example. In an open-plan approach to a school library or children's library department, furniture, particularly shelving can be used as a means of defining space for particular purposes, for example, a study area, as well as acting as a noise buffer. Other factors that come into play when deciding upon the detailed library layout include:

(a) appropriate gangways between rows of shelving and between seating
(b) simplicity (but not necessarily an uninteresting layout)
(c) flexibility (a layout that is amenable to change)
(d) economic in operation (does not require too many parts of the library to be staffed)
(e) varied visual experience (through choice of furniture and its arrangement).

While there may be a conflict between utilizing space economically (to house as much library materials and seat as many users as possible), and having an interesting layout that helps also to define different areas of activity, more varied patterns of shelving and seating, particularly for carrels, should be considered. Figure 10.2 shows some examples of innovative shelving arrangements by Germany's EKZ which also offers a helpful illustration as to how they replace more traditional layouts.

By way of summary to this section it is useful to list the five freedoms that Walter Dziura advocates should be guaranteed by the layout of a media centre and which seem to have a wider applicability.

- The freedom for the user to sit – the provision of 'multiple seating choices to the user.'
- The freedom for the user to move – 'traffic patterns should make the best use of available space . . . The user should be able to move . . . without disturbing others using the facility.'

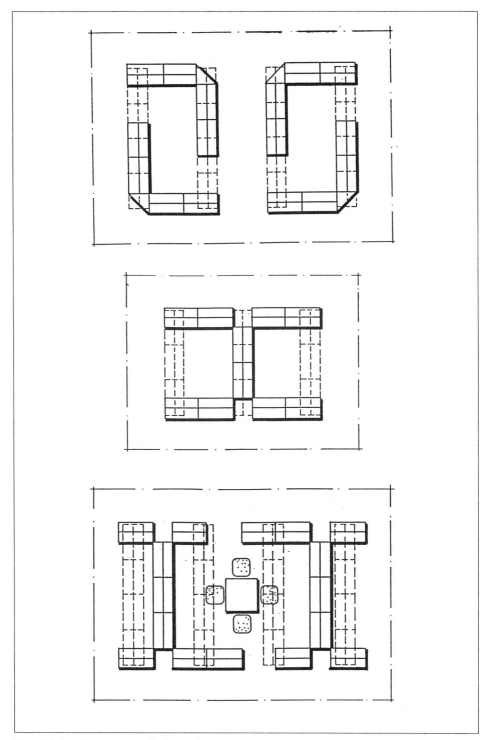

Fig. 10.2 *Innovative shelving layouts*
(Reproduced through the courtesy of EKZ GmbH)

- The freedom for the user to alter, vary, or change things – the ability to make minor changes to the environment. Also: 'How adaptable will the layout be to alteration in the current functions?'
- The freedom for the user to act and interact – a layout that provides 'immediate access to materials and equipment.'
- The freedom for the user to temporarily own – 'The design layout should provide ample opportunity for users to find and establish territory, keeping in mind that territorial right does not necessarily mean total isolation from fellow humans.'[14]

Such freedoms would seem to emphasize choice, ease of movement, access, interaction, and the ability to adapt and own, albeit temporarily, part of the library's space.

Constraints on interior space relationships and layout

The perfect accommodation for a school or children's library probably does not exist. For, as Infantino has written about the latter: 'we will probably never feel we know enough to plan the "perfect" children's room. But decisions must be made in any building or remodelling project and the "perfect" children's room will never be designed.'[15] However, good planning and design will endeavour to accomplish this, while constraints, leading to compromises of one kind or another, will inevitably conspire to prevent it. Compromise is particularly true when planning the interior arrangement and layout of the library. The shape of the building, the size of individual floors, the pattern of windows, architectural and structural features, and the location of the entrance will all affect the disposition of space and the interior layout. When remodelling or converting premises, existing lighting patterns, the distribution of electrical outlets, and floor loading may all affect what can be achieved by way of a layout, unless changes can be made as part of the conversion or remodelling.

A major problem and potential constraint occurs when converting a room or building that is of historical and/or architectural importance. Peggy Heeks suggests that: 'One should work with the character of the room or building which has to be adapted rather than against it and consider carefully the effect of change . . . In reaching decisions one should get a feeling for the room's potentialities and work, like the cosmetician, to disguise the defects and make apparent what is good.'[16] Modern library furniture, carefully chosen, will fit into historic locations, as witness the children's department at Castle Gates Library, Shrewsbury, or part of the school library at Old Palace School, Croydon. Covering up earlier decorative features and putting false ceilings into high Victorian or Edwardian rooms, however, invariably destroys their character and works against them rather than with them.

Mobile libraries

IFLA's *Mobile library guidelines* (and Eastwood's *Mobile libraries*) provide some suggestions in diagram form for the interior layout of mobile libraries, both bus and and trailer type.[17] Such interior arrangements are clearly influenced by the position of the entrance(s) and the counter, and where shelving (full and low height) and other storage fitments, can be placed along the interior walls of the vehicle. Although such layouts offer no guidance for vehicles whose clientele includes children nor for those dedicated especially to serve children, they provide useful models for consideration. Pybus states, however, that specialist mobiles, such as that for a Schools Library Service, require different design concepts. 'Schools Library Service vehicles, for example, require extra books not on display and they need to be able to carry a wide range of materials such as videos, films, charts, and they may need access to a catalogue of the Schools Library Service. The counter . . . need not be as formal as a public mobile library, but can be a collapsible shelf rather than a full counter.'[18]

Reading the architect's drawings[19]

At the appropriate stages in the design process, the school or children's librarian will need to examine promptly, and with attention to detail, the architect's proposals for a design solution, which will be in the form of drawings. This is one of the architect's methods of communication and, for a large building others may be used, such as a model, mock-ups of parts of the interior and a video presentation. While not universal, architects' drawing are increasingly created using computer-aided design hardware and software.

Even though the architect can be asked to clarify points about the drawings, it is vital that the librarian understands something about the range of drawings that will be provided and the conventions that are used, as regards symbols and scale for example, in order to fully appreciate what the architect is proposing. However, acquisition of this basic knowledge can lead to a sense of false security and, as noted earlier, should not prevent the librarian from asking questions about the drawings, even though impressed by their visual quality and apparent 'rightness' for what they portray. Does this room really have no windows? What does this dotted line mean? What sort of door is this? And other questions may be prompted by an examination and review of the plans.

In examining the architect's design for the building, it is important to examine all the relevant drawings in order to fully understand what is intended. The following list concentrates on those drawings that explain what the building will look like, how it is to be organized and arranged, and details of its interior layout, rather than those that relate to the details of its structure and mechanical, electrical and plumbing services.

Site plan

This plan shows the library's relationship to surrounding buildings (other school buildings, for example), streets and other features of the immediate environment for the public library, and the direction of north. It will thus show how people will make their way to the building and the orientation of the library in respect of weather conditions.

Perspective

This is an impression of how the main facade of the library will look from the outside, both physically (materials, scale, etc.), and in its intended setting. It can be particularly important to the architect in selling the 'look' of the proposed library and in helping the librarian understand significant details of the building, such as the entrance and the treatment of the main façade, as well as its overall nature. The school or children's librarian might ask how well the building conveys its purpose, if solely for pupils or young people, or whether clues to the existence of such facilities within a building are conveyed by the perspective view of a school or public library, if this had been required of the architect.

Floor plans

A plan is a view of the building seen from above showing width and length of enclosed spaces, structural features and objects; in a building of several floors there will be one for each level. When fully developed (from the block diagram described above), a floor plan will show the layout and arrangement of the furniture, fittings and shelving. Children's and school librarians are usually fairly at home with such plans, and they are likely take up most of their time, but to understand them fully they must be considered along with other drawings.

Sections

Usually more than one section is given and these provide a view of the interior of the library at points that will have been indicated on the plan drawings (for example AA, BB, CC). The sections or views result from cutting through the building, as though with a knife (from A to A or from C to C), and removing one of the pieces; one section may be at right angles to the other. Sections are useful in giving a feel of the internal spaces and for showing the height of individual levels, height under galleries, and the vertical relationships and communications between the interior features of the building. The areas chosen for sections usually provide details about more complex parts of the library building.

Elevations

Elevations are views of all the outside walls of the building as though seen from directly opposite and are useful in showing the external pattern and height of doors and windows, downpipes and other service-related aspects, and decorative features. In some situations, the appearance of what is proposed for the front of a building may differ considerably to that for the back or sides. Elevations of the interior walls may also be provided.

Other matters

Drawing description

On the right-hand side of each of the architect's drawings there will be space for: the title of the project; the name of the architect; title of the drawing (for example ground floor or section AA); the scale; date of completion of the drawing; and a space for notes, such as references to other drawings, details of agreed changes, and the explanation of symbols. The librarian should take in this information before attempting to read the drawings.

Scale information

For floor plans the scale is usually that of 1 cm = ½ metre (usually expressed as 1 :
50 or 1 : 5); the equivalent scale for older building designed in the imperial system is
¼ inch to 1 foot. Other plans may use scales of 1 : 100 (or 1 : 1, that is 1 cm = 1 m),
or in older buildings ⅛ to 1 foot. When examining drawings it helps to have a ruler
that converts architectural scales to actual measurements.

Architectural symbols

To extract the most information from an architect's drawing it is necessary to
appreciate the meaning of the various symbols used to indicate doors, windows,
types of interior partitioning, lifts, stairs, and to ask questions about those which are
unclear. The range of symbols used for library furniture and equipment – shelves,
tables, carrels, chairs, etc. – is usually fairly obvious; items for which there may be
no conventional symbol may be accompanied by a description on the drawing.

Reviewing the architect's plans[20]

Acquiring the knowledge to understand plans is one thing, reviewing plans in order
to check that space requirements and functional relationships and other criteria have
been met is another. This is a time-consuming job which is helped, therefore, by
setting aside enough time to do it thoroughly, making sure that all the relevant plans
and other documentation, such as the brief, are to hand, and that there is enough
space to work in. It helps to pin the set of plans up on a board or spread them out on
a table (preferably the former), rather than trying to refer to them as a sheaf of
documents. Before beginning a detailed review of the drawings, Holt suggests
familiarization with the drawings in a general way, identifying entrances and the
main features of the library, and goes on to say that: 'It takes time to become familiar
with the drawings; do not despair.'[21] Whether a building project is only concerned
with the school library or the children's department, or whether they are part of larger
school or public library projects, the school or children's librarian should have the
opportunity to familiarize themselves with and review the plans, and, in the larger
project, to comment on the relationship of the library to the proposed school or other
public library departments. Opportunities should be found to discuss the outcome of
such reviews (from concept to completion drawings) with the architect, possibly
devoting design-team meetings to such work.

The work of examining the drawings can begin by reviewing them in respect of
what was asked for in the brief; a summary list of spaces and their sizes in that
document will make this an easier task. This job is made even easier if the architect
marks the plans with the size in square metres of each area on the drawing. In order
to visualize how the sizes of individual areas will look in reality, it is useful to have
a number of yardsticks, such as the sizes of areas in the old library or that of
classrooms of differing sizes. Having checked that the architect has provided the
range of required spaces of the requested sizes, and no changes are needed, the
librarian should assess their location one to another in terms of brief's preferred
relationships.

Following an assessment of what has been provided and where, the librarian should endeavour to 'use' the building by, for example:

(a) 'following' traffic routes through the building – is it easy to understand the arrangement of the library and for users to find their way around? Is there enough circulation space, particularly around the issue counter area? Will there be unacceptable traffic through quiet areas – perhaps to reach group study spaces or a computer room?

(b) 'sitting' at a table – what might the librarian (acting as a pupil or young person) see, hear or feel like?

(c) 'working' at the issue desk – is supervision satisfactory? Will there be enough space for staff?

(d) 'sitting' in an office: Will staff be adequately accommodated?

In other words, the librarian should work hard to visualize the building from different locations and from the various points of view of both library staff, pupils or young people. Some particular points worth considering are:

1   Orientation of the building – the effect of sunlight and the potential for heat gain or loss.

2   Placement and number of windows.
    (a)   whether adequate, inadequate, overprovided or inappropriate for particular spaces.

3   Changes of level.
    (a)   have the problems of the disabled or young mothers with children been taken into account?

4   Noise problems.
    (a)   how will noise from the movement of staff and users, conversation and the use of machinery affect purposive use of the library?

5   Traffic flow.
    (a)   are the width of gangways adequate (measure them; do not depend on whether they look right), and is congestion likely at certain places at certain times?

6   Shape of spaces – partitioning of large areas around the perimeter for offices, study carrels, workrooms or other spaces may make for an irregular central space that may be less flexible at certain points.

7   Staircases – are they in the best place?

8   Galleries or balconies – is it clear what they will be used for? Are there implications for access and supervision? Should they be open or enclosed to keep out noise if they are to be used as a quiet area?

9   Security – will security to non-public parts of the building be compromised?

It is important that questions, queries and comments resulting from a review of plans are formally noted and communicated to the architect. The results of their subsequent discussion should also be recorded. If significant changes are to be made to the architect's proposals, they should be made early on in the design process (schematics) rather than later when much of the earlier work would be aborted.

Aids to library planning and design

Normally design and drawing can safely be left to the architect. However, there are those instances already referred to, usually small-scale installations or refurbishments in existing buildings, where the librarian is expected to do both. In such instances, the first step is to acquire or create a scaled plan of the space which is to be used for library purposes. While plain paper can be used for this purpose, graph paper makes matters easier at a latter stage when drawing in shelving, seating, etc. However, even assuming that the analysis of space relations and the creation of block diagram has been carried out, drawing is a time-consuming and inflexible way of trying out various permutations and arrangements of furniture and equipment within those spaces. Consequently, many librarians make scaled cut-outs in thick card of library shelving, furniture and equipment, and experiment with different arrangements on the outline plan created earlier before committing themselves to a final drawn solution, which might then be given to a library supplier. The use of magnetic boards and strips, or of commercial layout planning equipment, such as Modulex, are similar, if more expensive tools, which can and have been used by librarians to plan an interior layout.

Increasingly librarians have access to drawing or CAD drawing software, such as Visio, and, providing it allows the librarian to work to scale, will offer a flexible approach to determining the best interior layout for a small library or department. Like all such tools, it takes time to learn to use, and there is always a danger of not arriving at a decision because of the ease with which new solutions can be drawn and printed out for discussion amongst those concerned.

Where computer-aided design is used by architects and by library equipment suppliers, it is much more sophisticated and usually has a 3D capability to it. This allows the client to have a greater understanding of the spaces being created (see Figure 10.3) and also the opportunity via the computer to 'walk' through them. The

Fig. 10.3 *3D drawing of a library layout*
(Reproduced through the courtesy of Don Gresswell Ltd)

interactive nature of CAD is also a feature; the architect or library equipment supplier can sit down with the librarian in front of a computer screen and quickly examine possible changes to layout etc. without becoming irrevocably committed to them. But whether using cardboard cut-outs on an outline plan, or drawings created by hand, or CAD, the opportunity should not be missed to allow future users to comment on what is planned, as well those involved in the team charged with carrying the project through.

References

1 Cohen, A. and Cohen, E., *Designing and space planning for libraries*, New York, Bowker, 1979, 64–6.

2 Brauer, R. L., *Facilities planning: the user requirements method*, 2nd edn., New York, Amacom, 1992, 99.

3 Idem, 217.

4 The preparation of bubble diagrams is described by Brauer, op. cit., in his Appendix B, 216–4.

5 Cohen, A. and Cohen, E., op. cit., 73–8; Holt, R. M., *Planning library buildings: from concept to completion*, Metuchen, NJ, Scarecrow Press, 1989, 46–52; Thompson, G., *Planning and design of library buildings*, 3rd edn., London, Butterworth, 1989, 39–44.

6 Anderson, P., *Planning school library media facilities*, Hamden, Conn., Library Professional Publications, 1990, 107, 128, 147, 169, 178.

7 Carter, K., 'Images of information in a 21st century high school', *School library journal*, **40** (2), 1994, 26.

8 Ibid., 26.

9 While, G., 'The return of Andrew Carnegie: a very personal blueprint for the design and layout for a modern children's library', in *Never too young: book 1: library services to pre-school schildren and their carers*, (ed.) J. Heaton, Newcastle under Lyme, Youth Libraries Group, 1991, 66.

10 Cohen, A. and Cohen, E. op. cit., 68–9.

11 Idem, 69.

12 Anderson, op. cit., 153, provides an example of the block diagram approach for renovated AV services.

13 Cohen, A. and Cohen, E., op. cit., 78.

14 Dziura, W.T., 'Media center aesthetics: focus on design, color scheme and furnishings', in *Reader in children's librarianship*, (ed.) J.Foster, Englewood, Colo., Information Handling Services, 1978, 371–2.

15 Infantino, C. P., 'Exchanging experiences/interchanging ideas', *Illinois libraries*, **60** (10) 1978, 912.

16 Heeks, P., *Administration of children's libraries*, London, Library Association, 1967, 39.

17 Pestell, R., *Mobile library guidelines*, The Hague, IFLA, 1991, 45–56; Eastwood, C. R., *Mobile libraries and other public transport*, London, Association of Assistant Librarians, 1967, 145, 151.

18 Pybus, R. L., *Design and construction of mobile libraries*, 2nd edn., [London], Branch and Mobile libraries Group of the Library Association, 1990, 29.

19 For a more detailed discussion of this section *see* Holt, op. cit., 167–201

20 For a fuller discussion *see* Holt, op. cit., 201–8, 233–4; Anderson, op. cit., 180–5.

21 Holt, op. cit., 204.

11 FURNITURE AND EQUIPMENT

Selecting furniture and equipment[1]

In making choices about what to buy, the librarian will be greatly helped by as full information as possible of what is available on the market, and a clear idea as to the precise purpose for which furniture and equipment is required. There is a great variety of shelving, storage and display units for library materials of all types, as well as a multiplicity of tables and seating and other items of furniture and equipment. While the aesthetic qualities of furniture and equipment are very important, their functionality (the ability to do the job), and to meet other criteria discussed below, must be taken into account.

A visit to the annual Library Resources Exhibition and other trade fairs, exhibitions and centres (see Appendix 1), and obtaining suppliers' catalogues will provide the librarian with a good idea of what the market currently offers. The names and addresses of relevant companies are given in Appendix 2. In addition to information gathering, the librarian will naturally seek the advice of the architect (who will be concerned with the way that what is selected will harmonize with the building) and the design team, as well as the specialist members of the library staff, such as those responsible for work with children and young people. While the choice of furniture will be dictated by decisions regarding policy, for example the range of formats to be provided in a school library or one for children and young people, operational methods (manual or automated systems, for example) and the ages and needs of the users, other factors will need to be taken into account.

A fundamental one will be the amount of money available, as this will affect the quality of the materials and the standard of fitting that can be afforded, and whether the furniture is to be custom-made or purchased 'off the peg'. The budget may dictate that steel, or a mixture of steel and wood shelving, can be afforded rather than all wood, if that is preferred. Furniture and equipment usually amounts to about 10–15% of building costs. As indicated in Chapter 3, it is important not to leave the selection and ordering of furniture and equipment to the last moment, not only so that the library will open on time but because the allocated budget may be eroded by earlier calls on it. Additionally, it may be difficult for suppliers to meet substantial, and by then urgent orders, without adequate notice.

The overview of furniture and equipment for both school and children's libraries provided by Colin Ray,[2] is now somewhat dated, but it covers basic features and dimensions of such items as shelving and display furniture and can, therefore, be a useful place to start investigating the topic.

Shelving and other furniture

When choosing shelving and furniture, the librarian should take into account such matters as:

1 Durability – good quality, sturdy furniture, particularly seating, should be acquired as it will subject to the demands made on it by children and young people and is unlikely to be replaced in the immediate future. In addition, the finish (laminate or linoleum, for example), to work and study table tops, the tops of low bays of shelving, counter tops, and the furniture in a children's activity area and elsewhere should take into account the hard wear such surfaces will receive.

2 The ease of cleaning and maintenance – as regards children's libraries, Fleet comments that 'Upholstered chairs are usually more comfortable than wooden ones, but they must be in a spongeable material, or . . . of a fabric . . . that . . . can easily be removed for regular cleaning.'[3] However, vinyl rather than fabric upholstery might be easier to maintain, if possibly less attractive.

3 Flexibility – for example, does a shelving system accommodate a number of formats and allow for a variety of uses?

4 Modularity – can furniture, such as a counter, be easily altered or extended?

5 Compatibility – this may be a minor matter in some instances, but will the chosen items complement any existing furniture and shelving? Associated with this factor is the question of availability – will the chosen furniture range be available well into the future if further matching items are required?

6 Aesthetics – what contribution will the furniture and equipment make to the appearance and ambience of the library?

7 Safety and stability – there should be 'no sharp corners, rough edges or small pieces which could be removed and swallowed'.[4] Shelving, in particular, freestanding shelving, for example, must be strong (thus able to support the heaviest reference works) and stable. Do the fillings of beanbags and other soft furniture meet the appropriate health and safety standards?

8 Ergonomics – will tables, carrels and chairs allow both staff and users to work comfortably and with no detriment to their health and safety?

9 Space saving – where there is a need for furniture that will save on space – with regards to periodical display for example – then this factor too will be important one in selection.

Some of these matters are discussed more fully below.

Aesthetics

The crucial contribution that the choice of furniture makes to the desired ambience of the school library or that for children and young people has been discussed earlier. The choice of all steel or all wood shelving, or a mix of the two, is further complicated by questions of colour and types of wood finish, although natural wood finishes outsell colour. There is bound to be an element of personal, subjective opinion about any choice and the librarian must be prepared to accept that situation. Equally subjective are opinions about the preferred general style of shelving: British and Scandinavian librarians seem to like a fairly enclosed form, while French and German colleagues appear to like something less solid and more 'see-through'.

Flexibility

Flexibility in library shelving implies the capability to adjust the height of individual shelves, as required, and to change the fittings used in the basic bay so that they can be utilized for a different purpose or purposes – to house a kinderbox below and a display board and shelf above – for example. Equally, such shelving should be hospitable to the storage and display of a variety of formats, possibly in an integrated fashion, unless a completely different policy, and thus a different style of display unit is required for the separate display of videos, CDs and cassettes, for example. Seating at tables that can be grouped and arranged in different patterns to cater for individuals, or small and large groups of children, also provides flexibility over the provision of a smaller number of larger tables.

Modularity

Furniture that is modular, such as an issue desk, that is made up from standard components, and thus can be reassembled in a new location or easily added to, is to be preferred to the single fitted or fixed piece of furniture. Modern library shelving also often has this characteristic.

Ergonomics

Reflecting a body of research, Michelle Robertson states 'that in a well designed learning environment, a greater level of learning and more effective information handling occurs than in a poorly designed educational environment'. She goes on to say that: 'Humans adapt to a wide variety of conditions relatively well, but this adaption takes a physical and mental toll.'[5] Other than furniture design, which is considered in terms of the computer workstation, the issues that she addresses have been considered in Chapter 9. While there are matters that relate to the design of the computer hardware, the major points that need to be considered here as regards the workstation furniture are:[6]

    (a) Table design – to include perhaps a separate adjustment for the keyboard and, more particularly, wire management.

    (b) Table surface – in lighter colour with dull matt finish; large enough for documents to be consulted – a document holder is helpful.

    (c) Ergonomically designed chair – adjustable, and with good support to lower back, for example.

These points would seem to demonstrate that it is unhelpful, uncomfortable and potentially dangerous for modern information technology to be dumped on any old furniture without any consideration given to the ergonomics of using it.

Range and dimensions of shelving and other furniture

Over the years a number of standard dimensions have evolved for library furniture, especially with regards to library shelving and tables, and these will have a strong influence on how many books, for example, can be accommodated on a shelf and the numbers of people at a table. However, along with other publications, the Library Association's *Guidelines for children and young people* makes the point that the height of furniture, such as shelves and counter, should relate to the age of the children for whom they are intended.[7] Where a children's department caters for a range of age-groups then furniture, such as chairs, should be provided in various sizes. Some adult seating will be needed also in areas catering for very young children and where a collection is provided for parents and carers. The dimensions of furniture and shelving are likely to vary to greater or lesser degree from one supplier to another, but some common measurements are given below.

Shelving

Shelving for books and periodicals is usually 90 cm (900 mm) or 1 metre (1,000 mm) long, although other lengths, such as 750mm or 1,200 mm may be on offer. Shelving can be wall fixed or freestanding, the latter single or double-sided. Freestanding shelving is also known as island shelving. Standard shelf depths are of 200, 225, 250 and 300mm; shelves of the latter depth will probably be needed for large picture books. Very deep shelving of 400 mm is also available from some manufacturers. The heights of individual bays of shelving will depend on whether they are wall fixed or freestanding, the placement of the lowest shelf, and the number of shelves per bay, which can vary from two to seven; bay heights can thus range from 915 mm to 2,300 mm. Bays of shelving with two to five shelves, however, are likely to be used in public areas for children and additionally those with six shelves in facilities for young people or students. They are likely to be of the following height:

two shelves	915 mm
three shelves	1,200 mm
four shelves	1,500 mm
five shelves	1,800 mm
six shelves	2,100 mm

Learning resources in schools makes the following recommendations about the overall maximum height of wall shelving in different schools:

secondary schools	1,950 mm
middle schools	1,500 mm
primary schools	1,200 mm

and that island stacks be 1,200 mm or 1,500 mm in height. Other recommendations are also given about the length, depth, etc. of school library shelving and the amount that should be given over to display, one-sixth in a secondary school, for example, if space permits.[8] It is wise to check manufacturers' catalogues for the dimensions of their shelving, to see whether they follow the norm closely or not, and whether other useful sizes are available.

The amount of shelving and other display and storage equipment needed will, amongst other things, depend on the capacity of the shelving and equipment itself. The following published general guidance is offered[9]:

children's books – 30 to 36 per 900 mm (3 ft) run of shelf
reference books – 18 per 900 mm (3 ft) run of shelf
picture books – 36 to 42 per 900 mm (3 ft) run of shelf
periodicals – 3 (one year of monthly issues) per 900 mm (3 ft) run of shelf
face-on display of periodicals and picture books – 3 to 4 per metre of shelf space.

It is wise to check the above figures, which are probably a little on the low side, with the material that will actually be accommodated. It is usual to base calculations on shelves that are only 75–85% full, because shelves that are jam-packed make it difficult to shelve and extract books, to provide space for new books to be interfiled, and are not as attractive.

Choice of shelving can take into account a number of features, such as:

(a) The ease of guiding.
(b) The effectiveness of the book support.
(c) The availability of a pull-out shelf for note-taking.
(d) Whether end panels can be used for display.
(e) The storage of periodical back numbers under a lift-up shelf.
(f) The availability of corner display, shelf or seating units.
(g) Whether glass doors can be fitted.
(h) Whether there is the option of a writing surface fitting; at sitting height it can be used for reading or writing and at standing height for an OPAC terminal.

Books may also be displayed in a variety of other ways, for example:

(a) In decorated storage cube carousels for ordinary and picture books.
(b) In mobile spinners on castors.
(c) On paperback display towers.
(d) On paperback display carousels.
(e) In wire wall racks and freestanding wire display units for books, including paperbacks; usable also for periodicals and leaflets.
(f) On picture book tables with lectern slopes on either side.
(g) In kinderboxes (usually about 600 x 600 mm), in natural or coloured wood.
(h) In folding bookcases on castors, each unit consisting of two halves of three adjustable shelves.

Display and storage of non-book materials

The storage of audiovisual materials, non-book items, such as posters, and other objects, like toys and realia, can pose problems. The librarian can look for a flexible book shelving system that can also accommodate a variety of other media or opt for different and separate storage methods. For example, sound cassettes, CDs, videos and computer software can be stored in racks or browser units, or on carousels or spinners – freestanding or wall mounted. Display systems can be locked (requiring staff assistance for access), or open access ones, with or without the contents of the container. Where contents are displayed in the containers they can be protected by the use of security boxes, which helps overcome the need for additional storage and improves retrieval time. A double-sided browser unit, 900 mm wide, can, for example, house 500 CDs or 700 cassettes or a mix of both.

Other storage arrangements could include:

(a) Stands, wallracks or towers with hang-up plastic bags to display both print and non-print media, audiovisual material, toys, games and computer software – useful in both the school learning resource centre, for teaching or project packs, and the children's or youth library. A kit is available so that standard library shelves can be converted to take hang-up bags.

(b) Storage units (350 mm wide x 700 mm high x 470 mm deep), on castors for mobility, housing plastic trays containing, for example, school library materials or toys and games.

(c) Cupboards or storage units with a good number of compartments, rather than shelves, and upright and horizontal divisions at varied intervals to give a variety of different sized storage spaces, that can be used for toys, videos, posters or to house plastic storage trays.

Tables and seating

Standard sizes for rectangular library tables include 900 mm x 600 mm for one person, 3,350 mm x 600 mm for a single-sided table for four persons, and 2,500 mm x 1,200 mm for six people, three each side. Bearing in mind the different heights that might be required in libraries for children and young people, one manufacturer[10] offers the following sitting/working heights for tables and chairs for four different age groups:

Age	Table height	Seat height
5–7	550mm (21⅝ ins)	320mm (12½ ins)
7–9	600mm (23⅝ ins)	360mm (14 ins)
9–13	650mm (25½ ins)	390mm (15 ins)
13–adult	700mm (27½ ins)	445mm (17 ins)

Another supplier offers tables at three heights of 500, 550, and 630 mm, and seats at heights at 280, 330 and 370 mm, thus also catering for the 3–5 age group. The need for some tables to be able to accommodate children and young people in wheelchairs needs also to be taken into consideration, as does the design of carrels, counters, computer workstations and other items of furniture.

Tables may also be available as quarter-circle, half-circle, round, or square, as well as the more usual rectangle. Trapezoid tables allow for many different configurations to accommodate groups of varied size. Bench-type furniture can be used to accommodate a row of OPACs or terminals for other IT uses.

Other seating options include:

1 Integrated table and seat with animal side panels (desk height 500 mm; seat height 250 mm)

2 Colourful aphablocks for use as seats or decoration (300 mm cubes).
3 Wooden chairs in a variety of primary colours.
4 Soft seating, for example,
    (a) vinyl foam furniture (various shapes for sitting in/on)
    (b) beanbags
    (c) play cushions in animal shapes.
5 Coloured plastic 'one-piece' chair and table.

Carrels

A variety of sizes of carrel are available, for example 900 x 900 mm or 700 x 900 mm, with side panels at a height of 1,200 mm; the work surface should be at least 600 x 900 mm (2 ft x 3 ft). Carroll suggests, however, a minimum of 760 mm x 1,000 mm (30 ins x 39.37 ins). Pierce deems neither size entirely satisfactory where non-print hardware, microform readers, etc. will be used and suggests 1,125 mm x 750 mm (45 ins x 30 ins) as adequate but not excessive. Peter Stubley suggests that a study workstation for computer use should be 900 mm wide and 1,100 mm deep. The standard table or carrel height for adults is between 700 mm and 760 mm; the lower figure is perhaps more suited to the younger student. A study carrel may be equipped with an optional shelf, light, socket outlet, and cable access hole in the worktop.

Various patterns of arrangement for tables and carrels have been devised – octagonal, staggered, at right angle to the wall – and some of these arrangements, for three, four, six and larger numbers of students, are illustrated in Ellsworth and Wagener's *The school library*.[13] The variety of possible arrangements of tables and seating – for example, in an horseshoe or hexagonal arrangement – in rooms for small groups from four to a dozen students, is also discussed and illustrated in the same work.[14] The DES publication, *Designing a medium-sized public library*, provides some guidance on the layout and spacing of shelves, carrels and seats, for example in a cruciform pattern or along a wall, but this is not geared specifically to children's departments.[15]

Counters

In order that issue counters do not intimidate young children, they should be at sitting height 720–725 mm (29 inches) or 800 mm (32 inches), rather than the high, stand-up issue counter of 960–975mm (39 inches). To cater for wear, counters should have a linoleum inset. The ability to accommodate computer terminals and their wiring is usually a modern-day requirement. Where counters serve both adults and children, a mix of heights can be requested to accommodate all age groups. In small school and children's libraries an appropriately sized office desk perhaps with an additional work unit, would probably be better than a counter, whether 'off-the-peg' or custom-built.

Much detailed information about shelving (dimensions, capacity, etc.), seating, carrels, tables and other furniture is to be found in Thompson's standard work.[16]

Other furniture

A range of other furniture for the school or children's library could include:

(a) Catalogue cabinets, which are apparently still popular in spite of modern counterparts: allow 1,000 cards plus guide cards per drawer. Cabinets are available in units from 1 to 30 drawers which can be placed on tables or on leg bases 660 mm (26 ins) high. Another version consists of a basic four-drawer unit to which extension units can be added.

(b) OPAC stations designed for stand-up or sitting use.

(c) Freestanding decorative 'fences', 660 mm high, to define a children's area.

(d) Modular partitions (1,300 mm high x 650 mm wide x 25 mm deep), for dividing a room or creating a play area, made in light, fire-retardant materials and available in three versions – decorative, opaque, translucent.

(e) Puppet theatre with write-on/wipe-off panels and shelf for props.

(f) Lockable exhibition cases, tall and low (990 mm high), wall mounted and freestanding.

(g) Book trolleys – available in wood or metal, single or double-sided, long (750 or 840 mm) or short (440 or 508 mm), with slanted and/or flat shelves

(h) Mobile shelving – it is claimed that this can increase storage capacity by up to 100%; standard versions are seven or eight shelves high with shelf depths of up to 450 mm. Lower and more flexible versions, i.e. which can be easily relocated, are available and can be used in public spaces. A possibility for the larger school or children's library.

Furniture systems for children

Some of the furniture that might be selected for a school, children's or young people's library will not be special to those types of library service but will also be found in an adult library. The furniture systems described below, however, have been specially designed for children and are thus particularly suitable for areas for young children in public libraries and/or for primary or junior school libraries. They endeavour to be both attractive, interesting, functional and fun. References indicate suppliers from whom the various systems are available.

Daillot children's furniture[17]

This system enables the creation of integrated shelving, reading and creative play areas, in a variety of configurations, which are designed to encourage reading through the provision of a stimulating environment. Special reading areas can be designed for a particular library or stand-alone items bought, for example, a reading house, a forest reading table and bench (each has decorated end panels), reading steps or stages, reading towers, or an octagonal enclosed reading area with sofa seats. Distinctive features of the Daillot furniture are the enclosed spaces that can be created, giving children the privacy and secrecy they like, and that books, as in the reading house, can be displayed in and on the furniture.

Modulsystem[18]

The modulsystem, devised by EKZ in Germany, is a unique but simple furniture system that provides space for the display of books, toys, and games in libraries (Figure 11.1). It consists of three basic building modules – an open box, an open cube

Fig. 11.1 *Modulsystem configuration*
(Reproduced through the courtesy of Don Gresswell Ltd)

(which can be divided in various arrangements), and a diagonal cube – that can all be joined together by large plastic nuts and bolts. The diagonal and open cube have a depth, width and height of 294 mm; the open box has the same depth but twice the width and height.

Various configurations, both simple and complex (Figure 11.2), can be created at will and changed when necessary, for example a reading bridge, train, snake or small enclosed children's area. End panels, worktables, storage cupboards, book browser trays and additions to create a Wendy house, or other featured item, provide even greater variety, usefulness and complexity of the finished arrangement. This is a modular system that encourages creativity in its use in a library as either a major or minor component of the furniture used for shelving and display. It is available in various colours, although natural wood is the most popular choice in the UK.

Oblique children's library furniture[19]

Oblique is a flexible, multicoloured furniture system, with a high percentage of face-on display, for presenting reading materials to children (Figure 11.3). There are three types of shelving in addition to the basic units, which consist of fixed shelves (both flat and sloping), and are available as single- or double-sided units in three widths

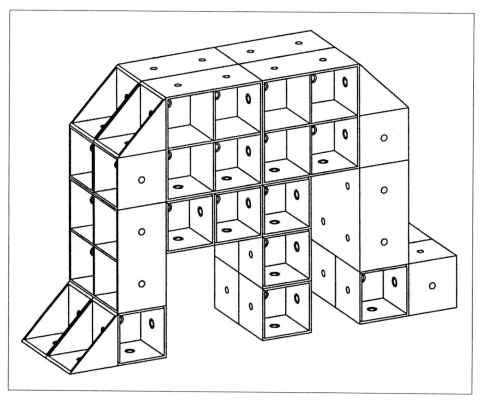

Fig. 11.2 *Modulsystem configuration*
(Reproduced through the courtesy of EKZ GmbH)

(500, 700 and 900 mm) and three heights (550, 750 and 1,000 mm). The other three types of shelving are:

1   Single-sided adjustable shelf units (1,500 mm high), for use against walls, with a depth of 280 mm, and available in two widths, 700 and 900 mm.
2   Kindertrolley – a 600 mm square kinderbox on castors with a height of 300 mm.
3   Tray storage units on castors (width 1,040 mm and three heights, 1,940, 1,440 and 940 mm), providing accommodation for trays of teaching or learning materials, for example those related to National Curriculum subjects.

Other Oblique furniture includes a browser table, drawer unit, hang-up towers for plastic storage bags, book trolley and reading table.

Fig. 11.3 *Oblique children's library furniture in Underhill Infants School, Barnet*
(Reproduced through the courtesy of Don Gresswell Ltd)

Executive and Bibliotec systems[20]

These two systems are colourful, modular, display shelving on non-traditional lines for children, that include guiding. They are available in three heights (1,200, 1,500, and 1,800 mm), to accommodate picture books, paperbacks, and other formats, and in a variety of configurations (single- and double-sided, wall fixed), that permit a great deal of face-on display. Apart from the use of the tilted or tiered shelf in many units, a distinctive feature is that end panels and backs of some units can be fitted with 'displaywalls'; useful in the latter case, amongst other possibilities, for creating window displays where children's areas are located at the front of a library.

KidZstuff and Themeboard[21]

This furniture has been designed for the younger element in the school or children's library. A variety of shelving, display shelves, browser boxes, tables and seats can be assembled from seven basic units (with a common width of 600 mm), and linked in different arrangements. KidZstuff is available in beech or oak with a red or blue diamond link but other finishes are available.

From the same company comes the idea of the Themeboard, which can be seen as ideally suited for making a contribution to an environment for children. The Themeboard is a large, colourful, graphic wall unit (4,800 mm x 1,200 mm) portraying a theme, such as the sea, that can be mounted as a single unit or as part of frieze made up from two or more boards. The graphics are built up from multilayered board and cut-outs which gives the Themeboard a three-dimensional character. The units would be good for the space above shelves in the children's library or can be used to cover complete walls, as end panels, or to create partitions.

Play and display furniture

A number of library furniture suppliers offer furniture in the colourful and simplified shape of a train, lorry, bus, or boat, which is able to store and display a limited number of books, and that young children can sit in or on while they read. Some such items, such as a barge, may be especially designed to reflect a local theme or association. Play and display furniture will often form the centre-piece of the area for young children and, depending upon its size, may take up a great deal of floor space. Associated with this trend is the decorated kinderbox; kinderboxes with end panels with animal or transport themes or simply decorative shapes. Some such kinderboxes include seating and may be preferable to larger play and display furniture where space is limited. A range of library furniture for children, including the categories described in this paragraph, is shown in Figure 11.4.

Equipment

Where the selection of mechanical and automated equipment is concerned, similar criteria are involved as those for furniture, such as, need, cost, durability, and safety. The school or children's librarian will be particularly concerned also with such matters as, ease of operation, portability, efficiency, economy, warranty, maintenance costs, and obsolescence – what is the likely life of equipment before it will be

Fig. 11.4 *A range of library furniture for children*
(Reproduced through the courtesy of Point Eight Ltd)

outmoded? In some instances it may be worth considering the leasing or renting option.

Suppliers

As discussed elsewhere, there are a number of companies who specialize in supplying libraries with shelving, counters, study furniture, seating, etc. and one or several suppliers can be used to meet the school or children's library's main shelving and furniture requirements. Items, such as microfilm readers, computer hardware, or equipment for exhibition and display, or office purposes will probably come from other specialist suppliers. Many of these library supply companies advertise in the professional press and there is a published directory.[22]

Unless there are good, usually aesthetic, reasons, it is probably best if library furniture and equipment is not architect- (nor librarian-) designed. Such furniture is likely to prove more costly (and possibly impracticable) and ignores the expertise and experience built-up over the years by the specialist library suppliers. As discussed earlier, some suppliers will assist in the planning of the library interior if requested. If asked, suppliers can adapt current products or cooperate in developing new ones to meet particular requirements; the scale of the project will determine how viable either of these approaches might be. Such situations can serve as product development opportunities for the supplier and any such product might be offered more widely on the market.

Checklists of furniture and equipment

Designing and renovating school library media centers lists furniture and equipment requirements area by area, as well as providing a basic equipment checklist – ranging from a portable amplifier to a wireless microphone – as an appendix.[23] *Guidelines for school libraries* provides useful guidance on furniture as regards sizes, and, where appropriate, capacity; checklists of equipment are also provided.[24] The Library Association's guidelines on the provision of learning resources accommodation in schools look at basic furniture needs and also provide checklists for audiovisual, office and reprographics equipment.[25]

Children and young people: Library Association guidelines for public library services, provides a very basic annotated list, including such items as shelving, tables and chairs, display facilities and notice boards.[26] *Libraries designed for users* also has a list of furniture and equipment which covers shelving and storage, the staff work area, audiovisual equipment and teenage centre requirements.[27] The equipment needs of the disabled child are described in two publications by Margaret Marshall, and include cassette players and talking book machines, a Kurzweil reading machine, and access to computers. The latter may be the easiest or only means of written communication for some children.[28]

Mobile libraries

The *Mobile library guidelines*, and other similar publications, offer little by way of guidance on road vehicles for children, however, their more general information may be of interest. The guidelines state that, while wooden or metal shelving can be used on mobile libraries, the former poses fewer stress and stability problems than metal and should not rattle when the vehicle is under way. The guidelines make the following recommendations for shelving:

1   It should be adjustable, and tilted to keep books in place.
2   Side shelving tilted between 10 and 15 degrees (1:12 to 1:18) to the horizontal.
3   The back wall shelving tilted between 15 to 20 degrees (1:18 to 1:23) to

overcome inertia – a British recommendation differs on this and the previous point.[29]

4   It should be three times stronger than static shelving to prevent timber from splitting due to a moving load.

5   It should be constructed in separate bays not in excess of 762 mm (30 ins) to give additional strength.

6   Shelving should begin at 305 mm (12 ins) from the floor

7   For the distance between shelves and shelf depth the guidelines offers the following general suggestions:

Category	Height between shelves	Shelf depth
paperbacks	203 mm (8 ins)	152 mm (6 ins)
oversize books	368 mm (14.5 ins)	229 mm (9 ins)
other	254 mm (10 ins)	229 mm (9 ins).[30]

The guidelines recognize that children's books and easy books require special shelving and that browser boxes are ideal but that space considerations may restrict their use. They continue by stating that: 'Provision should be made for the same range of materials that exist in a static service point and may include periodicals, audio cassettes, video cassettes, compact discs, posters, computer software, games and toys.'[31] However, the guidelines recognize that the range of storage options that can be used is dependent on the available space and the formats to be displayed.

For the mobile library counter the following alternatives are suggested:[32]

width – between 500 mm (20 ins) and 625 mm (25 ins)
height – sitting, 711 mm (28 ins); sitting/standing, 914 mm (36 ins)
length – depends on available space.

This chapter shows that much thought has gone into the creation of furniture for young school pupils and the youngest users of the public library. Older pupils and young people will clearly be served by much of the furniture available for adults but little attempt seems to have been made to create library furniture that might have a special appeal to this particular group. Also, while the design of library road vehicles in general has received a reasonable amount of attention in the professional literature, those for children, whether as one of many groups of users or as the sole user group of a vehicle, has not. As this book has shown, road vehicles for children are more varied than the available literature would suggest, and therefore the needs of children and young people are worthy of more special design consideration in guidance issued by the library profession.

References

1   A full treatment of the topic is given in Brown, C. R., *Selecting library furniture: a guide for librarians, designers and architects*, Phoenix, Ariz., Oryx Press, 1989, 66–71, where some attention is given to children's furnishings.

2   Ray, C., *Library service to schools and children*, Paris, Unesco, 1979, 32–41.

3   Fleet, A., *Children's libraries*, London, André Deutsch, 1973, 45.

4 Esson, K. and Tyerman, K., *Library provision for children*, Newcastle under Lyme, Association of Assistant Librarians, 1991, 2–3.

5 Robertson, M. M., 'Ergonomic considerations for the human environment', *School library media quarterly*, **20** (4), 1992, 211.

6 Idem, 213–4.

7 Library Association, *Children and young people: Library Association guidelines for public library services*, London, Library Association, 1991, 15.

8 Kinnell, M. (ed.), *Learning resources in schools: Library Association guidelines for school libraries*, London, Library Association, 1992, 30–1.

9 Thompson, G., *Planning and design of library buildings*, 3rd edn., London, Butterworth, 1989, 138; Carroll, F. L., *Guidelines for school libraries*, The Hague, IFLA, 1990, 28–9.

10 Remploy Lundia.

11 Pierce, W. S., *Furnishing the library interior*, New York, Dekker, 1980, 44–5.

12 Stubley, P., 'Equipment and furniture to meet the requirements of the new technology', in *Library buildings: preparations for planning*, (ed.) M. Dewe, Munich, Saur, 1989, 109–10.

13 Ellsworth, R. E. and Wagener, H. D., *The school library: facilities for independent study in the secondary school*, New York, Educational Facilities Laboratories, 1963, 56–69.

14 Idem, 70–2.

15 Department of Education and Science, Architects and Building Branch, *Designing a medium-sized public library*, London, HMSO, 1981, 24, 26, 28, 48–50.

16 Thompson, op. cit., 133–92.

17 Don Gresswell Ltd.

18 Ibid.

19 Ibid.

20 Point Eight Ltd.

21 Reska Terrapin Products Ltd.

22 McSeán, T., *Library Association directory of suppliers and services*, 2nd edn., London, Library Association, 1994.

23 Klasing, J. P., *Designing and renovating school library media centers*, Chicago, American Library Association, 1991, 14–16, 75–7.

24 Carroll, op. cit., 27–31.

25 Kinnell, op. cit., 30–1, 34–5.

26 op. cit., 14–6.

27 Lushington, N. and Mills, W.N., *Libraries designed for users*, Syracuse, New York, Gaylord, 1979, 170–8.

28 Marshall, M., *Libraries and the handicapped child*, London, André Deutsch, 1981, 164–8; *Managing library provision for handicapped children*, London, Mansell, 1991, 104–5.

29 A 1 in 7 slope for the sides and 1 in 9 for the rear are advocated in, Pybus, R.L., *The design and construction of mobile libraries*, 2nd edn., [London], Branch and

Mobile Libraries Group of the Library Association, 1990, 31.

30 Pestell, R., *Mobile library guidelines*, The Hague, IFLA, 1991, 25–6. A further dscussion of these figures is given in Eastwood, C. R., *Mobile libraries and other public library transport*, London, Association of Assistant Librarians, 1967, 161–5.

31 Idem, 26.

32 Idem, 27. A further discussion is given in Eastwood, op. cit., 158–61.

12 CASE STUDIES

This chapter provides brief accounts of recently completed libraries in schools and for children and young people in the UK. They provide useful exemplification of much of what has been said in earlier chapters and potential models for those involved in planning or replanning their space resource.

Whitgift School Senior School Library, Croydon, Surrey
School background

Whitgift School is an independent day school for about 1,000 boys aged 10–18. The school, which dates its foundation to 1596, moved to its present extensive parkland site at Haling Park, South Croydon, in 1931. The 1931 buildings have been enhanced in recent years by a number of improvements and additions, including a major new building of 1990, containing the new senior school library, which replaces an earlier one of 1,350 ft^2 (125 m^2).

The school is divided into junior and middle schools and a sixth form. The junior school is for the 10–13 age group and much of its work is based in a purpose-built classroom block with its own library. The latter is a pleasant, well-equipped, but rather formal library in a converted classroom. There are plans to extend the present building and relocate and develop the junior school library.

In the third, fourth and fifth year, boys are in the middle school and then the sixth form offers two years of A-level and other studies. A sixth-form centre provides both an area for quiet study and a social base; it has 40 seats in the work area and another 40 in the social area. Facilities include a radio, television, drinks machine and a microwave. There are offices in the centre for the head of sixth form and for the sixth-form art tutor and science tutor. The school is establishing close links with European and international schools and boys are actively encouraged to study foreign languages.

Academic departments are housed in their own areas in classrooms, many with separate libraries or resource centres. A separate careers department provides a comprehensive range of information to pupils on all aspects of higher education and careers.

The new building at Whitgift School

At a cost of over £10 million, a major extension, almost doubling the size of the school's buildings, was provided to the 1931 buildings in 1990. This new building provides an integrated facility for teaching science and technology, art, crafts and design, and geography with a library at its heart. The building comprises a large, single-level central space for a complex of workshops, linked to, and surrounded on three sides, by two-storey wings. The various departments have their own computing facilities and many areas are networked to the computer workshop and to the computer centre.

The Senior School Library

The library (4,964 ft²: 461 m²) is located on the first floor of the new building, and adjacent to it, although not under the library's control, are the computer centre and archives department (together totalling a further 1,378 ft²: 128 m² of space). Of these three components, two (the library and computer room) are now accommodated somewhat differently to what had been originally planned. The computer centre was to have occupied the end of the longish rectangular section of the library (but it was felt that the library would benefit more from the available natural light), and the library was to have utilized the computer centre's present location as part of the library floor area. This earlier plan would have given the library a somewhat more compact and more easily supervised layout. The present arrangement also means that the library is used as a thoroughfare to the computer centre, with pupils passing in front of the study area to the right of the entrance.

The librarian of the senior school library is a head of department and is assisted by the junior school librarian for part of each day and by a clerical assistant for 25 hours a week. The library is open during term time from 8.30 a.m. to 9 p.m.

Entrance area and staff accommodation

The entrance to the Raeburn Library, as it is known, is well identified, and double wooden doors with glass panels lead to an enclosed, glazed bag deposit area for students. The divisions in the wooden bag deposit furniture are too small, however, to take the modern pupil's holdall and so these tend to get placed on the floor or on top of the furniture. Passing through the 3M security system, the low library counter, at which staff are able to sit, is straight ahead, with workroom and stack area behind, and the glazed librarian's office to the left. In the library proper, and to the left of the security system, are display boards and a photocopier for pupil use.

Reference and study area

To the right of the security entrance is the reference and study area (Figure 12.1) with shelving for reference books, local history books (to draw attention to the archives department close by), eight study tables and thirty-two chairs, and seven architect-designed carrels, placed at an angle to the far wall. The carrels each have an electrical point and task lighting. An exhibition case and low display stand help mark this area off from the rest of the library. In the wide corridor alongside the computer centre, five carrels are located on one side for audiovisual use (tapes, slides and videos), and on the other side glass fronted shelving displays school archival material and memorabilia.

Fig. 12.1 *Whitgift Senior School Library: counter and reference and study area*

Main library area

To the left of the entrance is the main body of the library (Figure 12.2) containing a newspaper and periodicals area, an informal reading area for fiction as well as study tables for use with information books related to the curriculum and pupils' interests. Seating is incorporated into some shelving, and both study and casual seating are arranged less formally than in the reference and study area. A total of 90 seats is provided in the library as a whole. As in the reference and study area, shelving is of white metal with light oak end panels and bay guiding. It is thought that the bookstock will grow to a total of 20,000 volumes; it is about 18,500 at the moment. Although the library's stock is largely book-based at present, a multimedia collection is being established to include audio and video cassettes, and software packages. The information technology equipment described below is located to the right of the issue desk, in front of the librarian's office.

The generous height of the ceiling in all library areas, with flush light fittings, gives it a spacious feeling, and the wall space, painted duck egg blue above the wall shelving in the main library, is used to accommodate uplighters. The ceiling over the counter is a little lower. Heating equipment is located along one wall of the main library area under the windows, which are equipped with vertical blinds. The opposite and end wall are shelved. Otherwise, bookcases are freestanding with low, oversize and periodical bookshelves down the centre of the room. The informal shelving arrangement has created a number of alcoves accommodating seating, that to the rear of the room, by the emergency exit, has caused supervision problems and the table and seating have been removed.

Fig. 12.2 *Whitgift Senior School Library: main library area*
(Reproduced through the courtesy of Library Furnishing
Consultants Ltd)

The colour scheme employed in the library is of light wood and white metal shelving with dark-blue upholstered integral seats; casual seats have a patterned upholstery on light-coloured wooden frames. Study tables and carrels are also of light-coloured wood and study seats are green and blue upholstery on light wood frames. The carpeting is a blue/green/white tweed effect.

Information technology

An automated issue system and catalogue are in operation and the BBC's Domesday Survey, an interactive video which provides a picture of Britain in the 1980s, is also available and has been used for a variety of project and other work. There are two CD-ROM workstations, one of which is for multimedia CD-ROMs. Campus 2000, giving access to commercial and educational databases, has had its subscription dropped due to cost and lack of use, but it may be reinstated as there is potential for renewed interest. The computer centre, accessible from the library, provides wordprocessing facilities on 28 PCs linked up to the Econet system. The centre can be occupied by a class or individuals, such as sixth formers writing an essay, and is available during the lunch period and after school.

Archives department

The archives department holds the foundation's muniments and records, school records, photographs, memorabilia, ephemera and local history material. It consists of two offices – the planned search room has been divided in two – and an environmentally controlled storage area. This is a somewhat different arrangement to that proposed at one stage, when all the non-public areas were to be allocated to the archives department. It is felt that space provision is probably inadequate for the present and possibly for the future. The archives department is staffed by the school archivist, with some assistance, and is open three days a week to researchers, but there is limited current pupil use of this material.

Some design aspects

The senior school library is a single open space whose flexibility is hampered to some extent by the nature and location of the windows. Its proximity to the archive department and computer centre are considerable assets, although access by pupils to the latter can cause noise and disturbance. The shelving and furniture has been carefully chosen and arranged to provide an attractive and varied interior that allows pupils to use the library and its varied facilities in an easy and enjoyable way. The bag deposit area does not seem to work effectively and a better use might be found for this space in the future.

Building, furniture and equipment details

Architects: Hugh Wilson & Lewis Womersley
Shelving, seating, tables and counter: LFC and others; some items architect designed
Library Management System: Microlibrarian
Security system: 3M

Park Community School Library Resource Centre, Havant, Hampshire
The school and its community

Park Community School was built in the 1960s as part of the Leigh Park estate development, reputedly one of the largest housing estates in Europe. The school has a population of 666 pupils aged 12–16 and this number is due to increase to 850, 11–16-year-olds, in September 1994. A growing range of community and adult education activities, coordinated by the community development officer, ensures heavy use of the site and buildings and close links with local organizations and individuals.

As part of an upgrading and enlargement of the original school, a substantial addition was made to the rear of the old school building in 1989–91. A feature of this modern addition is a concourse running its entire length, giving access to the library resource centre (LRC) on one side (Figure 12.3), a theatre on the other, and to other parts of the school. Not only is the concourse a communication route through the school but, as some seating is provided at various points, it is an area where pupils can socialize.

Fig. 12.3 *Park Community School: entrance to library resource centre*

The Library Resource Centre

The LRC and its staff form part of the curriculum support team, which has the shared task of providing full resource and information services for teaching staff and pupils to meet curriculum requirements, and is answerable to the deputy head with responsibility for the curriculum. Therefore, alongside the school resources and information officer (SRIO), in charge of the LRC, there is an information technology coordinator and a media consultant; the latter responsible for advice and assistance on non-IT resources. There are four LRC staff under the direction of the SRIO: two resource technicians, responsible for production and equipment respectively; two resource assistants, one responsible for reprographics and the other the library.

Within its two main responsibilities, of providing and managing resources for learning and teaching, and identifying and promoting appropriate learning experiences and practices, the curriculum support team sees its day-to-day work as being concerned with the provision of:

(a) information sources, including the library
(b) general equipment requirements, including audiovisual and computers (items associated with a particular subject course are the responsibility of the appropriate coordinator)
(c) production facilities, from recording (radio and television) to reprographics.

The staff emphasize a team approach and the need for liaison, communication and discussion with teaching staff. An excellent series of 'resources papers' is produced by the team, for distribution to teaching staff, that keeps teachers informed of the resource services and facilities available to them.

Location of and access to the LRC

The LRC is located on the ground floor and access for pupils is from the concourse, or from a three-storey block of the original school; there is another entrance for staff only. That part of the LRC facing onto the concourse is completely glass-fronted, a constant reminder of its existence and providing good opportunities for display.

During term time the LRC is a open from 8.15 a.m.–9 p.m. (4 p.m. Fridays); a book trolley service is arranged to support evening groups. In school holidays it is generally open from 9 a.m.–3.30 p.m. During lesson periods, unaccompanied pupils and small groups, with written permission from their teachers, are encouraged to use the LRC. Whole classes visit by arrangement, but this does not exclude other pupils from using the centre at the same time.

Accommodation

The LRC (approximately 277 m², excluding office/workroom) consists of three major spaces, of which the main library constitutes the new part of the group. The LRC is reasonably centrally placed and accessible from all parts of the school complex.

Main library

This area (approximately 153 m², Figure 12.4), contains reference, fiction and non-fiction collections, as well as small collections of local studies and easy reading volumes. Magazines are displayed on stands in an area to the right of the entrance with casual seating. To the rear of the library, behind the issue desk, which is large enough to provide staff workspace, there are offices for the LRC staff and an adjacent careers office. Adjacent to this office is a round study table and seating. There is space for pupils' bags to be left behind the issue desk.

To the left of the entrance is a study area which also houses a television with teletext. Along the rear wall of this area pupils have computer facilities providing access to the LRC catalogue, CD-ROMs (a newspaper, encyclopedia and database, with other acquisitions imminent), careers databases and some e-mail and desktop publishing, using an Archimedes A5000. Wordprocessing, using ten Cambridge Z88 laptop computers, is provided in the special collections room. As at Whitgift School, the subscription to Campus 2000 has been discontinued but is under review; alternative means exist for some of its services.

There are three computer rooms in the school, two of which are networked, supplemented by a range of smaller installations within subject areas and the LRC. The intention, therefore, is that the LRC facilities complement rather than replicate those provided elsewhere.

Display boards are available in the main library for use in connection with current topic work and boards are also maintained in other parts of the school. A microfiche reader is available in the library office.

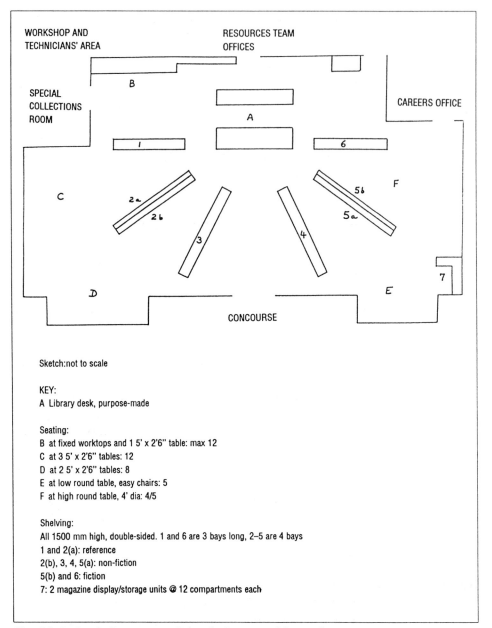

Fig. 12.4 *Park Community School: the main library layout*
(Reproduced through the courtesy of Roger Hawkes, Park Community School)

The use of glass in the main library, for much of the side walls, as well as the concourse frontage, and the inconvenient location of ventilation control panels on what little side wall space there is, means that shelving is somewhat crowded towards the centre of the area. However, as the newer of the three LRC rooms, its high, partially glazed, pitched roof; exposed red structural metal beams; black framed glazing to the concourse; grey and white wall surfaces, and other details, contrast it strongly and colourfully with the two other rather ordinary spaces of the original school building.

Shelving, which is arranged in a kind of radial pattern out from the issue desk, is of white coloured metal, with wooden shelves and canopy. The low casual seats are upholstered in red, and study tables are black wood on metal frames, with their seating of charcoal upholstery on silver metal frames. There are 40 seats in the main library, plus 20 in the Special Collections Room; this is a total of 60 – more or less the standard in respect of the school's current population. The carpet is coloured grey throughout the area.

Special collections room

This room (approximately 56 m^2), houses the main collection of non-book material, that includes slides, film strips, illustrations, folders of newspaper and magazine cuttings on particular topics, and video and audio items. There is also a staff library, and a careers library and display boards in this area. Some equipment, such as the two Apple Macs for desktop publishing, is for staff use only, but most is generally available, and includes video, filmstrip and slide viewing facilities, and a Z88 printer.

Workshop and technicians' area

The workshop and technicians' area occupies approximately 68 m^2. The workshop is an open access area for staff and pupils, with appropriate small equipment to hand. Reprographic, presentation and finishing facilities are provided for both staff and students. There are three photocopiers, one on open access to staff, a second, operator-controlled bulk copier, which also collates and stitches material, and a colour machine, located in the workroom, operated by resources staff only, for which an increasing amount of work is accepted for neighbouring schools. In addition there are stapling, trimming and shredding facilities. The workshop also handles staff requirements for laminating and binding, and for items such as booklets, OHP transparencies and posters. The technicians' area, beyond the workshop facilities, is out of bounds to pupils.

Some aspects of design

The fact that the LRC consists of three separate rooms, with a number of entrances and no security system, could pose problems of security and supervision. However, the positioning of the issue desk and the creation of windows in the dividing walls between rooms, combine to ease the situation by providing good sight lines etc. The coming increase in pupil numbers may exacerbate this, as well as requiring a review of patterns of use and the possible introduction of controls if necessary, especially at break times. In adjusting to this new situation, it may be necessary to also review how space is being used – in the special collections room for example, and whether it is necessary to place shelving against glazed walls in the main library, in order to increase capacity and/or free floor space in the centre of the main library.

Building, furniture and equipment details

Architects: school addition: Architect's Workshop, Winchester
Shelving: Remploy Lundia
Seating and tables: various office suppliers
Library management system: Elrond, Head Software International

Hulbert Middle School Resource Centre, Waterlooville, Hampshire
The school and its building

Although located in an area of housing, Hulbert Middle School, opened in 1982, has almost a rural feel to it, as it is built in the former grounds of a big house. It has a roll of 400 children aged 8–12 but this age range is to be changed to 7–11 in 1994/95. The school building was constructed under a single, wide-span pitched roof.

Internal changes of floor level, responding to the slope of the site, define three separate teaching areas: upper and lower schools divided by a central zone with hall, shared facilities and two-storey staff rooms contained by brick walls. The building enjoys generous daylight and natural ventilation in spite of the deep plan and generous overhanging eaves which protect the south-facing windows from overheating in summer.[1]

The resource centre

Small collections of books are available for children's use in classrooms in Hulbert Middle School but generally resources are centralized over parts of two floors of the building and are the responsibility of a teacher-coordinator. The ground floor houses an open-access fiction library in a largish alcove created by shelving, with stock categorized into genres (the area marked 7 in the plan, Figure 12.5, to the right of the centrally placed stairs). The fiction library, which has 3 tables and seating for 12, is also used as a general group work area. Opposite this, one of the class base/tutorial rooms (marked 6 in the plan), has been turned into a reading room housing the school's reading schemes. Low wooden shelving along the wall outside this room displays books on loan from the Schools Library Service. The resource area to the left of the plan (also marked 7) houses three-dimensional resources, such as science and maths equipment.

Rather steep brick-enclosed stairs, impossible for a disabled pupil, lead up from the lower resource areas to another resource centre area (53 m²) on the first floor. This is more like a gallery, in that it is defined by a low brick wall and is open to the pitched roof. The non-fiction collection is located here and school staff pass through this area to their staff lounge, previously located elsewhere in the school. This access route to the staff lounge divides this upper area into two parts: a book and study area to the right of the stairs and storage for other resources to the left.

The book and study area on this upper level is a small rectangular space, and the school was helped to make the best possible use of its limitations with a layout suggested by the shelving supplier. The shelving for books is of red metal, with three or four wooden shelves, the upper shelf angled to allow face-on display. Some are arranged against the low enclosing wall of this space, while some double-sided bays

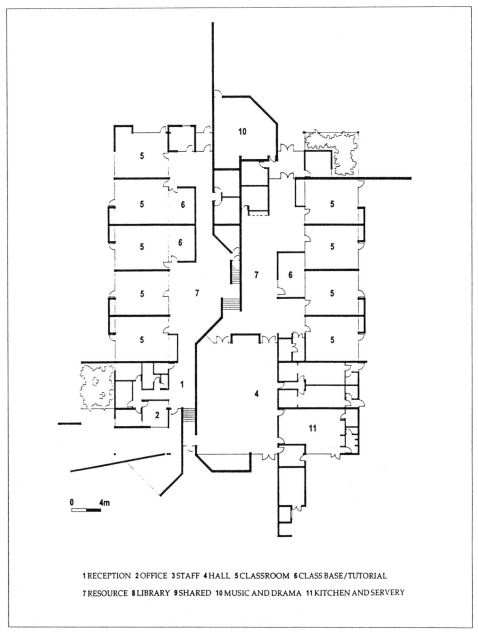

1 RECEPTION 2 OFFICE 3 STAFF 4 HALL 5 CLASSROOM 6 CLASS BASE/TUTORIAL
7 RESOURCE 8 LIBRARY 9 SHARED 10 MUSIC AND DRAMA 11 KITCHEN AND SERVERY

Fig. 12.5 *Hulbert Middle School, Waterlooville (1982)*
(Reproduced through the courtesy of the Architects Dept., Hampshire CC)

are placed at right angles to it. In this area there is seating for eight pupils, on red upholstered chairs with black metal frames, at appropriately sized red formica topped tables. There is also a red beanbag in one corner of this fairly crowded area. There is limited wall space for display purposes here but more in the ground floor resource areas. Additional shelving and storage for tapes in hang-up bags and charts has been installed along the wall to the right leading from the stairs. As with the fiction library below, this upper area is carpeted brown and there are plenty of potted plants in both locations.

To the left of the stairs, a locally made counter top has been installed, to follow the angled line of the wall, with shelves and divisions below for resource boxes, posters, slides, videos and computer packages, including a computerized weather recording station (Figure 12.6). Computer software is held by the IT coordinator and is available on request when packages are borrowed from the centre. Topic boxes are for year groups and are regularly weeded and updated.

A desk is provided for the part-time (mornings only) library assistant, rather than a counter, but there is need for sufficient workspace. A TV is provided in this upper area – there is space in front of it for a small number of viewers – and off-air recordings are made when required. A photocopier is also available.

In the area at the bottom of the steps, leading to the lower resource areas, there are resource centre dedicated computers with software provided by the teacher/IT coordinator.

Use of the resource centre

During their first term at the school, children come to the resource centre in groups of four to learn from the library assistant about its use and facilities. And, as part of the school's English policy, all children receive further training in library skills. Otherwise pupils visit as needs arise during the working day. The resource centre is not available, however, as a work area during break or lunch time, nor in the

Fig. 12.6 *Hulbert Middle School: staff desk and non-book resources*

afternoon unless supervised by an adult. The library assistant is available to support children's use of the centre and, as noted earlier, to develop their library skills. Using a card made out in their name, and kept at the library assistant's desk, children issue their own books, and they may be given permission to take books home overnight. Staff and children are able to borrow a book or collection of books for use in the class and staff are encouraged to get children to use the resource centre to find books for themselves.

The Schools Library Service van brings exchanges to its loan stock twice a year and children help in the selection of new titles. The public library mobile library also visits the school every Monday.

Some design aspects

This is a school of bustle and activity (with music playing in the background), a major part of whose learning resources are helpfully located in central and accessible areas on the ground floor, through which pupils regularly pass. The quality of the building and the feelings of spaciousness and light provide an enviable school and resource centre environment for all concerned.

There is no doubt, however, that the resource area on the upper level, while a colourful, visually attractive and inviting space, is limited in what it can accommodate in terms of pupils, books and other resource materials. Expansion could only occur at the expense of the pleasant accommodation occupied by the staff lounge.

Building, furniture and equipment details

Architects: Architects Department, Hampshire County Council
Shelving: Remploy Lundia
Table and chairs: supplied through Hampshire County Supplies
Other items: Don Gresswell Ltd

Croydon Central Library: Children's Library
Croydon Central Library

Opened in late 1993, the new Croydon Central Library on Katharine Street, is built behind part of the facade of the Grade II Victorian town hall and public library, which will itself be converted for cultural and other purposes as part of this major project. The spacious entrance area to the library, incorporating part of the old building, will thus eventually also provide access to a museum, exhibition galleries, cinema, cafe, and other facilities, to be opened in 1995, thus creating an enviable multicultural centre for Croydon. The rear part of the library complex provides a new and contemporary street facade to Mint Walk and staff and delivery access to the building.

The new library at 6,000 m² is one of the largest public libraries built in recent years, and 264.4 m2 is occupied by the children's library. This compares with the 140 m² provided in the old building. The number of visitors in the old premises was over 540,000 in 1992–3 but, in the six months since the opening of the new library, the number of visitors was 556,227 (an increase of 109%).

The new library has been designed to take full advantage of information technology and has full raised access floors to facilitate its implementation.

Location of the children's library

The new library has four public floors linked by lift and escalator. Above these is the library administration floor. In designing the building, particular attention was paid to the needs of the disabled and young. This concern is evidenced by the location of the children's library on the ground floor (other than the tourist information, the only public department on entry level), and access to it. As the entrance to the whole complex is below street level, a ramp has been provided in addition to the broad stairs. On entering the library, a return books counter is immediately to the left (part of an office, counter, and enquiry points grouping), and inside, beyond the double, automatic entrance gates, is the entrance to the children's library on the right (Figure 12.7). Probably because of it's ground floor location, the children's library has an unusually high ceiling, with flush lighting, that adds to the feeling of spaciousness in the department.

Decorative features

Because of its colourful nature, decorative features, and varied furniture, all visible though glass panels dividing the children's library from the entrance area, it immediately creates an impression on the visitor. An impression not just of colour and variety but of spaciousness and accessibility. The bottom part of the above mentioned glazed panelling is, in fact, filled in, but each has a porthole in it and other decorative features, thus setting a nautical theme for the department. This theme is repeated in a book browser unit designed like a ship, and such features as a lighthouse, and creatures created by the artist-metalworker, Jon Mills, and located at the top of structural columns. There are also porthole windows adjacent to alcove seating (Figure 12.8).

Layout and arrangement of the children's library

To the left of the entrance to the children's library is the pre-school area, which is partially enclosed by shelving, linked by specially created panels providing a physical but not visual barrier to the area. Books in this section are stored in units with display shelving above and kinder boxes below. Others are housed on more conventional shelving under headings such as 'first books', and 'starting to read'. There are beanbags in this area as well as casual seating for adults. Fronting this section are books and journals for parents. Within the pre-school area are also an activities room with sink, and a baby changing room and toilet.

In the centre of the department are four OPAC terminals (Figure 12.9) quite close to the staff desk with office behind. The rest of the shelved part of the children's library includes fiction and information books (with round tables and chairs nearby), sound tapes (mainly spoken word), and books for young adults housed on standard shelving and spinners. Bay guiding is located on the tops of shelving and spinners.

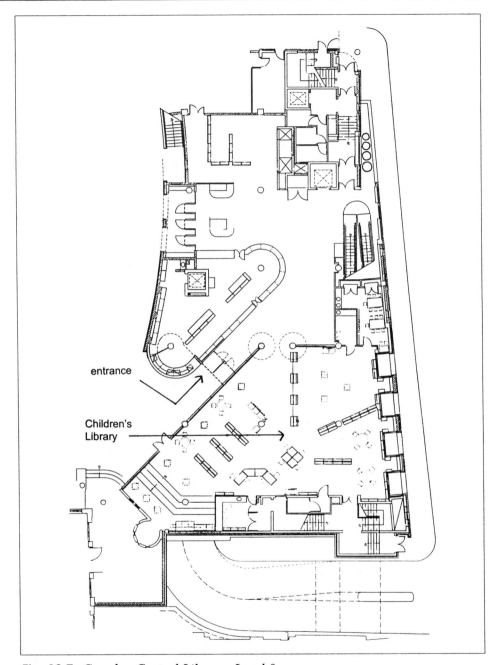

Fig. 12.7 *Croydon Central Library: Level 0*
(Reproduced through the courtesy of Don Gresswell Ltd)

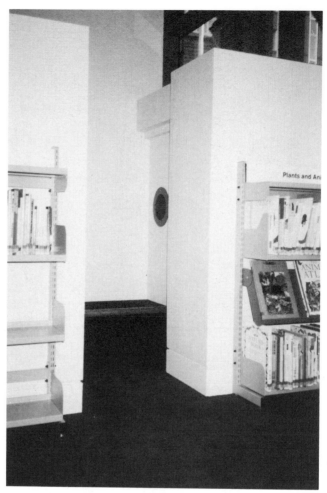

Fig. 12.8 *Croydon Central Library: alcove seating*

To the rear of the department, and visible from the main library entrance area, is the boat book browser unit (Figure 12.10), and carpeted auditorium steps, where children can sit and read or plug in headphones to listen to a tape. This performance area will accommodate up to 60 children for events and library visits. At the top of the steps is the storytelling tower where small groups of children can sit on cushions to listen to a story.

The young adult spinners, containing fiction arranged by genre and children's paperback books, are in wood and the rest of the more traditional shelving has yellow and green metal shelves with wooden end panels. The pre-school area makes use of yellow and green steel shelving, colourful kinderboxes (using a fish pattern), and low seats and tables, making use of yellow, green and red. All this is against a carpet of deep blue – another maritime allusion.

Fig. 12.9 *Croydon Central Library: OPAC terminals*

Some aspects of design

The children's library is clearly visible to all users of the library service and readily accessible to its users. However, its location is rather separate and isolated from the rest of the library departments, although this can often be the case in large libraries. One might question, therefore, whether this location was the best solution or a necessary compromise.

The children's library houses material for teenagers but the space allocation, decoration and facilities might seem to favour the younger child. The emphasis on play and story type activities might also tend to obscure the educational role of the department; information technology is confined to the provision of OPACs, for example. While there are further materials and facilities for young adults (and other children), elsewhere in the library, no separate, special provision has been made for this age group in this large library. However, there is a space within the building which could be used for that purpose should this be felt necessary at a later date.

Building, furniture and equipment details

Architects: Tibbalds Colborne Karski Williams Monro (TCKWM)
Shelving, tables, chairs and other furniture: Don Gresswell Ltd
Library management system: Libs 100 plus (Geac Computers)
Security system: Checkpoint Systems
Signage: Pentagram Design; Don Gresswell Ltd (bay guiding).

Fig. 12.10 *Croydon Central Library: boat book browser unit*
(Reproduced through the courtesy of Don Gresswell Ltd)

Petersburn Library and Drop-in Centre, Airdrie
The community and its library

Monklands District Council's Petersburn Library and Drop-in Centre opened in November 1991. Previous branch libraries in the Petersburn area had been housed in converted premises and so the new building was its first purpose-built community library. Partly funded through the government's Urban Aid programme, the facility has developed as an informal learning environment related to community needs and interests, as well as carrying out the more traditional library roles. It has also been designed especially to attract, accommodate and serve teenagers and young adults.

The library part of the building (137.75 m²) consists of an open-plan ground floor, partially covered by the mezzanine floor above. The ground floor consists of adult lending and reference areas, with separate sections for children and teenagers. There is also a library counter with workroom-cum-storeroom behind. The mezzanine floor is an area for information and for quiet study. There are study carrels, career and job information, computers for learning packages, wordprocessing and desktop publishing, and a photocopier.

Because the Petersburn/Craigneuk area has one of the highest teenage populations in Scotland a drop-in centre is an adjoining feature of the building. The drop-in centre has its own entrance but can also be accessed from the foyer to the library, which also links with the adjacent community centre.

Children's section

The section for children occupies a rectangular space to the left of the issue desk and the stairs leading up to the mezzanine floor. Reference, non-fiction, story and Ladybird books, along with 'easy reads' and talking books, are housed on shelving round the walls of the area. The wall shelving is four shelves high and some bays have sloping top shelves for face-on display. The space above the wall shelving is used for display, although no special surface seems to have been provided for this purpose. However, notice boards are available in the foyer for advertising community events, public information, etc. The central floor space of the children's section is given over to a more informally arranged display furniture for nursery books, fairy tales and a dinosaur nursery display feature. There is limited seating at a table – enough for four children.

The children's section or the drop-in centre, as appropriate, is used for storytimes, school visits (including library skills sessions), a junior writers' workshop, clubs (including one for computers and another for teenage girls), and meetings of a studio users group. The library participates in a local playscheme, a toy library in a local school, and special library events that included the visit of a graphic novel artist, a Halloween day for younger children, and a library poster competition organized with local primary schools for National Library Week.

A Creche Workers Support Group meets locally and services creches in a number of places including the library when it puts on an event. Creches are held in the library or drop-in centre depending upon which half of the building the event is to be held in. Both are formally registered as creches. For most daytime events a room is booked in the adjoining community centre.

Teenage section

The teenage section occupies a corner at the rear of the ground floor; an alcove formed by the wall of the workroom and bays of shelving. It displays the best in teenage fiction, graphic novels, non-fiction (books on pop stars, sport and fashion), music videos and music CDs. A group of chairs occupies the centre of the floor space making for a fairly formally arranged teenage area.

Drop-in centre[3]

It is expected that teenagers will use the facilities of the main library but the drop-in centre (67.7 m²) offers additional attractions to meet the social and educational needs of young people (Figure 12.11). The development of the centre and its activities has taken place in close consultation with its users, and the library's staff includes a youth development worker, assistant youth development worker and studio technician, all full-time. Community Education students, from the closest training college (Jordanhill), were on placement with the centre in mid-1994. The centre is open to those who are 16 to 25 years old but, because of demand, opens especially for the under-13s on Saturday mornings. There are requests for longer opening hours; the centre currently opens till 8 p.m. on two nights but closes at 5 p.m. on two days. The drop-in is closed Saturday afternoons and Sundays and on Mondays the space is used for library organized events and activities.

Fig. 12.11 *Petersburn Library: Drop-in Centre*
(Reproduced through the courtesy of Lindsay McKrell, Petersburn Library)

Services and facilities
The drop-in centre offers the following materials, facilities and services to young people.

   (a) an attractive meeting place

   (b) a computer section with a wide choice of computer games

   (c) a small library of music books and sheet music

   (d) magazines – fashion and music; magazines for younger readers are kept in the teenage section of the library

   (e) soft drinks vending machine

   (f) the latest hi-fi equipment; the non-stop satellite music channel MTV; user-led record, compact disc and music video collections

   (g) pop videos

   (h) a music tuition service

   (i) a youth information point

   (j) an acoustic guitar lending library

   (k) a custom-built recording studio, with guitars, amplifiers, drums, keyboard and microphones available

   (l) Scotvec training courses in video recording and editing, and sound engineering

  (m) assistance in seeking employment (job vacancies boards) and training. Help with job applications is provided.

As part of the centre's development, a video editing suite has been adapted from a cleaner's store in the plant room, and office space created in the void in the mezzanine behind the study gallery. These have been operational since October 1993.

Range of accommodation

The main entrance to the drop-in centre leads to a long rectangular area that accommodates the computers along one wall and has plenty of red upholstered casual seating and low tables where people can listen to music, watch videos or satellite TV, or browse through books and magazines. Magazines are displayed on a mobile bookstand, and leaflet racks and notice boards are also available. The drop-in has its own toilet facilities, unlike the library. To the left of the entrance is an eight-track recording studio, which can also be used as a rehearsal room for bands, and its control booth. There is a large hall and meeting room in the adjacent community centre to host events organized by or for teenagers. Since this is run by a separate council department, a charge is made to the Libraries Department for such lets.

Decor, etc

The centre is decorated with posters of pop groups and films, and a large pop art wall mural, planned, designed and painted by a group of regular drop-in users. Posters of local events and community group activities are also displayed.

Some aspects of design

The success of Petersburn with teenagers might be said to be due to the lack of much else to do and youth unemployment that is 10% above the national average. But this would be to underestimate the thought and resources that have gone into making provision for teenagers, the concern of the staff that it should meet their needs and the attitude they have to their users. By making varied provision for teenagers in an open-plan library, which also offers a variety of other services that teenagers might want to use, young people can still feel part of the community in general while the adjacent drop-in centre allows them to socialize in and enjoy an environment and facilities that have been created especially for them whenever they so wish. This seems to be library provision that is satisfactorily meeting the needs of teenagers in an appropriately accessible and designed building.

Building, furniture and equipment details

Architects: Director of Technical Services, Monklands District Council
Shelving and counter: Don Gresswell Ltd
Tables and chairs: Don Gresswell Ltd
Library management system: Bookshelf
Security system: Modern Security System
Recording studio etc: ABC Music, Surrey

Centre for the Child: Birmingham Central Library

The children's library in Birmingham Central Library was referred to in Chapter 2 as an outstanding example of children's provision in the early 1970s. In April 1991, however, the central children's library was destroyed by fire and the aim of the present project, which is due to be completed in late 1994, is to rebuild it as the Centre for the Child in the city, bringing together a range of resources and services to meet the needs of children and their carers. These needs will be met by the rebuilt library's concern for reading and literacy (in its broadest, modern sense); the child's care and welfare, education, leisure and recreation, and the opportunities that will be provided for children with disabilities. For parents and carers there will be books for loan, information, help, advice and support. The need for modern, satisfactory library accommodation for this group is demonstrated by the 1,125,000 visits that were made to the Central Library in 1992/93 by children and young people.

Influencing the development of the Centre for the Child have been the requirements of the Children Act, to provide services and access to information about those services, especially for those in need; the Education Reform Act, with the demands of the National Curriculum; Birmingham City Council's corporate childcare strategy, with its emphasis on the corporate provision of services, and its commitment to the Educating Cities Charter, which, amongst other things, is concerned with the education, advancement and development of all citizens, starting with children and young people.

Location

Not only is it intended to rebuild the central children's library, but, in its manifestation as the Centre for the Child, to relocate it within the Central Library building. Rather than its former basement location, the new centre will be located on the ground floor, close to the main entrance to the Central Library. Alongside the centre will be the Business Information Department, which will operate over two floors, as it will incorporate the former basement children's library area.

Space limitations

The design for the Centre for the Child has tried to take on board as many of the needs of parents and their children, especially those with a disability, as possible. However, with a finite amount of space, inevitably some compromises over design matters have had to be made. This was one of the factors which prevented the establishment of a creche within the centre. The issue of space for parking buggies and prams is being considered separately within the Central Library as a whole, as part of the plans to make it a more child-friendly building.

Range of spaces

The following areas and rooms are proposed as the principal features of the centre:
   (a) Children's lending library – to include: baby and toddlers' area (designed with families and small children in mind); beginning to read area; reading recovery area (to support work begun in school); teenage area (offering a relaxed environment and a gateway to other central library services).
   (b) Childcare information bureau – providing information on childcare in its

widest sense, to include such issues as child development and play, day childcare providers, and events and facilities in Birmingham. It will form a key element in the wider role of the Centre for the Child as an information centre for parents.

(c) Homework and study area – this, together with other areas, to support children and young people as independent learners.

(d) Open learning centre.

(e) Activity/meeting rooms – a moveable room divider gives flexibility to use the room as one or two spaces.

(f) Disability resource centre – to give children and their carers better access to library services, books, stories and information.

(g) Parent and baby room for changing and feeding.

(h) Unisex disabled toilets.

(i) Corporate and other display areas.

(j) Counter.

(k) Staff workroom, office, kitchen and toilet.

For details of the preliminary proposals for the layout, see Figure 12.12.

Resources and equipment

The following resources and equipment are proposed for the centre:

(a) Information and story books of all kinds, for all ages, and in a variety of languages.

(b) Magazines.

(c) Computer hardware and software.

(d) Cassette players and talking books.

(e) Reading machines and induction loops for children with disabilities.

(f) Open learning materials in book, tape and disc forms.

(g) Toys and play equipment.

Some noteworthy features of the centre will be:

(a) A child-friendly environment with all appropriate safety features.

(b) Furnishings designed to encourage parents and children to share books together.

(c) For those children with disabilities, a wide range of equipment, from computers to hand-held magnifiers, reading machines, and induction loop systems.

(d) A variety of information and electronic technology.

(e) A childcare enquiry and advice service which will include a telephone helpline.

Planning the Centre for the Child

The planning of the centre exemplifies many of the points made in the earlier chapters of this book, as does its design for the later chapters.

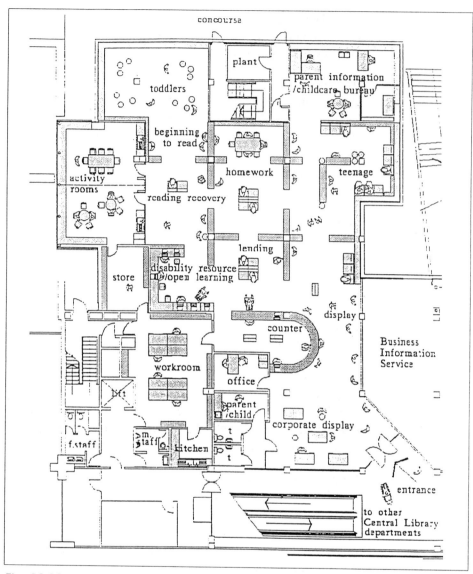

Fig. 12.12 *Centre for the Child: preliminary layout plan*
(Reproduced through the courtesy of the Leisure & Community
Services Department, Birmingham City Council)

The role of the centre

Rebuilding has been used as an opportunity to rethink the role of the former
children's library and this has led to the development of an eight-point philosophy,
influenced by both national and local issues, as well as the requirement to meet the
diverse needs of the individual child. This philosophy highlights the importance of
the child by providing a central place for resources and facilities to assist reading
skills, foster independent learning, and provide help for children with disabilities.
Also it aids parents and carers with their children's development, care and education,

and acts as a gateway to city council services for children and those carers. It will provide a child-centered focus, enabling council departments to work corporately to meet the needs of children and their parents.

Planning alternatives

Consideration has been given to possible planning alternatives. Either to rebuild the centre in the old location within the central library building, which was physically and visually remote and with limited expansion opportunities, or to relocate it within the building, which, while more costly and complicated, would provide a better location and easier accessibility, a more attractive environment, and sufficient space to house the new, wider roles of the centre. Relocation was chosen and, with some new building work, 505 m² (317 m² + 188 m²) will be available in the new position, as opposed to a possible 298 m² in the former location.

Consultation with users and others

Initially, after the fire, there was discussion about the future of the central children's library with colleagues both within the library service and other council departments with responsibility for children. Subsequently, active users were given a form to complete on their visit to the temporary children's library or sent one through the post. This asked both parents and children to say what they liked about the former children's library and what they would like to see when it was rebuilt. On the whole, responses fed into the process, confirmed and supported the ideas emerging from other discussions. Since then consultation has gone further, and has involved working with a group of 7–11-year-olds, and a model of the proposed centre, to get their ideas as to what should be included. Further groups of children are being consulted as to the best ways of promoting the centre to children across the city when it opens. Further consultation is being undertaken with parents and families to identify what activities they want to see taking place in the centre and when are the most convenient times for family use.

Sponsorship

In order to make the project a true partnership, the Libraries and Learning Division of Birmingham Leisure and Community Services Department are endeavouring to raise about 10% of the estimated budget for the proposed centre through sponsorship. Funds raised in this way will be accepted as a general contribution to the project; for specific equipment, furniture or resource, or for a particular area of the centre. Sponsorship will be acknowledged in a variety of ways within the finished centre.

Team planning

Staff of the library service's children, youth and education team set up a steering group for the Centre for the Child, with the principal officer occupying the chair. The steering group invites additional people to attend its meetings when special issues need consideration. Separate meetings are conducted with the architect and these have been used to discuss and develop the original brief and to deal with other matters, such as lighting and electrical plans, interior design, and room data sheets. It is expected that the steering committee will consider the question of drawing-up performance measures and indicators for the centre in order to gauge its success in achieving its objectives.

An innovative centre

The Centre for the Child will aim to meet the needs of children and young people aged 0–16. It will also work closely with other departments of the Central Library to support the work they carry out and the services they provide for older teenagers. A promotional plan for the centre is being developed as part of the ongoing forward planning process. Activities will be specifically targeted at priority groups, such as disabled children, to ensure that awareness of the facilities is raised and that they are used. The Centre for the Child is both innovative and unique in its concept. From the tragedy of the fire will emerge a positive and exciting resource for the children of Birmingham and their families.

References

1 Weston, R., *Schools of thought: Hampshire architecture 1974–1991*, Winchester, Hampshire County Council Architects Department, 1991, 96.

2 Woof, N., 'Broad brief for Croydon suppliers', *Library Association record trade supplement*, **95** (12), 1993, 9–11.

3 'Monklands attracts teenage drop-ins', *Library Association record*, **94** (5), 1992, 297.

Association of Library Equipment Suppliers (TALES)
c/o OCLC Europe
7th Floor, Tricorn House
51–53 Hagley Road
Edgbaston
BIRMINGHAM B16 8TP
Telephone: 0121-456 4656

An informal trade association for organizations supplying products and services to libraries and information units.

Branch and Mobile Libraries Group of the Library Association
Hon. Secretary
Mrs V Warren ALA
Wealdon Area Libraries
Hammonds Drive
Lottbridge Drove
EASTBOURNE BN23 6PW
Telephone: 01323 417629

Specialist group of the Library Association. Produces the periodical *Service point* and other publications.

British Educational Equipment Association
20 Beaufort Court
Admiral Way
LONDON E14 9XL
Telephone: 0171-537 4997

Trade association, organizer of exhibitions, and valuable source of information about equipment, materials and books.

Building Centre
26 Store Street
LONDON WC1E 7BT
Telephone: 0171-637 1022

Provides a source of ideas and information for buildings; exhibition of building materials and a literature service.

**An Chomhairle Leabharlanna
(Library Council)**
Research Library
53/54 Upper Mount Street
Dublin 2
IRELAND
Telephone: 00-3531-6761167

Maintains a library
equipment centre and trade
information database.
Produces a number of fact
sheets.

Cimtech Limited
University of Hertfordshire
45 Grosvenor Road
ST ALBANS
Herts AL1 3AW
Telephone: 01707-279691

UK's leading centre in
the techniques and
technologies of
information management.

**Council for Educational Technology
for the UK**
Sir William Lyon's Road
Science Park
COVENTRY CV4 7EZ
Telephone: 01203-416994

Central organization for
promoting the application and
development of educational
technology. Produces the
*British journal of educational
technology* and other publications.

**Department for Education,
Architects and Building Branch**
Room 5Q3 Sanctuary Buildings
Great Smith Street
LONDON SW1P 3BT
Telephone: 0171-925 5889

Produces a series of
publications to assist in
the design of educational
buildings which give basic
information, advice on
meeting statutory
obligations and examples
of good practice.

**International Federation of
Library Associations and
Institutions (IFLA)**
Headquarters
P O Box 95312
2509 CH The Hague
NETHERLANDS
Telephone: 00-3170-3140884

Special interest sections
include: public libraries;
children's libraries;
school libraries; library
buildings and equipment.

Library Association
7 Ridgmount Street
LONDON WC1E 7AE
Telephone: 0171-636 7543

The Library Association's library
and information service is
administered by the British Library.

Library Information Technology Centre
South Bank Technopark
90 London Road
LONDON SE1 6LN
Telephone: 0171-928 8989

Europe's foremost centre of expertise in library and information technology. ·

National Playbus Association
Mobile Projects Unit and
Playbus Unit
93 Whitby Road
Brislington
BRISTOL BS4 3QF
Telephone: 0117-277 5375

Provides information and advice; produces a number of publications and information sheets. Offers a design and conversion service through a trading company.

Play Matters – National Toy Libraries Association
68 Churchway
LONDON NW1 1LT
Telephone: 0171-387 9592

Provides an information service and publishes *Ark* and *What toy*.

Pre-School Playgroup Association
61–63 Kings Cross Road
LONDON WC1X 9LL
Telephone: 0171-833 0991

Promotion of playgroup and mother and toddler groups; information service.

School Bookshop Association
6 Brightfield Road
LONDON SE12 8QF
Telephone: 0181-852 4953

Concerned with the promotion of children's books; publishes *Books for keeps* – the children's book magazine.

School Library Association
Liden Library
Barrington Close
Liden
SWINDON SN3 6HF
Telephone: 01793-617838

Publishes *School librarian* and many useful publications, including those on the design of school libraries.

University of Wales, Aberystwyth
Information and Library Studies Library
Llanbadarn Fawr
ABERYSTWYTH
Dyfed SY23 3AS
Telephone: 01970-622417

Maintains a database of library buildings backed by a collection of plans and/or other documentation for each building.

**We Welcome Small Children National
Campaign**
93A Belsize Lane
LONDON NW3 5AU
Telephone: 0171-586 3453

Women's Design Service Interchange
15 Wilkin Street
LONDON SE1
Telephone: 0171-709 7910

Youth Libraries Group of the **Library Association** Hon. Secretary Ms T Kings, BA, ALA 48/49 Greenhill WIRKSWORTH Derbyshire DE4 4EH Telephone: 01602-412121	Specialist group of the Library Association; publishes *Youth library* *review*, posters, a video and other publications.

Exhibitions and fairs

Computers in Libraries International
Annual meeting and exhibition, organized by Mecklermedia, London.

International Federation of Library Association and Institutions (IFLA)
Annual general meeting at locations around the world includes an exhibition of services and
suppliers for libraries.

Library Resources Exhibition
Annual exhibition of services and suppliers for libraries, normally at the National Exhibition
Centre, Birmingham.

Libtech, the International Library Technology Fair
Exhibition of IT products for libraries in the UK held annually at the University of Hertfordshire.

Online/CD-ROM Information Exhibition
A large exhibition of electronic information services and products. Held annually in London in
association with the International Online Information meeting.

Under One Umbrella Conference
Library Association's biennial conference; location can vary. Includes an exhibition of services and
suppliers for libraries.

SUPPLIERS OF SHELVING, FURNITURE AND FITTINGS

The following list of UK suppliers has been compiled mainly from the *Library Association directory of suppliers and services*.[1] Major suppliers of shelving, furniture and fittings in Australia, Europe and North America have also been added for readers outside the UK. It should be noted, however, that appearance in this list does not imply endorsement by the author or publisher.

United Kingdom

Apollo Space Systems Ltd
Apollo House
Wharf Road Industrial Estate
PINXTON
Notts NG16 6LE
Telephone: 01773-812800
Fax: 01773-580286

Balmforth Engineering Ltd
Finway
Dallow Road
LUTON
LU1 1TE
Telephone: 01582-31171
Fax: 01582-454103

Community Playthings
ROBERTSBRIDGE
East Sussex
TN32 5DR
Telephone: 01580-880626
Fax: 01580-882250

Learning Curve Sigma
Education and Library Furniture
P O Box 223
ALTRINCHAM
Cheshire WA14 3DX
Telephone: 0161-928 5945
Fax: 0161-928 5945

Ateka Tape Racks
Unit 8   Station Road
Industrial Estate
HAILSHAM
East Sussex BN27 2ER
Telephone: 01323-845880
Fax: 01323-843366

Bruynzeel Storage Systems
Pembroke Road
Stocklake Industrial Estate
AYLESBURY
Bucks HP20 1DG
Telephone: 01296-395081
Fax: 01296-86807

Don Gresswell Ltd
Bridge House
Vera Avenue   Grange Park
LONDON N21 1RB
Telephone: 0181-360 6622
Fax: 0181-360 9231

Libraco
Crown House
23 Crown Road
Shoreham   SEVENOAKS
Kent TN14 7TN
Telephone: 01959-524074
Fax: 01959-525218

Library Design and Engineering Ltd
44 Gloucester Avenue
LONDON
NW1 8JD
Telephone: 0171-722 0111
Fax: 0171-483 2374

Librex Education Company
Colwick Road
NOTTINGHAM
NG2 4BG
Telephone: 0115-950 4664
Fax: 0115-958 6683

Peters Library Service
The Kit Shop
120 Bromsgrove Street
BIRMINGHAM B5 6RL
Telephone: 0121-666 6646
Fax: 0121-666 7033

Remploy Lundia
Ashton Road
OLDHAM
Lancs OL8 3JG
Telephone: 0161-626 4119
Fax: 0161-652 2705

B Serota Ltd
Acme Works
Rendlesham Road
LONDON   E5 8PS
Telephone: 0181-985 1736
Fax: 0181-985 5109

Library Furnishing Consultants Ltd
Phoenix House
54 Dennington Road
WELLINGBOROUGH
Northants NN8 2QH
Telephone: 01933-442777
Fax: 01933-442764

Lift (UK) Ltd
Triangle Business Park
Wendover Road
STOKE MANDEVILLE
Bucks HP22 5BL
Telephone: 01296-615151
Fax: 01296-612865

Point Eight Ltd
Shaw Road
DUDLEY
West Midlands DY2 8TP
Telephone: 01384-238282
Fax: 01384-455746

Reska Terrapin Products Ltd
Mount House   Bond Avenue
Bletchley MILTON KEYNES
MK1 1SD
Telephone: 01908-371001
Fax: 01908-365352

United Kingdom: mobile libraries

Bailey's Bodybuilders Ltd
Tunstall Road Industrial Estate
Tunstall Road   Biddulph
STOKE ON TRENT
Staffs ST8 7BD
Telephone: 01782-513671
Fax: 01782-522079

Leicester Carriage Builders
Marlow Road
LEICESTER LE3 2BQ
Telephone: 0116-282 4270
Fax: 0116-263 0554

R Hind Ltd
Durranhill Industrial Estate
CARLISLE
Cumbria CA1 3NQ
Telephone: 01228-23647
Fax: 01228-23647

G C Smith (Coachworks)
Long Whalton
LOUGHBOROUGH
Leicestershire LE12 5BY
Telephone: 01509-842451
Fax: 01509-844443

W B S Keillor Ltd
Alma Place
Bucklershead
DUNDEE
Telephone: 01382-350567
Fax: 01382-350496

Europe
Denmark
Dansk Biblioteks Center as
Tempovej 7–11
DK-2750 Ballerup
Denmark

France
Borgeaud Bibliothèques
Siège Social
122 Rue de Bagneux
92120 Montrouge
France

Germany
**Einkaufszentrale für
 Bibliotheken GmbH (EKZ)**
Bismarckstrasse 3
72764 Reutlingen
Germany

Netherlands
NBLC Systemen BV
Postbus 1104
1300 BC Almere-Stad
The Netherlands

Sweden
Bibliotekstjänst AB
Tornavägen 9
S-22100 Lund   Sweden

Finland
Kirjastopalvelu Oy
Särkiniementie 5
SF-00210 Helsinki
Finland

Nelco
Nelco
Siège Social
20 Avenue du Prèsident Allende
Zone Industrielle Mozinor
(Porte 22) 93106 Montreuil Cèdex
France

**Schulz Bibliothekstechnik
 GmbH Speyer**
Friedr-Ebert-Str 2a
D-67346 Speyer
Germany

Norway
A/L Biblioteksentralen
POB 6142 Etterstad
N-0602 Oslo 6
Norway

North America
Brodart
1609 Memorial Avenue
Williamsport
PA 17705
USA

Gaylord
P O Box 4901
Syracuse NY 13221-4901
USA
(Has an International Department)

Australia
Nova Library Pty Ltd
35 Gilbert Park Drive
Knoxfield 3180
Australia

**Queensland Library
Suppliers Pty Ltd**
P O Box 1345
Fortitude Valley
Qld 4006
Australia

S&M Supply Company Pty Ltd
P O Box 3311
Sydney   NSW 2001
Australia

Reference

1   McSeán, T., *Library Association directory of suppliers and services*, 2nd edn., London, Library Association, 1994. A classified and alphabetical guide to suppliers in the UK library and information world that provides useful guidance on where to obtain the myriad requirements when setting up or renovating a library service.

BIBLIOGRAPHY

Abramo, P., 'Communicating with environments', *Illinois libraries*, **60** (10), 1978, 875–6.

Akin, L. and Dowd, F. S., 'A national survey of portable library structures: what works and why', *Public libraries*, **32** (5), 1993, 267–9.

Allies, B., 'Library and resource centre, Millfield School', *Architects' journal*, **173** (17), 1981, 791–806.

Amdursky, S. J., 'Re-creating the children's room: a renovation project at Kalamazoo Public Library', *School library journal*, **39** (2), 1993, 25–8.

American Association of School Librarians and Association for Educational Communication and Technology, *Information power: guidelines for school library media programs*, Chicago, American Library Association, Washington DC, Association for Educational Communication and Technology, 1988.

American Association of School Librarians and Association for Educational Communications and Technology, *Media programs: district and school*, Chicago, American Library Association, 1975.

American Association of School Librarians and the Department of Audiovisual Instruction of the National Education Association, *Library standards for school media programs*, Chicago, American Library Association, 1969.

American Library Association, *Standards for children's services in public libraries*, American Library Association, Chicago, 1964.

Anderson, B., 'Designs on a new toy library', *Ark*, Spring 1992, 12–13.

Anderson, M. J., 'Service for the eighties: trends in society today which will affect public library service to children tomorrow', *Illinois libraries*, **60** (10), 1978, 850–4.

Anderson, P. A., *Planning school library media facilities*, Hamden, Conn., Library Professional Publications, 1990.

Atherton, B., *Adapting spaces for resource-based learning*, London, Council for Educational Technology, 1980.

Baker, D. P., *Library media program and the school*, Littleton, Colo., Libraries Unlimited, 1984.

Barnes, M. and Ray, S., *Youth library work*, London, Bingley, 1968.

'Benefits beyond the curriculum', *Architects' journal*, 20 October 1993, 37–47.

Benne, M., *Principles of children's services in public libraries*, Chicago, American Library Association, 1991.

Bennett, J., 'Trends in school library media facilities, furnishings and collections', *Library trends*, **36** (2), 1987, 317–25.

Bisbrouck, M. F., *La bibliothèque dans la ville*, Paris, Editions du Moniteur, 1984.

Bock, D. J. and LaJeunesse, L. R., *The learning resources center: a planning primer for libraries in transition*, New York, Bowker, 1977. (*Library journal* special report series 3).

'Books and buses: the librarians' roadshow' *PLG news*, (15), 1983, 11–13 illus.

Bradford Education Library Service, *The effective junior and middle school library: a guide to its planning, policy, management and monitoring*, Bradford, Bradford Education Library Service, 1990.

Brandenburg, M. and Hart, L., 'The dream team: administrators, architects and library/media specialists', *Ohio media spectrum*, **42** (4), 1990, 5–10.

Branscombe, F. R. and Newson, H. E. (eds.), *Resource services for Canadian schools*, Toronto, McGraw-Hill Ryerson, 1977.

Brauer, R. L., *Facilities planning: the user requirement method*, 2nd edn., New York, Amacon, 1992.

Brown, C. R., *Selecting library furniture: a guide for librarians, designers and architects*, Phoenix, Ariz., Oryx Press, 1989.

Brown, R. A., 'Students as partners in library design', *School library journal*, **38** (2), 1992, 31–4.

Buchanan, G., 'By design: it's all in the details', *School library journal*, **36** (2), 1990, 25–7.

Cambridgeshire County Council Education Service, *Provision of learning resources in secondary schools: guidelines for good practice*, Cambridge, Cambridgeshire County Council Education Service, 1988.

Capital Planning Information, *Library and information provision in rural areas in England and Wales*, London, HMSO, 1993.

Carroll, F. L., *Guidelines for school libraries*, The Hague, International Federation of Library Associations, Section of School Libraries, 1990. (IFLA professional reports, no. 20).

Carter, K., 'Images of information in a 21st century high school', *School library journal*, **40** (2), 1994, 25–9.

Charlton, L., *Designing and planning a secondary school library resource centre*, [Swindon], School Library Association, 1992.

Chartered Institution of Building Services, *CIBS lighting guide: libraries*, London, Chartered Institution of Building Services, 1982.

Chase, B., 'Drawing strength: skillful design . . . and a little trickery', *School library journal*, **36** (2), 1990, 21–5.

Chekon, T. and Miles, M., 'The kid's place: Sacramento PL's space for children', *School library journal*, **39** (2), 1993, 20–4.

Cohen, A. and Cohen, E., *Designing and space planning for libraries*, New York, Bowker, 1979.

Cohen, A. and Cohen, E., 'Remodeling the library', *School library journal*, **24** (2), 1978, 30–3.

Dailey, S., 'Establishing an atmosphere for success', *Indiana libraries*, **8** (2), 1989, 99–103.

Department of Education and Science, *Educational design initiatives in city technology colleges*, London, HMSO, 1991. (Building bulletin, 72).

Department of Education and Science, *Public library service points*, London, HMSO, 1971.

Department of Education and Science, *The public library service: reorganisation and after*, London, HMSO, 1973.

Department of Education and Science, *The school library*, London, HMSO, 1967.

Department of Education and Science, Architects and Building Branch, *Designing a medium-sized public library*, London, HMSO, 1981.

Department of Education and Science, Architects and Building Group, *Access for disabled people to educational buildings*, 2nd edn., London, Department of Education and Science, 1984. (Design note, 18).

Department of Education and Science, Architects and Building Group, *Accommodation for the 16–19 age group: NAFE: designing for change*, London, Department of Education and Science, 1980. (Design note, 22)

Department of Education and Science, Architects and Building Group, *Area guidelines for secondary schools*, London, Department of Education and Science, 1983. (Design note, 34).

Department of Education and Science, Architects and Building Group, *Area guidelines for sixth form, tertiary and NAFE colleges*, London, Department of Education and Science, 1983. (Design note, 33).

Department of Education and Science, Architects and Building Group, *Crime prevention in schools: closed circuit TV surveillance systems in educational buildings*, London, HMSO, 1991. (Building bulletin, 75).

Department of Education and Science, Architects and Building Group, *Educational furniture for the 16–19 age group: specification and design*, London, Department of Education and Science, 1982. (Design note, 30).

Department of Education Circular 1982/87, Northern Ireland.

Devon Education and Devon Libraries, *Resources for learning: a handbook for the evaluation of secondary school library resource provision and use*, Exeter, Devon County Council, 1990.

Dewe, M., 'Trends in UK public library buildings during the 1980s', in *Petrification or flexibility*, Stockholm, Swedish National Council for Cultural Affairs, 1992, 31–7.

Directory of dual use libraries, 2nd edn., Ipswich, Suffolk County Information and Library Service, 1985.

Dixon, J.K., 'Experiencing architecture: the Young People's Library Department in Las Vegas', *School library journal*, **37** (2), 1991, 30–2.

Doll, C.A., 'School library media centers: the human environment', *School library media quarterly*, **20** (4), 1992, 225–30.

Dyer, H. and Morris, A., *Human aspects of library automation*, Aldershot, Gower, 1990.

Dziura, W. T., 'Media center aesthetics: focus on design, color scheme and furnishings', in *Reader in children's librarianship*, (ed.) J. Foster, Englewood, Colo., Information Handling Services, 1978, 369–75.

Eastwood, C. R., *Mobile libraries and other public transport,* London, Association of Assistant Librarians, 1967.

Edmond, D. and Miller, J., *Public library services for children and young people*, London, British Library, 1990.

Edmonds, L., 'Sorry about safety?' *Illinois libraries*, **60** (10), 1978, 868–74.

Edwards, R. P. A., *Resources in schools*, London, Evans, 1973.

Ellis, A., *Library services for young people in England and Wales 1830–1970*, Oxford, Pergamon, 1971.

Ellsworth, R. E. and Wagener, H. D., *The school library: facilities for independent study in the secondary school*, New York, Educational Facilities Laboratories, 1963.

Esson, K. and Tyerman, K., *Library provision for children*, Newcastle under Lyme, Association of Assistant Librarians, 1991.

Fasick, A. M. (ed.), *Guidelines for children's services*, The Hague, International Federation of Library Associations, 1991. (IFLA professional reports, no. 25).

Fleet, A., *Children's libraries*, London, André Deutsch, 1973.

Fowler, L. B., 'Facilities design: what I learned along the way', *North Carolina libraries*, **49** (3), 1991, 137–40.

Fraley, R. A. and Anderson, C. L., *Library space planning: a how-to-do-it manual...*, 2nd edn., New York, Neal-Schuman, 1990.

Gagnon, A., *Guidelines for children's services*, Ontario, Canadian Library Association, 1989.

Gillespie, J. T. and Spirt, D. L., *Administering the school library media center*, New York, Bowker, 1983.

Goldsmith, S., *Designing for the disabled*, 3rd edn., London, Royal Institute of British Architects, 1984.

Gordon, C., *Resource organisation in primary schools*, 2nd edn., London, Council for Educational Technology, 1986.

Griffith, R. L., 'Doing your homework', *Illinois libraries*, **60** (10), 1978, 860–3.

Habley, K., 'The many uses of color in the library rooms serving children', *Illinois libraries*, **60** (10), 1978, 891–8.

Harrison, K. C. (ed.), *Library buildings 1984–1989*, London, Library Services Limited, 1990.

Harrison, K. C., 'Public libraries in London', in *British librarianship and information science 1966–1970*, (ed.) H. A. Whatley, London, Library Association, 1972, 437–45.

Harrison, K. C. (ed.), *Public library buildings 1975–1983*, London, Library Services Limited, 1987.

Harrod, L. M., *Library work with children*, London, André Deutsch, 1969.

Hart, T. L., *Creative ideas for library media center facilities*, Englewood, Colo., Libraries Unlimited, 1990.

Head, J. and Barton, P., *Toy libraries in the community*, London, Eltan, 1987.

Health and Safety (Display Screen Equipment) Regulations, 1992.

Heeks, P., *Administration of children's libraries*, London, Library Association, 1967.

Hendry, J. D., 'JILL's pure brill', *Library Association record*, **88** (2), 1986, 78–9.

Herring, J. E., *School librarianship*, 2nd edn., London, Bingley, 1988.

Hewitt, J., *Toys and games in libraries,* London, Library Association, 1981.

Holt, R. M., *Planning library buildings and facilities: from concept to completion*, Metuchen, N.J., Scarecrow Press, 1989.

Huntoon, E., 'Their turn – kids speak out on library facilities', *Illinois libraries*, **60** (10), 1978, 876–80.

Illinois Association for Media in Education and International Association of School Librarianship, *Indicators of quality for school library/media programs*, (International edition), Illinois, 1985.

Infantino, C. P., 'Exchanging experiences/interchanging ideas', *Illinois libraries*, **60** (10), 1978, 908–13.

International Federation of Library Associations, Section of Public Libraries, *Guidelines for public libraries*, Munich, Saur, 1986. (IFLA publications, no. 36).

International Federation of Library Associations, Section of Public Libraries, *Standards for public libraries*, Munich, Verlag Dokumentation, 1973.

IT and school buildings, London, National Council for Educational Technology, 1990.

Jones, A. C., 'Dual purpose libraries: some experiences in England', *School librarian*, **25** (4), 1977, 311–18.

Jones, P., *Connecting young adults with libraries*, New York, Neal Schuman, 1992.

Kaspick, A. M., 'Planning a new youth services department; or, beauty's more than skin deep', *Illinois libraries*, **70** (1), 1988, 22–4.

Kelly, T., *A history of public libraries in Great Britain 1845–1975*, 2nd edn., London, Library Association, 1977.

Kingham, P. 'Something for nothing: every school's dream', *School librarian*, **41** (3), 1993, 98–9.

Kinnell, M., (ed.), *Learning resources in schools: Library Association guidelines for school libraries*, London, Library Association, 1992.

Klasing, J. P., *Designing and renovating school library media centers*, Chicago, American Library Association, 1991.

Konya, A., *Libraries: a briefing and design guide*, London, Architectural Press, 1986.

Kurtz, W. M., 'Changes, changes', *Illinois libraries*, **70** (1), 1988, 19–21.

Lambert, L. S., 'How to survive library renovation', *School library journal*, **38** (2), 1992, 38–9.

Lamkin, B., 'A media center for the 21st century', *School library journal*, **33** (3), 1986, 25–9.

Lewins, H. and Renwick, F., 'Barriers to access: libraries and the pre-school child in one English county', *International review of children's literature and librarianship*, **4** (2), 1989, 85–106.

Library and Information Services Council, *School libraries: the foundations of the curriculum*, London, HMSO, 1984.

Library and Information Services Council (Wales), *The report of a working group on libraries in maintained secondary schools in Wales*, Cardiff, Library and Information Services Council (Wales), 1990.

Library Association, *A charter for public libraries*, London, Library Association, 1993.

Library Association, *Children and young people: Library Association guidelines for public library services*, London, Library Association, 1991.

Library Association, *Library resource provision in schools: guidelines and recommendations*, reprinted with supplement, London, Library Association, 1977.

Library Association, *Public library buildings: the way ahead*, London, Library Association, 1960.

Library Association, *Unsupervised children in libraries: guidance notes*, London, Library Association, 1991.

Library Association, Community Services Group in Scotland, Teenage Sub-Committee, *Library service to teenagers*, [Glasgow], Library Association Community Group in Scotland, 1985.

'Library Association statement on sixth form college libraries', *Library Association record*, **81** (8), 1979, 399.

Library bus: a report on the Bradford books and information library bus, Bradford, City of Bradford Metropolitan Council, Libraries Division, 1982.

Library of the 1980s: Swedish public library buildings 1980–1989, Stockholm, Swedish National Council for Cultural Affairs, 1990.

Lindsay, M., 'Mobile libraries – forward or back?', *New library world*, **79** (939), 1978, 167–8.

Lockyer, K. G., *Critical path analysis and other project network techniques*, 4th edn., London, Pitman, 1984.

Lourie, J. E. and Nagakura, M. (eds.), *School libraries: international developments*, 2nd edn., Metuchen, N.J., Scarecrow, 1991.

Love, L., 'Teenagers and library use in Waltham Forest', *Library Association record*, **89** (2), 1987, 81–2.

Lovejoy, S., *A systematic approach to getting results*, Aldershot, Gower, 1993.

Lueder, A. C. and Webb, S., *An administrator's guide to library building maintenance*, Chicago, American Library Association, 1992.

Lushington, N., 'Designed for users', *Wilson library bulletin*, **58** (6), 1984, 424–6.

Lushington, N. and Kusack, J. M., *The design and evaluation of public library buildings*, Hamden, Conn., Library Professional Publications, 1991.

Lushington, N. and Mills, W. N., *Libraries designed for users*, Syracuse, N.Y., Gaylord Professional Publications, 1979.

McCormick, E., 'Revitalising the children's area', *American libraries*, **17** (9), 1986, 712–14.

McDonald, A., *Moving your library*, London, Aslib, 1994.

McSeán, T., *Library Association directory of suppliers and services*, 2nd edn.,

216

London, Library Association, 1994.

Manley, W., 'The Tempe Public Library: a model for the 1990s', *Wilson library bulletin*, **64** (4), 1989, 22–5, 158.

Marshall, M. R., *Libraries and the handicapped child*, London, André Deutsch, 1981.

Marshall, M. R., *Managing library provision for handicapped children*, London, Mansell, 1991.

Marshall, P., 'Children and young people: guidelines for public library services', *International review of children's literature and librarianship*, **6** (3), 1991, 201–9.

Maryland State Board of Education, *Standards for school library media programs in Maryland*, Baltimore, Maryland State Board of Education, 1987.

Maxwell, E., 'The planning and design of children's libraries', *Library management*, **14** (7), 23–35.

Meadows, H. J., *Performance assessment in public libraries*, Branch and Mobile Libraries Group of the Library Association, 1990.

Ministry of Education, *Standards of public library service in England and Wales*, London, HMSO, 1962.

'Monklands attracts teenage drop-ins', *Library Association record*, **94** (5), 1992, 297.

Montanelli, D. S., 'Space management for libraries', *Illinois libraries*, **69** (2), 1987, 130–8.

Morgan, S. M., 'The role of public libraries in lending toys: a review of recent developments', (M.Lib. thesis), University of Wales, 1991.

Morris, B. J. *et al.*, *Administering the school library media center*, New Providence, N.J., Bowker, 1992.

Morris, C.W. *et al.* (eds.), *Libraries in secondary schools*, London, School Library Association, 1972.

National Playbus Association, *Annual report 1992–3*, Bristol, National Playbus Association, 1993.

New York Library Association, *Standards for youth services in public libraries in New York State*, New York, New York Library Association, 1984.

New Zealand Library Association, *Standards for public library service in New Zealand 1980*, reprinted with additional policy statements in 1988, Wellington, New Zealand Library Association, 1988.

Nicholson, J. and Pain-Lewis, H., 'The teenage library in Bradford: an evaluation of Xchange', *Journal of librarianship*, **20** (3), 1988, 205–17.

Nielsen, G.S., 'Bogskib ohoej!', *Bogens verden*, **68** (7), 1986, 383–4.

Nova Scotia School Library Association of the Nova Scotia Teachers Union, *Nova Scotia school libraries: standards and practices*, Nova Scotia School Library Association of the Nova Scotia Teachers Union, 1987.

O'Brien, P., 'Dazzling center opens in Dallas', *American libraries*, **20** (6), 1989, 591–2, 594.

Office of Arts and Libraries, *Keys to success: performance indicators for public libraries*, London, HMSO, 1990.

Ohio Department of Education, *Quality library services K–12*, Colombus, Ohio, Ohio Department of Education, 1986.

Ontario Department of Education, *School media centres*, Ontario, Ontario Department of Education, 1972.

Orton, G. I. J., *An illustrated history of mobile library services in the United Kingdom*, Sudbury, Suffolk, Branch and Mobile Libraries Group of the Library Association, 1980.

Owens, R., 'Clear-sited design', *Architects' journal*, **195** (22), 1992, 28–39.

Owens, R., 'Sparkbrook surprise: Nelson Mandela School', *Architects' journal,* **191** (14), 1990, 35–41, 46–9, 51–4.

Park, L. M., 'The whys and hows of writing a library building program', *Library scene*, **5** (3), 1976, 2–5.

Pestell, R., *Mobile library guidelines*, The Hague: International Federation of Library Association, 1991. (IFLA professional reports, no. 28).

Pierce, W. S., *Furnishing the library interior*, New York, Dekker, 1980.

Prostano, E. T. and Prostano, J. S., *The school library media center*, 4th edn., Littleton, Colo., Libraries Unlimited, 1987.

Pybus, R. L., *The design and construction of mobile libraries*, 2nd edn., [London], Branch and Mobile Libraries Group of the Library Association, 1990.

Pybus, R. L ., *Mobile libraries in England and Wales: a guide to their construction and use*, 2nd edn., St Albans, Branch and Mobile Group of the Library Association, 1985.

Ray, C., 'Children's and young people's libraries', in *British librarianship and information science 1966–1970*, edited by H.A. Whatley, London, Library Association, 1972, 480–8.

Ray, C., 'Children's libraries', in *British librarianship and information science 1971–1975*, edited by H. A. Whatley, London, Library Association, 1977, 181–5.

Ray, C., *Library service to schools and children*, Paris, Unesco, 1979.

Ray, C., *Running a school library: a handbook for teacher-librarians*, London, MacMillan, 1990.

Ray, S. G., *Children's librarianship*, London, Bingley, 1979.

Ray, S. G., *Library service to schools*, 3rd edn., London, Library Association, 1982.

Robertson, M. M., 'Ergonomic considerations for the human environment: color treatment, lighting and furniture selection', *School library media quarterly*, **20** (4), 1992, 211–15.

Rogers, N. I., 'Getting involved; where do you fit in?' *Illinois libraries,* **60** (10), 1978, 854–7.

Rohlf, R. H., 'Best-laid plans: a consultant's constructive advice', *School library journal*, **36** (2), 1990, 28–31.

Rotherham, N. and others, *"If you can't measure it, you can't manage it": performance indicators for secondary schools*, Hertfordshire Library Service, 1991.

Sandler, C., 'Planning library media centers for the 21st century', *Media spectrum,*

18 (1), 1991, 9–10.

Sandlian, P. and Walters, S., 'A room of their own: planning the new Denver children's library, *School library journal,* **37** (2), 1991, 26–9.

Sannwald, W. W. (ed.), *Checklist of library building design considerations,* 2nd edn., Chicago, Library Administration and Management Association, American Library Association, 1991.

Saunders, L., 'Teenagers and library services', *Youth library review,* **16,** 1993, 15–17.

School Library Association, *School libraries: steps in the right direction: guidelines for a school library resource centre,* Swindon, School Library Association, 1989.

School Library Association, *School libraries: their planning and equipment,* London, School Library Association, 1972.

Scott, C., 'Coventry's state of the art mobile library', *Service point,* (52), 1991, 4, 6–7.

Scottish Education Department, *Standards for the public library service in Scotland,* Edinburgh, HMSO, 1969.

Scottish Library Association, *The school library resource service and the curriculum . . .,* Motherwell, Scottish Library Association, 1985.

Sernich, G., *Learning resource centres in Saskatchewan: a guide for development,* Regina, Saskatchewan Education, 1988.

Sever, I., 'Children and territory in a library setting', *Library and information science research,* **9** (2), 1987, 95–107.

Shaw, M., 'Top Valley: a joint use success story', *School librarian,* **38** (2), 1990, 51–2.

Shepherd, J., 'Children's librarianship and school libraries', in *British librarianship and information work 1981–1985,* (ed.) D. W. Bromley and A. M. Allott, London, Library Association, 1988, volume 1, 155–67.

Somerset County Council School Library Service, *Briefing notes on central library/resource centres in schools,* Bridgwater, School Library Service Resource Centre, 1988.

Spyers-Duran, P., *Moving library materials,* Chicago, American Library Association, 1965.

Statens Kulturråd, *Folkbibliotekslokaler: en handbok,* Stockholm, Statens Kulturråd, 1981.

Strasser, T., 'Lending ambiance to libraries', *School library journal,* **4** (10), 1988, 59.

Stubley, P., 'Equipment and furniture to meet the requirements of the new technology', in *Library buildings: preparations for planning,* edited by M. Dewe, Munich, Saur, 1989, 102–16.

Swisher, R. *et al.,* 'Telecommunications for school library media centers', *School library media quarterly,* **19** (3), 1991, 153–60.

Thompson, A., *Library buildings of Britain and Europe,* London, Butterworths, 1963.

Thompson, G., 'Building, equipment and conservation', in *British librarianship and information work 1976–1980,* (ed.) L. J. Taylor, London, Library Association,

1982, vol. 1, 25–34.

Thompson, G., *Planning and design of library buildings*, 3rd edn., London, Butterworth Architecture, 1989.

Todaro, J. B., 'Changing children's environments', *Illinois libraries*, **60** (10), 1978, 903–8.

Walling, L. L., 'Granting each equal access', *School media quarterly*, **20** (4), 1992, 216–22.

Walter, V. A., *Output measures for public library service to children: a manual of standardized procedures*, Chicago, American Library Association, 1992.

Weihs, J., *The integrated library: encouraging access to multimedia materials*, 2nd edn., Phoenix, Ariz., Oryx Press, 1991.

Weston, R., 'A schooling in community values', *Architects' journal*, 2 September 1992, 22–5.

Weston, R., *Schools of thought: Hampshire architecture 1974–1991*, Winchester, Hampshire County Architects Department, 1991.

'Wheels around Birmingham', *Service point*, (55), 1992, 14–15.

While, G., 'The return of Andrew Carnegie: a very personal blueprint for the design and layout for a modern children's library', in *Never too young: book 1: library services to pre-school children and their carers*, (ed.) J. Heaton, Newcastle under Lyme, Youth Libraries Group, 1991, 62–7.

Willett, H. G., 'Looking at environments for children in public libraries', *North Carolina libraries*, **49** (3), 1991, 150–5.

Withers, F. N., *Standards for library service: an international survey*, Paris, Unesco, 1974.

Woof, N., 'Broad brief for Croydon suppliers', *Library Association record trade supplement*, **95** (12), 1993, 9–11.

Wozny, J., *Checklist for public library managers*, Metuchen, N.J., Scarecrow, 1989.

Wyatt, G. and Cassels-Brown, R., 'A new library for St Paul's School, [Concord, New Hampshire]', *School library journal*, **38** (2), 1992, 35–7.

'Yoker Youth Library', *Service point*, (57), 1993, 7, 9.

INDEX